Why We Suffer

*A Western Way to Understand
and Let Go of Unhappiness*

Peter Michaelson

Table of Contents

Introduction

Emotional suffering is one of humanity's greatest trials, and we spend a lot of time and energy trying to avoid this familiar pain.

Many of us are convinced our chronic unhappiness is caused by external factors or conditions, such as the insensitivity or cruelty of others and the demands of a cold, cruel world. This belief covers up how we unconsciously participate in much of our own suffering.

Some emotional suffering is unavoidable. We experience it when, for instance, loved ones become ill or die. But a great deal of our suffering is unnecessary. This suffering originates from the dynamic interplay of conflicting forces in the mysterious inner cosmos known as our psyche. In large measure, we suffer out of ignorance of how our psyche works. This book provides insightful knowledge about these inner workings, and the insight, once assimilated, greatly reduces emotional suffering.

It is our emotions, not our mental faculties, that produce the most trouble for us. Our emotional side often swamps our mental side, causing negative reactions and irrational convictions, leading to a loss of perspective, clarity, and purpose. We spend a lot of time, often unsuccessfully, trying to fight off the ingredients of unhappiness, which include fear, anxiety, anger, guilt, confusion, apathy, shame, hopelessness, loneliness, depression, and self-doubt. For many of us, life becomes an ordeal, a wearisome quest for elusive happiness. Even the healthiest among us can have regular bouts or periods of unhappiness.

The psychological knowledge in this book is a powerful remedy for our suffering. This information shows that our human nature is, in a sense, operating with old software. We need to be upgraded. Microsoft can't do it—only we can. For that to happen, we need new knowledge to see ourselves more clearly and objectively.

Most of us have personal problems or challenges we would like to resolve. Collectively, we also have challenging national and worldwide problems that need to be solved. We might not be up to the challenge if we're not conscious enough of our inner dynamics. This puts us in grave danger of having our technology outstrip our ability to handle it wisely. Handicapped by a lack of self-knowledge, how can we trust ourselves to avoid conflict and self-defeat? We will just fail repeatedly to learn from history.

This knowledge provided by this book enables us to see into the operating system of our psyche, where we discover a "software component" that is seriously flawed. This flaw, first discovered almost eighty years ago, is a grave danger to each of us personally and to all of us collectively. This book provides evidence for the existence of this *deadly flaw*, as I call it. I show how awareness of this flaw eliminates our negativity, upgrades our intelligence, makes us a lot happier, and protects and enhances our democracy.

This book penetrates the mystery of the deadly flaw and reveals its operating system. We journey to the deepest depths of our psyche. The deeper we go, the more trepidation we can feel. Our psyche has "secrets," repressed from childhood, that are associated with guilt, shame, old memories, and rejection of self. Instinctively, we have some fear of uncovering this repressed material.

So we stay more on the surface of consciousness, finding comfort in our cherished perceptions and beliefs that we use to orient us in the world and contain our fear. But these illusions and beliefs also serve as ball and chain, blocking our ability to penetrate reality and limiting our prospects for personal growth and happiness.

Our deadly flaw affects us on more than a personal level. There are many correlations, of course, between our human nature and the conditions of social and political life. This book illustrates many ways that our blindness on an inner level has led to crashes, pile-ups, and missed turns on the road of human destiny. Our deadly flaw is an instigator of self-defeat, and it also produces a restriction of our intelligence that impedes creativity, initiative, efficiency, and foresight. Clearing up this psychological problem will give us a better chance to survive, prosper, and grow our democracy in the centuries and millennia to come.

I reveal this deadly flaw right up front, in the next paragraph. First, however, be warned that people often react on hearing about it with mild horror because it is indeed an affront to our ego. Our first reaction might be a gasp of disbelief or a snort of derision. That's the kind of reaction Nobel-laureate George Bernard Shaw imagined when he wrote, "All great truths begin as blasphemies."

This deadly flaw causes us to be addicted emotionally to pain and suffering. We might laugh at such an assertion if it were presented as a humorous headline in a satiric newspaper: "Humans Discovered to be Addicted to Pain and Suffering." I provide plenty of evidence, however, that this is no joke. This book reveals the deadly flaw's configuration, provides evidence for its existence, explains how it develops inside us, suggests why it has eluded the smartest people, reveals how lethal it is, and shows how we can overcome it.

The deadly flaw is largely unknown for good reason. For starters, it can't be seen directly, like a tumor or an infection. Hard science has *not* identified it as an anomaly or a flaw in our brain. On top of that, the idea of it, as mentioned, is quite disagreeable and even annoying. Just thinking about it, especially how it applies to us personally, can activate a kind of psychological gag-reflex. Even as we begin on a mental level to recognize the possibility that it's true, we can remain determined *emotionally* to resist accepting it.

This book examines its major symptoms and traces them back to the source. These widespread symptoms include the emotional suffering of worry, anxiety, fear, and depression, as well as behavioral problems, shortcomings in creative and intellectual capacity, and malice and aggression toward ourselves and others.

Let me say again that I know some readers will feel this book's thesis is disheartening. You have my sympathy. It does take character and courage to consider this material with an open mind. This knowledge does challenge our idealized self-image, while exposing a primitive side of human nature. That's why our ego hates to consider this knowledge.

This book's revelations, however, are more humbling than dispiriting. The knowledge is revolutionary because it gives us the power to determine our own destiny. Finally, we can take charge of our life.

This deadly flaw in our human nature gets the best of us only if we fail to become conscious of it. It is an emotional condition with complex interconnections and dynamic mechanisms. When we expose this inner condition, we are beginning to eliminate or eradicate it. When it no longer contaminates our inner life, we feel, just for starters, our goodness and our value more acutely, as we are more respectful of the goodness and value of others.

A lot of good ideas are circulating for making ourselves and the world a better place. But good ideas aren't enough in themselves. The deadly flaw can keep good ideas from being acted on because it compels us, at best, to be indecisive, confused, and prone to dissension. At worst, it produces self-defeat and self-destruction. The negative effect consistently trumps good ideas, positive affirmations, and best intentions.

Presumably, more brainpower can help to solve our problems. A term in use these days—intelligence augmentation—refers to our ability to use the increasing complexity of new information media and systems to our advantage. In other words, we could get smarter through cognitive calisthenics as technological acceleration helps enhance our brainpower. At the moment, though, what brainpower we have is surely contaminated by some dark impulses, as evidenced by our unstable economic system, as well as by violence, war, and a nuclear-weapons standoff. We are polluting and plundering our planet, our democracy is threatened by lust for power, and the mental health of millions is tipping into the red zone. Human intelligence is straining under the burden of our emotional weakness.

The psychological knowledge in this book clearly shows how so many of our actions and behaviors arise from our subconscious emotional life rather than our more conscious mental life. Our resistance, denial, egotism, and psychological defenses are mainly responsible for keeping an understanding of this emotional side sealed off in the cellar of our psyche.

When it comes to learning about this inner condition, we can expect little help from the experts. Psychologists, psychiatrists, and psychoanalysts in academia and in the mental-health professions have not recognized this flaw, and many of them will denounce any claims to its existence. These are smart people, but they are not necessarily any more conscious than the rest of us, which means their self-knowledge is no greater than ours. Plenty of circumstantial evidence for this flaw's existence is presented in this book. This thesis is based on the work of Edmund Bergler, a psychiatric psychoanalyst and prolific writer who died almost fifty years ago (see Chapter 1). Hard proof of the flaw's existence is not available because science has not penetrated the mystery of human experiences such as compassion, love, despair, or unhappiness. Science doesn't know what brain processes produce our personal subjective experience, or whether brain processes even produce our consciousness.[1] Yet many scientists insist (emotionally and egotistically, in my view) that the psyche, the dynamic seat of personal experience, cannot possibly exist because biology, chemistry, and physics haven't detected it. As they ignore or ridicule the psyche, they condone or promote drug intervention for psychological distress, short-circuiting in many instances our noble if often painful quest for purpose, meaning, and happiness.

Making sense of this inner world of the psyche—what Carl Jung called "the spirit of the depths"—requires an intelligence based in empathy, introspection, and experience, along with an understanding based on observation of how our psyche operates.

We don't have to fear or detest our deadly flaw. We only need to be conscious of it. Our intelligence and goodness then come to the rescue. We are more intricate in our makeup than we ever imagined, and we have so much room on the upside for growth and progress. If we can accomplish what we have *with* the deadly flaw, imagine what we will achieve when we escape its clutches. It's a big part of the madness, mystery, and magic of being human.

I believe this flaw is the weak link in our democracy, causing us to fail at times from holding our political and economic leaders responsible for their corruption and for the injury they do to us. Even when we do speak out as citizens, we are often misguided in identifying the problems because we're not being insightful enough. Our deadly flaw causes us to be negative, and thus we bring too much anger, fear, resentment, and selfishness to the debate. It also means that we fail to produce from our midst a higher quality of political candidates.

I have been a psychotherapist in private practice since 1985, and I have known about the deadly flaw since that time. I have taught this knowledge to my clients and shown them how it applies to their own particular issues. Clinical cases involving my clients are provided in this text. Such cases can be quite complicated, yet the ones presented here are kept simple. All cases are written to protect individual privacy.

Readers can look upon this book as a treasure map of self-discovery that leads us, through the riddles and paradoxes of our psyche, home to ourselves. Inward exploration can be experienced as an exciting adventure. On this hero's journey, we pass through a dark underworld, as life philosopher Joseph Campbell described it, until we emerge renewed into the sunlight. The reward for making this passage is the fulfillment of our destiny and the discovery of our authentic self. Answering the call to self-development also means that, individually, we are doing our share for the sake of our world and future generations.

Chapter 1
The Essence of the Deadly Flaw

Thinkers over the ages have speculated about a flaw in human nature. They have identified it through concepts such as original sin, an enemy within, or a death instinct. My thesis contends that a hidden flaw does indeed exist. It was discovered in the last century by a relatively unknown psychoanalyst. Only a tiny percentage of the population have recognized or understood this flaw or even heard of it.

It's not just a characteristic of "bad" people. The innocent of the world, the good people, are carriers of this emotional quirk, as are the less noble among us. This flaw, however, gets the best of us only when it remains unconscious, hidden from our awareness in our psyche. It is analogous to a sabotaging virus, bug, or worm in a computer system. Even an excellent computer can be compromised by a troublesome quirk. Such a system operates better once that problem is removed. Obviously, the problem has to be identified before it can be removed. Here, briefly described in the next few paragraphs, is the essence of the problem.

It does feel like blasphemy to say that we like our suffering. It is outrageous to suggest that we're secretly interested in holding on to our negativity. Yet this is the paradox of this deadly flaw. It compels us to recycle our old hurts from our past, as it tricks us through our defenses into covering up our collusion in our suffering. These hurts consist of unresolved negative emotions from our past involving deprivation, refusal, helplessness, criticism, rejection, betrayal, abandonment, and a sense of unworthiness.

Because of this flaw in our human nature, *we decline on an unconscious level to let go of our entanglement in these negative emotions. Moreover, we also secretly look for ways to recycle or relive this negativity.* Our flaw compels us to indulge unconsciously, and sometimes semi-consciously, in unresolved negative emotions. This produces personal self-defeat and, by extension, national and worldwide dissension and disharmony.

Our fate as a species, I believe, is to be defeated by this quirk of human nature, while our destiny is to overcome it.

Is it any wonder people don't want to see too deeply into their psyche? It's like bingeing on humble pie. If this is true knowledge, how could we not already know it! If it's true, we must be pretty stupid not to have seen it sooner!

The problem is not stupidity. It's our incredible resistance to upgrading our consciousness.

I first learned about this peculiarity in human nature in 1985 from the writings of psychoanalyst Edmund

Bergler, MD. Bergler wrote twenty-five psychology books, many of them issued by major New York publishers of that time, including Harper & Brothers, Doubleday & Co., and Collier Books.[2] He also wrote hundreds of articles that were published in leading professional journals and popular magazines.[3]

Despite the brilliance of his writings, Bergler, an Austrian Jew who fled the Nazis in 1938, established a private practice in New York City and died there in 1962,[4] is completely ignored by modern psychologists and researchers. Many PhD graduates in psychology from leading American universities have never heard of him. No biography of him has been written. A new book of his, likely written in 1952, was published by International Universities Press in 1998, thirty-six years after his death.[5] No mention was made in the mainstream media of such a noteworthy publishing event, nor did any reviews of the book show up in my latest Google search.

All this rejection of him and his findings makes perfect sense: As mentioned, it is a psychological axiom that we are repelled and inwardly terrified by the deepest truths about us. For starters, we repress much guilt, shame, and painful memories from early childhood. The knowledge Bergler uncovered is forbidden. We sense danger in knowing about our own participation in our suffering. The knowledge shatters our sense of who we are. We are afraid of it because we don't know who we'll be without our illusions, defenses, and attachment to suffering. Losing that sense of identity feels like a kind of death. Better the sufferer we know than the mysterious stranger we don't.

We relegated Bergler to obscurity for the crime of discovering the truth about us. Through denial and psychological defenses, we're always repressing vital inner knowledge that would threaten our egotism and self-image. Thus, we avoid the mortification our ego experiences whenever we get an inkling of how ignorant we are of vital self-knowledge.

Bergler, a post-Freudian, agreed with classical psychoanalysis that we retain in our psyche those feelings and impressions from childhood of being deprived, refused, helpless, controlled, and taken for granted. As adults, we frequently interpret our experiences through these leftover emotions. Whatever is unresolved in us will continue to be experienced by us in a painful and self-defeating manner. In childhood, we also acquire impressions of being rejected, unloved, betrayed, and criticized. The infantile experience is extremely subjective, so that even a person who was loved as an infant and well cared for as a child can still be entangled in lingering impressions of having been refused, controlled, and unloved.

Bergler plumbed a new depth of understanding when he claimed that we are emotionally attached to these forms of lingering negativity. The realization first came to him in 1932,[6] and he elaborated on his theory of compulsive suffering over the next thirty years.

According to the theory, our defense system is designed to cover up our collusion or indulgence in this hidden negativity. Through our defenses, we often blame others for our negative feelings, convinced that their (alleged) ignorance and malice are the causes or sources of our failure, disappointment, self-doubt, envy, anger, or apathy. We convince ourselves we are the victims of injustice and cruelty. Few of us are eager to acknowledge that our emotional suffering is produced by our willingness to keep recycling it.

So the suffering principle is a powerful force, the antithesis of the pleasure principle. The flaw in our psyche, Bergler said, constitutes a "basic neurosis," a condition common to all humanity.[7] This dark side hides out in us all, and it can produce many varieties of self-defeat and suffering that include defensiveness, apathy, self-pity, self-absorption, as well as cruelty, greed, hatred, and violence.

It's now time for humanity to acknowledge this flaw, this quirk of our nature that for many of us becomes self-destructive. We can feel appalled about its existence, but we need not be devastated. Its exposure, really, is cause for celebration. Its existence is certainly not our fault. Nor is it our fault that we haven't previously exposed it. It is an infantile aspect of our psyche that developed in earliest childhood. In seeing it, we accept that we are a work in progress and that human suffering can be greatly abated. The challenge is to be mature and grown-up from this point on, and become conscious of how we generate and indulge in negative emotions. That's the first step to overcoming this self-defeating inner program.

Spiritual teacher and best-selling author Eckhart Tolle has identified our unconscious willingness to suffer, though he mentions it only in passing, without discussion of its origins or mechanisms. In *A New Earth*, he writes: "Whenever you are in a negative state, there is something in you that wants the negativity, that perceives it as pleasurable, and that believes it will get you what you want."[8] He also writes, "If in the midst of negativity you are able to realize 'at this moment I am creating suffering for myself' it will be enough to raise you above the limitations of conditioned egoic states and reactions."[9]

I'm not sure that realization is sufficient. I believe we have to understand clearly how we are creating our particular form of suffering before we can become free of it. *Why We Suffer* identifies the origins, mechanisms, forms, and variations of our willingness to suffer. As I explain in detail later, negative emotions such as anger, hatred, jealousy, greed, envy, and hopelessness are symptoms of the deadly flaw, not the flaw itself. While we can be conscious of these negative emotions, we are not likely to be conscious of the deeper negative emotions that are ingredients of the deadly flaw. A jealous person, for instance, knows he suffers for his jealousy. He is *not* likely to know, however, that his jealousy is on the surface and that the real problem is his emotional attachment[10] to feeling rejected, betrayed, or devalued. This is the hidden source of his suffering, the fact that he is secretly (unconsciously) willing to indulge in feeling rejected, betrayed, and devalued.

In the same vein, a hateful person knows about his hatred and often will acknowledge it. He's not likely to know, however, that his hatred is created through his emotional indulgence in feelings of being refused, controlled, rejected, devalued or otherwise victimized. His hatred blames others, and it thereby serves as a defense that covers up his indulgence in his unresolved negative emotions.

The more profound answers to the following questions help us get to the hidden elements of our deadly flaw: What am I angry about? What do I fear? Why do I fear that? What makes me feel sad? Why am I lonely? For example, a person who suffers from substantial feelings of loneliness is likely indulging unconsciously in one or more negative emotions: rejection, abandonment, and a sense of unworthiness. A jealous person is also indulging in these negative emotions. An envious person indulges in feeling refused or deprived. We have not been conscious of how we're choosing to circulate these unresolved emotions from our past.

The deadly flaw is, at least in part, the source of our instinct for violence and war. (The *Star Wars* creators were right to warn us about the power of the dark side.) Personal and national self-defeat and self-sabotage are the consequences of having this flaw. Historian Barbara Tuchman's *The March of Folly* chronicled how governments down through the ages have committed the stupidest, most painful acts of self-defeat, often in the form of warfare, with depressing regularity.[11] Tuchman's book ends with the debacle of Vietnam. But the folly continues with ongoing wars and worldwide financial and environmental crises.[12] Self-defeat of deadly magnitude is inherent in our flaw. The negative emotions that emerge from this source within us are so powerful that they contaminate our collective behavior, as they frequently override reason, decency, and common sense.

Our psyche features its own inner courtroom drama, with a prosecutor (our inner critic or superego) and a defense lawyer (our unconscious or subordinate ego). Verbal abuse and a kind of emotional terrorism are aspects of our inner dynamics. Through the insinuations and accusations of our inner critic, we are harassed and tormented. The inner critic produces self-aggression in the form of self-criticism. This aggression can escalate into self-rejection, self-condemnation, and self-hatred. Our deadly flaw facilitates our absorption of this aggression. In other words, we soak up the negativity, and then we spew it out at others as we allow it to produce self-defeat.

Two aspects of our psyche—inner passivity and inner or self-aggression—are primary ingredients of the flaw that's at the heart of human dysfunction. We have a secret or unconscious willingness to experience both passivity and self-aggression. These negative emotions are like default positions in our psyche, from where we invariably experience life painfully.

When we are at war with ourselves in the conflict between our inner aggression and inner passivity, the resulting malevolence is compulsively transmitted outward toward others, and becomes cruelty, indifference, and violence. If we had cruel or dysfunctional parents or an unfavorable genetic makeup, our deadly flaw can be more problematic and our negative emotions more intense.

This book traces the origins of the deadly flaw to childhood, and it shows how it hides out behind the defenses of adults. I provide examples of how it generates self-defeat on personal, social, national, and worldwide levels. Our flaw can defeat our attempts to establish harmony and peace both inwardly and outwardly. On the broader scene, the level of the emotional and mental health of the people of any nation, and hence their level of self-respect and mutual respect, correlates directly with the quality of their government and institutions. The challenge of bringing peace and prosperity to the world is tough enough without this flaw. With it, the people of the world are in danger of self-defeat on a grand scale.

Bergler said this flaw is "the lifeblood of neurosis."[13] He coined the clinical term, psychic masochism, to describe it. I avoid that clinical term and refer to it, more euphemistically, as the deadly flaw.

Another frequently used term in this book is unconscious or deep negativity, which is described in detail in the next chapter. Deep negativity provides the basic ingredients for the deadly flaw, while the deadly flaw itself is the essence of the dark side of human nature. Through the deadly flaw, we recycle deep negativity, indulge in the consequent suffering, go looking for more opportunities to suffer in this way, and cover up this painful, self-defeating activity with various defenses.

Bergler was aware of the enormous resistance to his ideas and understood that we are determined emotionally, through our denial and defenses, not to disturb the psychic status quo. He stated once that his books were time-bombs that might not go off until more than 100 years have passed. Faced now with dire challenges, we might be open-minded enough to explore his formula for decoding the human psyche in order to speed up that timetable.

In large measure, I explain Bergler in my own words. In some sections in this book I don't mention him at all, though he is behind the scenes all the while. In other places, I quote him extensively. I reference his work more frequently later in the text. Any misinterpretations of him that might be found here are due entirely to my lack of understanding.

I have written five previous books, all of them based on Bergler's theories. For many years I was a client (or patient) of a psychotherapist who practiced Bergler's analytic method. My understanding of his work has evolved over time, and this book, I believe, is more precise than my previous ones in communicating his ideas. His writing is quite clinical for the most part, and it is more technical and precise than Freud's. Nonetheless, many readers find it impossible to digest the material as he presents it. I have tried to simplify this knowledge and make it more accessible to the public.

Still, the deadly flaw does involve complicated inner dynamics, and a taste of that complexity is sprinkled throughout this book. For those who might object to the heavy mental lifting, keep in mind that people tolerate and embrace complexity in modern technology. We are more complex than any piece of technology we have ever created, and it would seem foolish and self-defeating not to match our understanding of technology with in-depth self-understanding.

Chapter 2
No Denying the Negative

There's no denying that we experience negative emotions. We don't just experience them, though—we *produce* them.

Most of us are willing to acknowledge that we have a negative side. We often admit to being too angry, too impatient, too needy, too demanding, too lazy, and so on. "I'll try harder in the future to do better," we frequently tell ourselves and others.

We can certainly see negativity all around us. The many wars of the last 100 years have been spectacles of vicious brutality. Going back further, history confirms the existence of our dark side. The clash of truth and falsehood, courage and cowardice, charity and greed, have been expressed dramatically in mythology, religion, and literature. This clash is depicted in the Greek tragedies, world poetry, Shakespeare's plays, Dante's *Divine Comedy,* and in the great novels of Dickens, Dostoyevsky, Conrad, and Melville. Our struggle for the pre-eminence of the positive over the negative is the essence of our best drama and perhaps the meaning or purpose of life.

The dark side of our nature is symbolically represented as a dragon in the legends of brave knights and beautiful damsels. The devil is another symbol of a sinister power that corrupts us and is fiercely opposed to our well-being. Luke Skywalker in the *Star Wars* movies faces his inner demons, who urge him to follow in the steps of his evil father, Darth Vader. Come into the dark side of the force, the father at one point coaxes his son. Luke must use all his inner resources to resist the seductive appeal of the dark side. Myths, poetry, and legends, as well as our best movies, tell us that true heroism involves the adventure of self-discovery, the liberation from a negative force, and the pleasure of our courage.

Negativity exists in the outer world, so why not within us as well? A black hole in outer space is a metaphor for our deadly flaw. Black holes can't be seen directly, but only by their influence on surrounding bodies and energy systems. No light escapes from them because of their extreme gravity. In a comparable manner, our deadly flaw can't be seen directly. Lurking in inner space, it can be recognized in our patterns of self-defeat, our inability to learn from history, our need for enemies, our appetite for violence, our weakness against corruption, and our addictions, fixations, phobias, passivity, and compulsions.

Our inner space may have other similarities with outer space. Physicists say that 98 percent of the universe is comprised of what is called *dark matter*, which emits nothing but bends time and space. Another mysterious commodity called *dark energy* is apparently involved in the acceleration of the expansion of the universe. Perhaps our deadly flaw swirls in our inner space with certain physical properties consistent with outer reality.

Often the dark side is right in our face. Jill, a client of mine in recovery from drug and alcohol abuse, revealed her struggle against this dark force in a session: "I'm feeling a build-up of pressure. I'm being tempted to get back to drinking and drugging. You know what it is? I want to be bad. I can really feel how much I want to be bad. It's fun and exciting and hard to resist."

Jill had felt criticized and disapproved of during her childhood. She had felt like a bad child, and she now remained entangled in those negative emotions. She was her own worst critic and her own worst enemy. Her impulse to drink and to take drugs was caused in part by her unresolved conviction that she was a bad person. Drug abuse was the means by which she acted out in a dangerous manner the negative sense of self that still possessed her. Whenever she relapsed, she experienced waves of self-condemnation and self-hatred that were held in place by her deadly flaw. She could also imagine that condemnation coming at her from friends and family members.

Her addiction to alcohol and drugs was a symptom of a deeper problem. Her deadly flaw, manifesting in part as an emotional addiction to self-criticism and self-condemnation, compelled her to act out being bad. In other words, she was fated to fall into some dark pit of behavioral dysfunction, and it just happened to be with alcohol and drugs. Other ways that people fall prey to the deadly flaw include career self-sabotage, relationship failure, gambling, public shame, anti-social behaviors, variations of criminality, risk involving health, and suicide. Jill's substance abuse and her accompanying emotional suffering—along with the ill effects upon her physical health, career, and relationships—were the prices she paid for her deadly flaw.

Most of us do acknowledge our negativity, and we understand that it can have a powerful hold on us. We recognize negativity at this level—in our anger, greed, and judgmental impulses, for instance—but we don't see it at a deeper level. We're only seeing superficial or conscious negativity. We're not accessing deep or unconscious negativity.

Three categories of emotions comprise this deep negativity. Note once again that deep negativity and the deadly flaw are not the same thing. The deadly flaw consists in part of negative emotions (deep negativity) *to which we are unconsciously attached.* That means we're secretly willing to feel these emotions, no matter how painful and no matter the consequences. If we weren't attached to these darker emotions, we would quickly let go of them because they're so painful. Instead, they hang around and torment us, sometimes all through our life.

Deep negativity consists of three categories of emotions. Each category belongs to one of the three primary stages of child development. Freudian theory, one of several major theories of child development, identifies these as the oral, anal, and oedipal stages.[14] Children have different emotional experiences, positive and negative, in each of these stages. Frequently, the negative emotions remain unresolved, and they are then experienced repeatedly in painful ways in the lives of dysfunctional adults and also, to a lesser degree, in the lives of those adults generally considered normal or relatively happy.

Negative emotions particular to the first 18 months of life (oral stage) include: feeling deprived, experiencing loss, feeling starved or empty, feeling denied, missing out, never having enough, never feeling satisfied, and feeling refused.

We have many possible defenses to cover up our secret willingness to repeatedly experience these negative emotions. As adults, the primary defense against unresolved issues from this stage, stated unconsciously in our psyche, goes like this: "I'm not looking to feel deprived or refused. Look how much I want to get. My desire for this object (or this person or this experience) proves that I really do want to get."

Toddlers often scream in loud protest when they feel denied or refused. Much of the time the child's sense of refusal is based on his or her misreading of reality. Refusal is usually not the parents' intent. Children with unresolved oral issues can grow up to be adults who feel dissatisfied and deprived, and who struggle with self-regulation. Greed, envy, and boredom are symptoms of this lingering oral attachment to deprivation and refusal.

Negative emotions particular to the period from 18 to 36 months (anal stage) include: feeling helpless, controlled, taken advantage of, violated, trapped, dominated, restricted, inhibited, held up, held back, made to endure inappropriate behavior, imposed upon, obligated, drained, and told what to do.

The "terrible twos" mark this stage when children, protesting loudly or stubbornly, resist the feeling of being restricted or forced to submit. One notable objection is to toilet-training. As adults, the primary defense we use to cover up our attachment to these unresolved negative emotions goes like this, "I'm not looking for the feeling of being helpless or controlled. Look at how much, through my behavior, I try to avoid that feeling. And see how angry I get when someone tries to control me."

Adults with this lingering issue can be stubborn, rigid, passive, passive-aggressive, as well as controllers of others or people who are especially sensitive to feeling controlled. They can lack self-regulation and struggle with addictions and emotional ups-and-downs.

Negative emotions particular to the period from two years to five years (oedipal stage) include: feeling rejected, betrayed, abandoned, criticized, unimportant, not wanted, excluded, neglected, left out, looked down upon, seen in a negative light, unfairly accused, not supported, not validated, condemned, and hated.

Children at this age can collapse into sullen misery when it appears to them that they have been criticized or rejected, even when such criticism or rejection is not present or intended. As adults, our primary defense or cover-up of the lingering effect of this stage goes like this, "I hate the feeling of being rejected or criticized. Look at how, in my behavior, I try so hard to avoid having that happen. And look at how angry or upset I get at those who reject me."

Adults with these issues can be very sensitive to feeling rejected, criticized, betrayed, or abandoned. They can be their own worst critics, judgmental and rejecting of others, as well as needy and lonely. They can suffer by feeling unsupported emotionally by others, and be quick to doubt their own value.

The negative emotions from these three stages linger in our psyche. As adults, most of us are entangled to some degree in several of these emotions. The deadly flaw operates, as mentioned, in the psyche of everyday people. It is also lodged in the psyche of people with serious mood, anxiety, and personality disorders, and resolution or healing for these individuals is more problematic.[15] Typically, we can have at least one emotional entanglement from each of the three stages. We also have many defenses and rationalizations to cover up the unconscious choices we make to experience repeatedly this deep negativity.

We can expect to feel more serenity and peace of mind, and much less defensiveness and reactivity, once we identify our emotional attachments to deep negativity. We begin to track and monitor these negative emotions as we see through the defenses that cover them up. We eliminate our flaw with three basic steps: Step 1, we acquire an awareness of our specific attachments and the defense mechanisms we use to cover them up; Step 2, we practice tracking and monitoring the presence of these attachments in our daily experiences, clued in by the things we are typically frustrated about, complaining about, and feeling upset about; and, Step 3, we recognize the unconscious choices we have been making to recycle unresolved deep negativity.

This practice of "tracking," mentioned above, involves recognizing and understanding one's underlying deep negativity at those times when their symptoms appear. A man, for instance, who has gotten angry at his controlling wife, might realize that his anger is a reaction to (and a defense against) his underlying willingness to embellish upon the feeling of being controlled. With this knowledge, he "tracks" the symptom (anger) back to his own secret willingness to feel dominated. He understands that he is feeling anger, or using anger, to cover up his indulgence in his own passivity. Now, as he takes responsibility for this dynamic within himself, he sees the essential dishonesty of his anger, how he is using anger to cover up his collusion in feeling controlled, and he's likely to

Chapter 3
Conflicts in Mental Health

How do experts in psychology account for human misery and how do they treat it?

Until the 1960s, psychoanalysis had been considered the gold standard of psychological insight and treatment. Psychoanalysis collapsed as the preeminent school of psychology for a number of reasons, among them the apparent ineffectiveness of its treatment. Concerns were expressed that the discipline was producing analysts who had not cleared out their own deeper issues. If so, their treatment would be less effective and they would not be able to guide their patients out of neurosis.[16]

Even before Freud's death in 1939, psychoanalysis had begun to splinter into numerous competing theories and treatment procedures. It now has at least twenty-two theoretical orientations.[17] Some practitioners, influenced by cultural imperatives and their own resistance, promoted the theories and systems with which they and their clients were emotionally comfortable. Outside of psychoanalysis, mental-health practitioners introduced a variety of methods as new frontiers of inquiry opened in social psychology, family systems theory, behaviorism, cognitive approaches, ego psychology, gender and racial considerations, as well as humanistic and evolutionary psychology. Meanwhile, psychiatric medicine, espousing hard science, attacked both the efficacy and the theoretical basis of psychology and psychoanalysis.[18]

As the theories of classical psychoanalysis were demoted, psychology, psychiatry, and neuroscience produced a wide range of competing ideas and findings. Consequently, experts disagree on the primary cause of unhappiness. Some say it is mainly due to bad parenting or learned behavior, while others attribute it to cultural or social influences. Others blame genetics, biochemistry, medical conditions, or inadequate evolutionary adaptations. For the most part, they emphasize how external influences victimize us, as they discredit the notion that the knowledge we might wrest from the unconscious mind can free us of negativity and self-defeat.

Medical drugs have become a path of least resistance for treating many psychological problems. Male impotency, for instance, which can often be treated psychologically, is now called male erectile disorder and regarded as a medical problem to be treated by pharmaceuticals. This medical mentality is also applied to common depression. (Psychological treatments for these problems, based on understanding the deadly flaw, are discussed in Chapter 18.)

Obviously, the use of pharmaceuticals for psychiatric problems has its place, and these medicines are appropriate and helpful in alleviating serious emotional disturbances, including acute depression, severe anxiety, and phobias. But medical drugs, the uses of which can be driven by economic forces,[19] do not provide a cure for our deadly flaw. Usually these drugs treat only symptoms, enabling patients to be "managed" or to cope. Such drugs do nothing to raise our intelligence or creativity, in contrast to psychological insight.

A survey has found that the U.S. population with a mental illness disability has more than tripled from 1.25 million individuals in 1987 to more than four million at present.[20] Robert Whitaker, author of *Anatomy of an Epidemic: Magic Bullets, Psychiatric Drugs, and the Astonishing Rise of Mental Illness in America* (Crown Publishers, 2010), attributes this rise to the widespread use of antidepressants and other psychiatric drugs. In an interview, Whitaker said, ". . . the literature is remarkably consistent in the story it tells. Although psychiatric medications may be effective over the short term, they increase the likelihood that a person will become chronically ill over the long term."[21]

The insistence of many experts that addictions and compulsions are caused by "bad" genes, biochemical imbalances, or a "disease" serves to absolve the individual, to some degree, of personal responsibility for self-destructive behaviors. Certainly, genetics and biochemistry can be influences in emotional distress and out-of-control behaviors. Yet we must not allow these influences to sentence us to a life as victims of our biology. Whether or not we are impaired by such influences, psychological insight can help us become emotionally stronger and rise above our negativity. We have to see more clearly how we produce that negativity and recognize how it undermines self-regulation and leads to self-defeat. As our psyche's operating system becomes more conscious, each person identifies his or her deep negativity, and then recognizes how and when it is recycled. This provides even the genetically impaired individual the ability to moderate if not override the unconscious compulsion to recycle that deep negativity.

Also blamed for addictions, depression, anxiety, and apathy are parents, culture, and social injustice. Overlooked is the fact that the influences of society and culture can't be objectively assessed without considering that humans are a work in progress. We can't blame our problems on the creeps, jerks, and brutes wandering the earth. Of course, there's cruelty, ignorance, and injustice in the world. Are we going to allow this to defeat us? By exposing our deadly flaw, we can effectively take responsibility for our part in what is negative and dysfunctional in human affairs. We don't blame others (although we will seek redress if their behavior is immoral or illegal) when we realize how unconscious we have been of our deadly flaw.

We ourselves can be insensitive, selfish, and ignorant at times, and most of us, certainly, can "go negative" with minor provocation. The more self-knowledge we acquire, the smarter, stronger, and more positive we become.

Our unconscious mind participates with life either in a negative, positive, or neutral way. Often we "go negative" without even realizing it because we don't recognize our deadly flaw. It's not always an event, a situation, or other people that pose a problem for us. Rather, a problem is created when we are "triggered" and then "go negative" due to our emotional weakness. For instance, one person accepts hard times as a challenge, while another experiences it as a disaster. One person is deeply offended when someone ignores him, while another in the same situation barely takes notice. In most cases, the difference is accounted for by the level of our emotional health, meaning the degree to which we hold on to our suffering and recycle it.

Some experts claim that addictions and compulsions are a result of learned behavior. They say, in other words, that adverse family or social factors have conditioned individuals to act in self-defeating ways, whether with substance abuse or other out-of-control behaviors. To insist, however, that learned behavior instigates self-defeating behaviors raises the question of why these behaviors can't be unlearned. Learning to do things the right way instead of the wrong way is one of our basic abilities. The brain is very "plastic" and can be remolded. However, we're likely to be unable to learn the right way when we fail to penetrate the unconscious dynamics of our psyche. To learn to do things the right way, we need to understand the dynamics that drive us to do things the wrong way.

In part, our attachments to these negative emotions are developed in early childhood because of how, as babies, we make flawed assumptions concerning the reality of our situation. Babies are also caught in a complex emotional bind between their passivity and aggression. Adults and parents, who easily project their own idealized self onto infants, fail to appreciate the irrational nature of a child's consciousness. What are we missing?

Babies and young children often feel that they do not get enough (food, attention, love), and they become focused on what they feel is missing, not on what they are given. Even when well treated, they can feel deprived and refused. They can resent the affection and benefits given to their siblings or peers. They also often feel that whatever happens, they have somehow caused it to happen.

During the "terrible two's" they typically become furious at being "forced" to submit to the requirements of toilet training and other forms of socialization. Over the next few years, they can be extremely sensitive to feelings of being unloved or unappreciated, even when they have affectionate parents. Babies and young children are unable to understand another person's point of view. Sometimes there is no awareness even of the existence of such a thing as another point of view. Just as it is with many adults, the child's highly subjective perspectives become the child's reality. Childhood perceptions and emotions linger on to become the template through which adults experience life.

Many mental-health authorities and teachers take the nurture side in the nature-nurture debate. They tell their clients or teach their students that a child is a sweet innocent who is damaged by various forms of parental neglect, ignorance, or abuse. Human dysfunction, they say, comes from parents' domination, their undue exercise of power and control, their failure to acknowledge us, and their other violations of our youthful sense of self. Presumably, our parents acquired this ineptitude from their parents, and so on back into the mists of history. Blaming our parents for our misery is pointless and unfair. This blaming is primarily for the purpose of covering up our unconscious compulsion to suffer.

It can be hard to let go of a feeling that a grave injustice has been done to us by our parents' failures to raise us wisely. However, we can drop this sense of injustice and its accompanying suffering, and we don't have to forgive our parents to do so. We only have to see that our painful sense of injustice is a result of our willingness to go on feeling deprived, refused, controlled, unloved, criticized, or betrayed. This is how our deadly flaw works: Unconsciously, we chose to hold on to some hurt or other, while believing that our consequential suffering is caused by external factors.

Often times we also believe that some personal failing or defect of ours (i.e. stupidity, laziness, selfishness) is causing our suffering. But the defect we identify is typically just a symptom of the deadly flaw.

Parents certainly do have a major influence on the future emotional health of their children. But the problem is more complicated than many realize. Each child, because of the self-centeredness with which he or she is born, comes into the world predisposed to misinterpret the actions and intentions of parents, other adults, and caregivers. Classical psychoanalysis says we are born with an acute self-centeredness that distorts reality. This self-centeredness is a major contributor to the creation of the deadly flaw.[22] It produces an illusion of power and self-sufficiency that may ultimately help infants survive, in an emotional way, the reality of their helplessness.

Indeed, the existence of acute self-centeredness makes sense when we think that infants, in whatever degree they can rationalize their existence, would feel as if they might indeed be the center of the universe. All they know is their own little bodies, their own little selves. As far as they know, nothing else even exists. They have a sense of "oneness," but it places them at the center of *their* universe, oblivious and even hostile to reality that contradicts their exalted perspective. They initially perceive their parents, for instance, as extensions of themselves, and they're not eager to let go of that self-glorifying illusion.

History reveals how humans have been determined to deny reality and to see the world through self-centeredness. Our ancestors, for instance, felt the sting of being humbled when they were informed that the earth is not at the center of the universe and that the earth goes around the sun and not vice-versa. Copernicus and then Galileo were scorned and humiliated for insulting human self-centeredness with their knowledge.

Later, we found out we aren't even masters in our own house, as Freud put it. Whatever is going on inside us—all those drives, complexes, motivations, and sexual fantasies—is not what we would have ordered from the menu. Once again we were humbled: We're not as smart and superior as we thought. In revenge, we have managed year by year to take Freud down a peg or two, although signs have appeared of a restoration of his reputation.[23]

Along came Edmund Bergler with another affront to human self-centeredness, to the effect that we are unwitting collaborators in our own suffering, masters of self-defeat. Even if it were true, we didn't want to know about it. This allegation of our complicity in our suffering was so insulting that we have pretended—in an unconscious, collective conspiracy—that Bergler never existed and never recorded those awful ideas.

Chapter 4
Hidden Origins in Our Psyche

I have cautioned more than once that the ideas in this book are emotionally challenging. Readers who have reached this point in the text are to be commended for enduring the insults to their ego. You're going to be tested again.

A word is employed over the next few pages that hits a nerve in our psyche. This word, masochism, is intimidating, and it insinuates some nasty business. However, there is *no* suggestion here that we are sexual masochists. The reference is almost exclusively to non-sexual masochism which provides another way of understanding our hidden collusion in unhappiness, suffering, and self-defeat.

Sigmund Freud saw this masochism in human nature but he couldn't convince the world of its pervasiveness. It was tragic and predictable that both his admirers and critics stayed clear of the one topic that might be his greatest single contribution to psychology. While his lesser insights were intently scrutinized, people danced around and away from his writings on masochism.

He believed that masochism was an important consideration for psychoanalysis. He first attempted to understand it through sexuality. In *Three Essays on the Theory of Sexuality* (1905) he called the tendency to inflict and receive pain during sex the most common and important of all perversions. He said such perversion (he used the word as a clinical, not moral, term) was common even among the healthy, and that both sadism and masochism commonly occurred in the same individual.

In his paper, "Instincts and Their Vicissitudes" (1915), he described masochism more fully, and he related it to sadism turning back upon itself as a passive experience. Freud also introduced the concepts of *primary* and *secondary* masochism, along with the categories *feminine* and *moral* masochism.

Influenced by the slaughter of World War I, Freud proposed the idea of a masochistic instinct in *Beyond the Pleasure Principle* (1920). He described it as a kind of sadism against the self, a destructive element in the psyche he called the *death instinct*.[24] This part of us, which is overtly acted out by terrorists, is in conflict with another drive, which Freud called Eros, the *life instinct*.

In another essay, "The Economic Problem of Masochism" (1924), he said of moral masochism: "The suffering itself is what matters; whether it is decreed by someone who is loved or by someone who is indifferent is of no importance. It may even be caused by impersonal powers or circumstances; the true masochist always turns his cheek whenever he has a chance of receiving a blow."[25]

In *Civilization and Its Discontents,* published in 1929 when Freud was 73, he followed up on the idea that masochism was an inherent feature in human nature:

The assumption of the existence of an instinct of death or destruction has met with resistance even in analytic circles. . . . To begin with it was only tentatively that I put forward the views I have developed here, but in the course of time they have gained such a hold upon me that I can no longer think in any other way. To my mind, they are far more serviceable from a theoretical standpoint than any other possible ones . . . I know that in sadism and masochism we have always seen before us manifestations of the destructive instinct (directed outwards and inwards), strongly alloyed with eroticism; but I can no longer understand how we can have overlooked the ubiquity of non-erotic aggressivity and destructiveness and can have failed to give it its due place in our interpretation of life. . . . I remember my own defensive attitude when the idea of an instinct of destruction first emerged in psycho-analytic literature, and how long it took before I became receptive to it.[26]

Freud recognized that self-aggression, "even when it arises without any sexual purpose," appears to be processed in a masochistic manner: ". . . we cannot fail to recognize that the satisfaction of the instinct is accompanied by an extraordinary high degree of narcissistic enjoyment, owning to its presenting the ego with a fulfillment of the latter's old wishes for omnipotence."[27] Future research and reflection, he wrote, "will no doubt bring further light which will decide the matter."[28]

Some of Freud's followers considered these observations to be an aberration or intellectual failing of his old age. Edmund Bergler, however, made the pursuit of this idea his life's work. He tracked the concept into the deeply repressed memories of the oral stage of childhood development, beyond where Freud had explored. (Freud's work focused on the later stages of childhood development, namely the oedipal stage and, to a lesser extent, the anal stage. These two stages are closer to the surface of one's consciousness than the oral stage.)

According to Bergler, the process whereby we learn to sweeten our suffering begins in the oral stage of development, the first 18 months of life. The child's consciousness in this stage is strongly under the influence of three aspects in the psyche: acute self-centeredness, aggression, and *libido* (the psychic agency that regulates the pleasure principle). Bergler deduced that a baby's acute self-centeredness is in part responsible for the formation of the deadly flaw that he called psychic masochism.

Through this acute self-centeredness (Bergler called it megalomania), the child is greatly affronted when food and attention are not available on demand. When the

49

child begins to experience unpleasant sensations, such as helplessness in waiting to be fed or attended to, the child "deduces" that this waiting, or sense of deprivation and refusal, must be what he wants.

(Note to readers: I'm trying my best to avoid jargon, but I'm unable to adequately explain this process without using the psychoanalytic terms, megalomania, libido, and libidinize. A further explanation is needed for how we acquire the deadly flaw, and I need these three terms to explain how it happens.)

Infants believe, through megalomania, that whatever happens is what they want to happen. They have no capacity to imagine being acted upon through the will of others. They typically don't acquire the feeling of being up against the will of others until the anal stage after 18 months of age. At that point, they usually fiercely resist the feeling of others imposing their will. For infants in the oral stage, others don't exist. They experience their world as oneness, with themselves at its center. Parents and caretakers are experienced as entities that operate under the auspices of the child's magical powers.

Some of what parents and caretakers are doing, however, causes unpleasant feelings for the child. The child can't differentiate time, so waiting to be fed can feel like eternity. "Since waiting and refusal are happening," the child feels, "it must be what I want." If the unpleasant waiting is what the child wants, according to libido's "reasoning," this waiting "must be

50

what I like, despite the disagreeable sense of deprivation and refusal."

This faulty deduction, employed to preserve megalomania, enables the child to "sugar-coat" or *libidinize* (meaning the ability in the psyche to feel or produce gratification or pleasure) the feeling of being deprived and refused. The child creates an emotional attachment to the feeling of being deprived or refused. An inner conflict develops: The child wants to get and to feel satisfied, at the same time that the feeling of deprivation and *not getting* remains a familiar, unresolved attachment. This attachment lingers in the psyche of adults, producing a sense of inner emptiness along with envy, greed, desire, cravings, and a weakened capacity for self-regulation.

The child's weaning can feel like another experience of deprivation and refusal, as well as another affront to megalomania. As mentioned, this megalomania, in conjunction with libido, has the power to enable the child to "libidinize" the unpleasant experience of the alleged or actual deprivation and refusal: "If this unpleasantness is happening, it must be what I *want*. Hence, I must *like* it." Here, the child misuses or perverts libido, the pleasure principle, in an attempt to protect the cherished megalomania. This act of using libido to turn displeasure into an acceptable feeling (though it's a second-rate pleasure at best) captures the tragic-magic moment when the deadly flaw first sparks to life.

Hence, our deadly flaw is created in a kind of fusion of aggression, megalomania, and libido—all inner biological dynamics with psychological aspects. Meanwhile, another troublesome inner dynamic is also sparking to life. The psyche's natural aggression is blocked by the child's physical limitations. This aggression needs release. As Freud deduced, it turns and flows against the child to become self-aggression, giving life to the superego or inner critic.

This process whereby painful emotions are "libidinized" (meaning, once again, that the emotions are made agreeable, acceptable, or desirable, if only unconsciously), originates in the oral stage, the first 18 months of life. This process is later repeated in the anal and oedipal stages of childhood development with other negative emotions. Bergler believed that the emotional affinity for deprivation that arises in the oral stage lingers throughout the lives of most of us, affecting us negatively to different degrees. It can become more painful and problematic as we age when it remains unconscious.

By the age of three or four, the flaw consists of secret attachments to unresolved emotions (from the three categories listed in Chapter 2): deprivation, refusal, and loss (oral); helplessness and passivity (anal); and criticism, rejection, betrayal, and abandonment (oedipal). Once these emotions are made pleasurable through the deadly flaw, they follow us through life, with our active though usually unconscious involvement in repeatedly triggering and experiencing them.

A person's discovery of his deadly flaw normally corresponds with his discovery of repressed negative emotions (deep negativity). The following clinical case helps us to understand just how unconscious we can be of important psychological facts and feelings relating to our early years. Uncovering these feelings and experiencing them again are emotionally intense, but the processes of recollection with their accompanying distress do not have to be particularly painful for us. We commonly feel sorrow and sadness in this process, and these emotions are often experienced with a kind of existential intensity that can be quite tolerable if we can provide for ourselves, from within, some degree of emotional support for what we are undertaking, including trust in this process of self-development.

Ralph, a successful businessman, came for psychotherapy at his wife's insistence. She was concerned about his alcohol consumption and about the deterioration of his relationship with his teenage son. His wife, Jenny, complained of Ralph's rigid mentality and what she called his no-fun approach to life.

Ralph's son, Joseph, felt that his father was excessively stern and restrictive. Ralph would become angry at Jenny for allegedly undermining his authority whenever she gave in to Joseph's requests. When Ralph was a boy, he endured his father's strong willed, very strict approach to raising children. He claimed now that the whippings and beatings he received from his father had been appropriate discipline.

In his third session, Ralph became emotional when he related an incident that had occurred several years earlier with his alcoholic older sister. When Ralph and Jenny were informed that his sister was considering suicide, they drove to another city to be with her. They found her in "dreadful shape—she had hit rock-bottom." The following day, Ralph signed a form that committed her to a state rehabilitation center. Everyone agreed, his sister included, that this was the right decision. Months later, she came out of that center, and had managed her life reasonably well since then.

Nevertheless, Ralph was tearful as he told how he had committed his sister to this recovery program. He said he was feeling intense guilt about having done so. We explored the roots of his sadness and guilt, and discovered underlying feelings of rejection and betrayal. Ralph was surprised to hear that his feelings of betrayal had less to do with his sister and more to do with his father. When he committed his sister, Ralph felt he had betrayed her. Because of his own issue with betrayal, meaning his own emotional attachment to betrayal, Ralph had identified with his sister and had imagined that she was feeling betrayed by him. It was exactly those feelings of rejection and betrayal that, as a boy, Ralph had felt in connection to his father and his father's treatment of him. He had completely repressed those feelings. "What's the point of looking into the past?" he had rationalized. "It's all over and forgotten." But the unconscious does not forget repressed feelings.

Ralph's secret attachment to rejection and betrayal had been covered up by guilt and sadness, which in turn were covered up by denial. Yet he was replaying these painful emotions with Joseph, inducing his son to feel rejected and betrayed by him. By replaying these negative emotions with Joseph, Ralph was secretly identifying with Joseph's plight and thereby recycling, unconsciously, his own unresolved feelings of rejection and betrayal. His inner determination to do this, against all common sense and common decency, is attributable to the deadly flaw, the process whereby we indulge in core hurts from our past. These are not hurts that were necessarily inflicted on us by others. These hurts refer to the affronts to infantile self-centeredness and the painful and self-defeating defenses we employ to cover up our collusion in deep negativity. We circulate these old hurts because, to use another term, we are *emotionally addicted* to them. Thus, experiencing these hurts is like an addiction, and recycling them is like a compulsion.

Predictably, in ironic reversal, Ralph had begun to feel betrayed by his son. In what is typical behavior when people act out the deadly flaw, he ratcheted up the intensity of his negative feelings. Before Joseph became a teenager, he had idolized his father. As a typical teenager, however, he became more interested in his friends. Because of his problem with betrayal, Ralph found it easy to hold on to feeling injured by Joseph's alleged disloyalty. Ralph had felt a generalized disappointment and anger toward his son, but had not been fully conscious of his experience of rejection and betrayal with respect to his son because of his own repression of those emotions. He simply felt annoyed, irritated, and angry at Joseph. In being harsh and strict toward his son, Ralph was compulsively dishing out the abuse he had passively endured from his father.

So Ralph's deadly flaw was his attachment to feelings of rejection and betrayal, which meant he was unconsciously willing to seek out and recycle these painful emotions in everyday life and in his encounters with his son. He hid this fact from himself through his belief, created by his defenses, that his son's behavior and attitude toward him was the legitimate cause of his distress. Unconsciously, he was using his son as a scapegoat for the negative emotions he himself was willing to experience. To make this defense work, he had to feel hostility toward his son.

It would be pointless and self-defeating for Ralph to blame his father for making him neurotic and causing him pain. Where would it end? As an adult in the years to come, Joseph would start blaming Ralph. Such blame only enhances the sense of being a victim. To evolve, we need to accept responsibility for our negativity. We have to "own" it, wherever it may have come from.

Why is that so hard? What's the big deal? We don't want to own it because, through our defenses, we're so determined to avoid the humbling awareness of our participation in negativity and suffering.

When he came to therapy, Ralph was like a fear-filled dental patient. "People are often nervous about looking into their emotional problems," I told him. "There is a universal reluctance to examine one's psyche because people are convinced they will find out they are bad or sick. This conviction is based on old childish impressions of being defective, flawed, or inadequate. The initial anxiety associated with self-discovery and the penetration of our defenses is soon replaced by relief and a sense of well-being."

Certain painful feelings come to the surface from out of deep negativity. Most people recognize these negative feelings in the form of anger, fear, sadness, jealousy, boredom, shame, despair, loneliness, confusion, procrastination, and so on. These form the suffering that we experience for our deadly flaw. These negative emotions, although often dreadfully painful, are secondary, meaning they are the symptoms or the consequences of the deeper primary negative emotions. That deep negativity hides in our psyche and often it is not felt directly at all.

The negative feelings at the surface of our awareness are also employed as defenses. As an example, take a person who's angry about being rejected, in this case a person who is particularly sensitive to feeling rejected.

He might say in his defense: "I'm not looking for the feeling of rejection. The problem is that I'm an angry person. That's the problem!" The angrier he becomes, the more "successfully" he covers up his deadly flaw (in this case, his attachment to rejection), and the more he manages to convince himself that his anger is his main problem or that others deserve to be recipients of his anger. When his anger is directed at the person who is allegedly rejecting him, it produces this defense: "I'm not looking for rejection. Look at how angry I am at the person who is rejecting me!" He will now, however, feel some guilt and shame for his anger, another price he pays for his cover-up.

Through our defenses, falsifying reality takes precedence over accepting truth. We choose self-defeat and suffering over recognition of an inconvenient truth—the existence and influence of our deadly flaw.

Chapter 5
Understanding Personality Traits

The deadly flaw contributes to the formation of our personality traits. In this chapter I show the influence of the deadly flaw on what personality researchers refer to as traits of neuroticism and what Bergler called character neurosis. Here we see our personality traits in a new light, one that exposes the deadly flaw. This is not to say that the deadly flaw is the only influence on personality traits (genetics is certainly another one). But I believe the deadly flaw is the primary *psychological* influence on the formation of personality traits.

Let's start with a perfectionist. This individual, for the most part, acquires this personality trait as a consequence of his or her attachment to the feeling of being criticized. The personality trait also serves as a defense against conscious recognition of this attachment to criticism. However, not every person who is attached to criticism becomes a perfectionist. Other traits arise from one's attachment to criticism, such as being defensive, bitter, cynical, and highly critical of others.

The defense of the perfectionist goes something like this: "I don't want to be criticized. Look at how hard I try to do everything perfectly." He makes this plea of innocence to his inner critic, which, at the deepest levels, is cognizant of his attachment to feeling criticized and has accused him of indulging in that negative feeling.

The perfectionist is inwardly defensive. He reacts defensively toward his inner critic, mostly in the form of defensive thoughts and considerations. He also suffers from anxiety, produced because he is "under the gun" of his inner critic. People who are defensive in their dealings with others are usually inwardly defensive and weak vis-à-vis their inner critic.

Our inner defensiveness wastes creative energy. For the perfectionist, some of the energy of his emotional imagination is wasted, or at least used non-productively, in fantasies in which he sees and feels himself being criticized by others. It is also wasted in the inner defensiveness through which he denies his deadly flaw, his secret interest in feeling criticized. In other words, much of his emotional energy is consumed in the rationalizations and visualizations he creates in order to defend against his secret attachment to feeling criticized. He would more likely be creative and successful without this loss or waste of psychic energy. Consider, too, that it is difficult to feel self-esteem when we are regularly being harassed and discredited by our inner critic.

It is exhausting being a perfectionist. It is also impossible to succeed at it, and it is a drain on self-esteem. The perfectionist also makes careless mistakes,

60

unconsciously concocted or provoked, to bring criticism down on his head from others and from his inner critic. In self-defeat, he unconsciously creates situations that bring experiences of criticism to the fore. He does this because his attachment to that criticism is unresolved, and thus he's secretly willing (unconsciously compelled) to suffer the experience of it.

Jealousy is another personality trait. The jealous person is anticipating, often unconsciously, being rejected or betrayed. For instance, he or she conjures up images of a partner or spouse being involved romantically with another person. Whether such betrayal is actual or imagined, the images the jealous person produces by means of the emotional imagination tempt this person to misconstrue reality, which propels him or her toward suffering and self-defeat.

The jealous person is always trying to "prove," often through sheer speculation or the flimsiest of evidence, that his imaginings are an accurate reconstruction of the facts. He wants to establish that the betrayal he suspects is happening is a real possibility, thus giving himself some cover for secretly wanting to indulge in such feelings as rejection, betrayal, and being unloved.[29] His real problem is his addiction to these negative emotions.

Often jealousy in itself drives the partner into the arms of another person. Because jealous people are looking for rejection, their partner will unconsciously provide for them that which they are tempted to experience. We don't need conscious communication to give to each other the suffering that we each are unconsciously willing to experience. We somehow intuit that the other person is unconsciously willing to experience some unpleasantness, and, through our own lack of awareness, we fall into the trap of providing it. Hence, a partner expecting to be betrayed and willing to experience betrayal will induce his or her partner to provide such betrayal. It's a cause for sorrow that such dynamics are unwittingly acted out by millions of us.

One woman had been torturing herself daily for more than a year with visualizations of her husband making love to his secretary. Her husband, in reality, was kind, loyal, and devoted to her. In spite of his reassurances, she continued to imagine that he was betraying her. Her problem was her expectation of (and attachment to) rejection and betrayal, feelings she remembered experiencing in childhood when she perceived that her father favored her younger sister over her. Determined to recycle that feeling, she had transferred her wish to feel betrayed on to her husband.

Greed, another symptom of the deadly flaw, also can influence and even define a person's personality. Clearly, such individuals are likely to be self-centered and insensitive to others. The greedy person is usually not aware of his or her attachment to feeling deprived, denied, or to losing out in some way. This person can be a worrier who imagines worst-case scenarios involving these possibilities. When people accuse Wall

Street financiers of simply being greedy, they are missing the deeper elements that produced the greed. As mentioned earlier, not only can greedy people have an attachment to deprival, they can also be lost to themselves in the sense of not feeling any intrinsic self-worth. Their deadly flaw holds them in a void, a profound sense of unworthiness, a depth of nonbeing, which they react to with egotism, narcissism, and a need for materialistic self-aggrandizement.

These underlying issues guide many of them into the business of making money for money's sake in the first place. They are desperate to bolster their sense of value, and money provides them a conviction of superiority, as well as a "security" that compensates for the insecurity of their self-doubt and shallow consciousness.

The people-pleaser, another low self-esteem personality, also strives to avoid recognition of his deadly flaw, his attachment to feelings of rejection and abandonment. He unwittingly rejects his own self in order to gain the acceptance and approval of others. Because he is so ingratiating, however, others lose respect for him. Soon his worst fears are realized because, in ignorance of his deadly flaw, he acts out that to which he is attached, meaning he creates actual rejection and abandonment.

Shyness is another personality trait involving low self-esteem. Shy people frequently visualize scenes or produce daydreams in which they are somehow being defeated, seen in a negative light, ridiculed, or humiliated. Their greatest fear is the occurrence of such an experience. Yet whatever they fear in this manner is what they are secretly attached to. Their anticipation of being ridiculed paralyzes any positive regard for themselves and their life. So, in lieu of the real thing, shy people produce conscious or subliminal visualizations to this effect—scenes rich with the feeling and sight of their humiliation.

They may alternate such scenes with ones in which they are triumphantly humiliating someone else or in which they are being acclaimed for some accomplishment or power. They can be determined injustice collectors, while harboring bitterness about the low regard in which they believe they are held, although through self-rejection it is they who hold themselves in the lowest regard.

Shy people have a dearth of exhibitionistic self-assertion. Their shyness in itself exhibits an admission that something forbidden has been seen. They can't distinguish between appropriate exhibitionism and negative exhibitionism. The sense is that all self-exhibitionism is bad or wrong. Given an opportunity to impress others, they might unconsciously feel, "I don't want to exhibit myself and make a fool of myself." In childhood, their parents might have disapproved of, as inappropriate or self-serving, any displays of intelligence or verbal self-assertion. Hence, behaviors such as displaying feelings or being spontaneous and expressive are felt by shy people to be bad or unacceptable. Such displays, they feel, will exhibit all that is faulty or unworthy about them. Their deadly flaw (primarily their attachment to being seen in a negative light) binds them to these old emotional impressions of themselves.

The bored person is another personality type who is under the influence of his visual drive or emotional imagination. Despite his existence in a dynamic and thrilling world, the bored person is like a magician able to create feelings of emptiness and nothingness out of thin air. He can be quite determined unconsciously to empty his emotional imagination of content and to shut it down, in order to heighten the sense of deprivation, refusal, and emptiness. When a person is chronically bored, he is preoccupied, even obsessed, with the impression that he is *not getting* or that he is being denied some sort of pleasure or satisfaction. His attachment to "not getting" is the core of his deadly flaw, a feeling he unconsciously creates through the meagerness of his imagination and visual intake.

Boredom is a widespread condition, a "quiet desperation" that most sufferers take for granted. They do not always register the sense of it with acuity or even complain about it. If the boredom is painful enough, however, they can certainly become chronic complainers. They may also become desperate fun-seekers and lose their powers of self-regulation, becoming reckless and compulsive, trying to avoid their boredom.

Obviously, a person who is chronically bored can greatly limit the possibilities for his life. The problem can be resolved by exposing boredom's roots in his attachments to the pain of deprivation and refusal. The opposite of boredom is concentrated enthusiasm in one field, or a pleasing interest, involving an ability to record and monitor one's satisfaction, in a range of different experiences.

Boredom itself is a defense. The following example shows how the defense works when boredom stems from a secret attachment to deprivation. The defense states (unconsciously), "I'm not looking for the feeling of deprivation. The problem is, there is nothing on this plate (in my world) that interests me." So the individual unwittingly declines, at a great price to his happiness, to record or appreciate the beauty and pleasure the world has to offer. Seeing through this defense is a major step in dissolving the visual block.

Boredom can also be an unconscious defense to ward off the inner critic, which looks for "incriminating" material to punish the individual. This defense consists of throwing the baby out with the bathwater, clearing the psychic chamber of its vitality. It's a preventive method of "proving" that "I'm a good person." If all "dangerous and incriminating" material is removed from the psychic chamber, the inner critic has no evidence with which to condemn the individual.[30] This defense may neutralize the inner aggression, but a life of boredom is the individual's end in this devil's bargain.

Being a funny person is usually an admirable quality. But it can have its not-so-funny side. Humor in itself is a source of much pleasure. It also is, Bergler wrote, "a necessary and healthy internal debunking process and therefore a fear-reducing process . . ."[31] He believed that humor is directed at "internal powers" more so than "external powers."[32]

The class clown or comic person, or the professional comedian, has made a fine art of deflecting or neutralizing reproaches from the inner critic by reducing them to absurdity. Because he practices inner protection through wit, irony, and sarcasm, his inner defensiveness, if he is verbally adroit, can carry over to his persona and can make him a star comic or at least a sparkling personality. While he can deflect or confound the inner critic in this manner, he can't overthrow it and emerge from under its authority.

Some self-esteem is gained through this personality trait, yet the individual's emotional life is unstable. Many famous comedians have died young from self-abuse or have committed suicide because their use of comic humor as a defense finally collapsed in the face of intense inner conflict.

The humorist often presents "artificial victims" to his inner critic. As substitutes for himself, his jokes describe bunglers who make fools of themselves.

Another variation is to make a fool or an object of derision of oneself. The defense works because the individual gets social approval—laughs—for it. This is the Rodney Dangerfield self-derision persona. He got laughs, as well as validation for his comic skills, because people are happy to see someone other than themselves—the victim who parodies himself—dangling on the butt-end of the joke. This applies, too, to the "insult comedy" of Don Rickles and the "big oaf" persona of Jackie Gleason. Many of Jay Leno's and David Letterman's jokes produce instant glee from the audience's feeling of "superiority" over the derided victim. The glee expresses our momentary triumph over our inner critic.

Personality traits of the negative variety (such as being an angry, needy, or greedy person), while symptoms of the deadly flaw, produce suffering in themselves. Simultaneously, the traits are also defenses covering up the flaw. For example, a greedy person suffers for his greedy feelings with guilt and with the chronic sense of being deprived. At the same time, the greed *covers up* or *defends against* his realization that the source of his greed is his emotional addiction to feelings of being deprived, refused, or denied. The greed provides "evidence" for his defense in its claim that he really wants to get, rather than to "not get." He may admit that he is indeed a greedy person, thereby employing the defense of pleading guilty to the lesser crime. But he will not likely volunteer the fact that he's emotionally addicted to deprivation, which in psychic accounting is the greater crime (the deadly flaw).

When chronic anger becomes a personality trait, the anger, too, is both a defense and a symptom. As a defense, reactive anger (say at being rejected or criticized) is expressed for the purpose of covering up one's deadly flaw, in this case one's unconscious willingness to indulge in feeling rejected or criticized. This anger is also a symptom because it becomes a painful and self-defeating experience in itself. Much more will be said about our defenses in later chapters.

Chapter 6
Contaminating Our Senses

We possess a function that psychoanalysis calls the *visual drive.* It refers to our ability and our tendency to imagine or to visualize events, situations, ourselves, and other people—whether in the past, present, or future.[33] Instead of using the clinical term, visual drive, I refer to this function as the *emotional imagination.* This term incorporates a consideration of the quality of our visual and imaginative experiences, as determined by the pleasure principle and by the deadly flaw.

The flaw regularly spoils our everyday experiences by contaminating our emotional imagination and our visual function. Instead of seeing clearly, we see, as in Corinthians, through a glass darkly.

Ideally, our emotional imagination is a source of inspiration, pleasure, and creativity. However, much of the time our perceptions and visualizations are colored or contaminated by the deadly flaw, which is determined to make its presence felt. We make an unconscious choice to surrender our emotional imagination to the negative side. Or, if we prefer to whitewash our role in these hidden dynamics, we might say that our emotional imagination has been hijacked by the deadly flaw. It's more truthful, I believe, to acknowledge that we're the ones who surrender our emotional imagination to the negative side. It helps us to overcome the deadly flaw when we take responsibility for our unconscious choices.

Most people are unaware of how they can be using their emotional imagination as a tool for creating defenses and for suffering. The emotional imagination becomes an inner torture machine, and we don't see our own connivance with this arrangement. It's not that we are weak-willed. The knowledge we need to avoid such suffering has simply not been widely available, mainly because of collective resistance to letting go of the old familiar model of humanity we know so well.

Those plagued by a renegade emotional imagination include worriers, cynics, perfectionists, jealous and envious types, many kinds of phobic people, shy people, the politically and religiously intolerant, racists, sexists, terrorists, and the bored and depressed. The careers and happiness of just about anyone can be impeded by a dysfunctional emotional imagination, including writers, in the case of writer's block.[34]

One way to understand our misuse of the emotional imagination is through a widespread activity people frequently engage in called *negative peeping*. This term is indeed a bit odd, with a quirky sexual connotation. But it usually has nothing to do with sex.

Negative peeping explains much of the negative operations of the emotional imagination. This peeping involves the use of our imagination or our eyes to produce and absorb scenes or impressions that feed, activate, and recycle our negative attachments. This peeping can also be employed to establish and strengthen defenses against attachments to negative emotions. Most people can fall prey at times to negative peeping. For many, it's an unconscious compulsion.

A person walking, say, through a mall or a park can be secretly peeping at people to whom he or she can feel inferior. At the same time, this person can be unconsciously noting those people to whom he or she can feel *superior,* which is still a negative way of perceiving since it involves a secret willingness to identify emotionally with the one who is seen as inferior. Hence, the peeper can be secretly identifying with the person who he sees as inferior, or the peeper can feel inferior to the one he sees as superior. The peeper's sense of self is trapped between these negative impressions, with nowhere to go. He is also peeping when he looks into the mirror and sees, in his own reflection, someone who he feels is flawed or defective in some way. That is how, through the deadly flaw, *he secretly wants to feel about himself.* Such peeping constitutes a compulsion to see oneself in a negative light. A vain person is someone who, on the surface, sees himself in a superior way. Deeper in his psyche, though, he is covering up attachments to being seen in a negative light or to the feeling of having little or no importance.

As another example, a person with anxiety about attending social events frequently imagines that others ignore him or look down on him at such events, though in reality that would likely happen only if he were to behave inappropriately. Before going to a social event, he may for several days or weeks peep into the future, visualizing himself at the event and being seen there by others in a negative light. This peeping can be unconscious or conscious. Even if it is conscious, the individual is unlikely to be aware that he is secretly wishing to be immersed in that feeling of being seen in a negative light. He is activating and recycling the painful feeling in advance of the event. Yet he doesn't see or understand the inner processing whereby he is generating his anxiety or tension.

One friend, a covert peeper, was a sharp-eyed reader of bumper stickers. He was quick to express indignation at the mentality of the various points of view. One day he angrily vowed to join the gun-control lobby after seeing three bumper stickers in one day that read, "God, Guts, and Guns." He didn't realize he was secretly looking for offense in these aphorisms.

Another peeper, a client, was a bird-watcher. She loved to camp on weekends alone on one of Florida's small deserted coastal islands and check out the bird life through powerful binoculars. On the mainland she was a workaholic who was convinced that people found her to be inadequate or unworthy. The deserted island became her great escape where no eyes could look at her. No one was around to see her as she felt herself to be on the mainland—fat and inadequate. Her peeping served as an inner defense that said in so many words: "I don't secretly indulge in the feeling of being looked at and judged. See how much I like it here where no one sees me. Besides, I am not passively attached to being seen critically; I am the one who actively does the seeing. And I like what I see." She felt thrilled in appreciating the birds, but by doing so in this instance she concocted a defense called a *magic gesture.* In this defense, she gave a feeling of value and worth to the birds for the purpose of claiming that such validation was what she really wanted for herself. All the while, of course, she was covering up the deep hurt of (and secret appetite for) feeling unworthy.

Another peeper I knew was a nudist. She too had a core issue involving an unconscious attachment to being seen as less than others. She was an attractive woman who nonetheless also felt her body was fat and unappealing. At the nudist beaches, she preferred to sit instead of striding about, as she watched and evaluated others on the basis of physical appearance and personality. Whenever she stood up and walked around, she became very conscious of the eyes of others upon her. It felt as if they were sizing her up as somehow lacking or disappointing. Not surprisingly, she felt more relaxed at an inland nudist camp where older, "more forgiving" people gathered, instead of at the Club-Med style colony on the coast where the young and beautiful congregated.

In her office, she found herself peeping at co-workers who frequently gathered together to gossip. She felt they ought to be punished. She peeped in order to identify with them being seen doing something "bad," thereby conjuring up an old feeling from her past. In college, she had been an alcoholic and drug user, and had been tormented by the feeling that her mother, teachers, and classmates saw her as a bad person. Although she no longer abused substances, she still had not worked out this self-defeating attachment to being seen in a negative light. Peeping served her defense in which she claimed she was actively doing the seeing, rather than admit she was "into" being passively seen as defective.

Via the emotional imagination, everyday "normal" people, in various degrees, seek out, promote, create, or misuse present-day circumstances to resurrect feelings associated with unresolved emotional pain from childhood. Doing this, we trap ourselves in the loop of the deadly flaw, and sentence ourselves to diminished self-respect. This happens because we compulsively circulate through our mind and emotions whatever is unresolved from our past, no matter how painful that is.

A primary element in low self-esteem is the feeling of being looked down upon by others as inadequate, unworthy, or flawed. When we are stuck in this painful self-centeredness, we are, through our deadly flaw, recycling within ourselves unresolved feelings involving rejection, criticism, and unworthiness. All of this

75

produces low self-esteem. Through our deadly flaw, we are prepared to entertain feelings of self-criticism, self-rejection, and, in severe cases, self-hatred. Hence, we're also seeing ourselves in a negative light, and our self-esteem is undermined from within. Instead of feeling self-esteem, we flounder in the inner critic's painful self-scrutiny.

Self-esteem is not real unless it includes respect for one's self *and* for others. Without self-respect, we compulsively look outward to feel disrespect toward certain people or individuals, believing in our self-deception that they somehow deserve our disrespect. This gives us a temporary illusion of being superior, but it blocks the development of our self-esteem. Meanwhile, the more we consciously strive to look good in the eyes of others (to the point of becoming, say, a people-pleaser instead of being our own authentic self), the more we secretly are expecting and experiencing the feeling of being seen and judged as being unworthy, having no value, or lacking in basic qualities.

Instead of seeing and appreciating another person, the typical negative peeper is instead "seeing" how he thinks that person is seeing him. He is entangled emotionally in what others are thinking and feeling as they look back at him. The faces of others are mirrors in which he sees himself, as determined by his deadly flaw. (This is what it means to be self-conscious in a painful way.) Even if the other person is being respectful, the peeper can still feel he is being looked down upon. If the other person is pleasantly curious about him and is asking personal questions of him, he might feel that the questioner is looking for (or will find) something bad to hold against him.

On a conscious level, he's often eager to be seen in a positive light, and he might be desperate for approval. This still covers up his expectation of being seen in a negative light—which, to repeat, is his *secret willingness* to experience himself in that old, unresolved way.

Some women peep at TV and fashion magazines to see images of "Miss Body Beautiful," the slender, buxom female ideal often produced by diet pills, cosmetic artistry, and plastic surgery. Men too, of course, can be wrapped up in physical self-image and dream of being Mr. Irresistible or the reality TV bachelor with bodybuilder muscles and a knockout personality. When men and women do this on a regular basis, they are recycling feelings of self-doubt and self-rejection. They may sense that they are caught up in some negativity, but very seldom do they realize their compulsive determination to seek out and recycle the unresolved emotions that percolate beneath their tension or anxiety. Without this awareness, they can't establish the inner power and consciousness to decline the temptation to operate from the limited intelligence of this old default position.

I remember one client, an office manager, complaining of the lack of respect he got from his assistant manager. Yet when this client looked at his assistant, he expected to see some form of disrespect coming back at him. In fact, the client gave off subliminal messages in his own eyes, face, and body language that reflected that expectation. So he got what he was looking for. His assistant knew it, too, even if unconsciously, and played into what was expected of her. These consequences reveal how we generate dissension and antipathy, and how we miss opportunities for enjoyable affection and respect.

Frequently in romantic encounters we are reacting in part to the approval of ourselves in the eyes of the "beloved." We see in those eyes the "confirmation" of all our virtues. That full and unqualified acceptance of us feels heavenly, for now we have this defense against our mocking, harsh inner critic: "I am not worthless and no good; see how much I am adored in my beloved's eyes." When a couple fails to get beyond the initial infatuation into deeper or more mature love, the bloom fades from the romance, eyes narrow with disappointment, and faces harden with rejection.

Worriers are obvious examples of negative peepers. They peer into the future and become agitated by the worst-case scenarios that their imaginations produce. It is appropriate to plan wisely for the future. But worriers absorb an unpleasant experience *in the present moment* for what has not yet occurred and may never occur. They frequently visualize situations in which they feel helpless and overwhelmed. Worrying becomes a problem for self-regulation of emotions and behaviors, and it is another example of our affinity for suffering.

Because their negative peeping is compulsive, worriers are consequently obsessively involved with what the future holds. Normally, the present moment offers us opportunities to experience pleasure, whether that is appreciating beauty, family, health, and prosperity. The pleasure is enhanced when it is registered or monitored by our consciousness, and at our best we can assimilate with some degree of satisfaction the fact or the wonder of our existence. But the unconscious agenda of worriers overrides the capacity to experience more pleasure. Enjoyment in the present moment is elusive when our secret game is to look for ways to recreate or replay familiar feelings of injustice, neglect, and deprivation, along with the helpless feeling of impending, unavoidable hardship or catastrophe.

Worriers cover up their unconscious participation in the negative experience by rationalizing that they are future-focused in order, ostensibly, to prevent bad things from happening. In reality, they have simply concocted, through negative peeping, a way to suffer in the moment, even when things many otherwise be going well for them.

Many people imagine, especially in troubling economic times, that the future holds only more hardship, loss, and deprivation. People can use tough economic times as an excuse to feel their attachments to deprivation and helplessness more intensely. A person who is constantly worried that something bad will happen to his investments is entangled in a secret attachment to loss and deprivation, possibly in combination with an attachment to the feeling of the helplessness to which he imagines such loss will reduce him. It is not logical to suffer now, in the present moment, for what might never happen (and is often *unlikely* to happen) in the future. We don't know what the future holds. If we are strong emotionally, we accept that uncertainty, and we take care of our responsibilities in the present, drawing from the present moment all the healthy pleasures we can and trusting that we can rise to future challenges.

Peeping becomes sexual with Peeping Toms and with people who consume pornography. A Peeping Tom ostensibly seeks the sight of naked women as he invades their privacy. Yet his compulsive behavior is really driven by his yearning to experience the female's alleged "refusal" to show or exhibit herself. He defends against this realization with acute disappointment when, as typically happens, he fails in his neighborhood prowling to observe nudity. People who are addicted to pornography can be reacting to a variety of secret attachments, including a willingness to feel passively blocked from experiencing sexual pleasure in a loving relationship.

While worriers peep into the future, others peep into the past, among them cynics, the embittered, and those full of regret or painful nostalgia. As they peep into the past, they conjure up the hurts and injustices—

real or imagined—that they have secretly endured and are willing to continue to endure. They mourn the opportunities they have missed. They hold on to grudges and grievances like aristocrats hold on to the family jewels. These unhappy memories fuel their unconscious willingness to scan the past to indulge in old hurts and injustices. Such people can be very offended if someone suggests they're suffering unnecessarily. They're convinced their suffering is validated by the "grievous" injustices they have endured or the "unforgivable" mistakes they have made.

Through negative peeping we can sometimes sabotage ourselves by refusing to see reality because reality has negative connotations for us. Jason, an oil painter, had struggled through his career trying to raise his skill level in order to be more successful. He realized that he had not been evaluating his own work objectively enough to spot the flaws and weaknesses in his paintings. In a session he said, with some amazement, "Months later I look at a piece and I say, 'How did I miss that flaw. Look at that hand. It's all wrong. How come I didn't see that before?'"

I knew from our earlier sessions that Jason felt his father had regarded him as a disappointment. He pointed to the fact that his father had been very concerned that he didn't have the talent to make a living as an artist. I told Jason, "You have an unconscious wish to believe that your paintings lack value and don't measure up. It's as if you see your artwork through your father's eyes. You immediately try to cover up or defend against your secret wish to see your art as inferior. Consciously, you claim that your paintings are good or good enough. Unconsciously, your defense contends, 'I don't want to see my work as flawed. I want to see it as good. See how much I like what I see.' With this defense, however, you lose your objectivity. You blind yourself to the defects because, emotionally, you see the defects in such a self-critical way."

Jason was highly critical of the art produced by his contemporaries. He felt aggressively critical when he visited art galleries or looked through art magazines. "Not only do you secretly want to see your work as lacking in quality," I told him, "but in your negative peeping you also wish to see the work of your contemporaries as better than yours. This impression deepens your willingness to feel unworthy, inferior, even valueless. To cover this up, you claim unconsciously, 'I don't passively want to see their work as better than mine. I aggressively see their work as inferior. I see all their defects, and I don't like what they produce."

Jason's misuse of his emotional imagination had prevented him from enjoying his work more and from improving his art. He hadn't been able to get past this creative block because of his deadly flaw. As he became conscious of his inner program of self-defeat, he became a more accomplished, successful artist.

Artistic and intellectual benefits are available through self-awareness as well as through successful sublimation. When the emotional imagination is successfully sublimated, or diverted into positive channels, this tendency can shift in time to intellectual curiosity. This curiosity, Bergler stated, "underlies the individual's characteristic interest in adding to his store of general knowledge, as well as to his understanding of intellectual problems."[35] Here, the pleasure principle is invoked to support an activity that is in our best interests.

Chapter 7
Born to Falsify

One of their great hurts my clients have expressed to me over the years concerns their sense that their parents failed to recognize or appreciate them at some deep, essential level. They felt taken for granted. Sometimes they even felt invisible.

More than likely, their parents experienced the same lack of recognition or appreciation from their own parents. We can't appreciate each other more fully if we don't know our own self more deeply. Self-understanding is a form of intimacy or connection with one's self. To establish that intimacy, it helps to know more about the experience of our early childhood beyond our first memories.

People don't remember those early months or the first few years of life. That time seems lost to us, like human experience before recorded history. But this vitally important time shapes the course of our lives. It's not that we have to remember a bunch of details about this period. Rather, we have to understand how we likely experienced it. How is it that we know so little about that experience? In this chapter we plunge into early childhood to understand more about the conditions that gave life to our deadly flaw.

It's true that babies do not speak up to verbalize their experiences (except for crying or laughing). But shouldn't psychology or science have produced by now a widely accepted explanation that represents the common experience of childhood? Details differ from person to person, but much of what each child feels is common to us all. Yet even college-educated people shrug their shoulders when asked what they might have felt in the period before their first conscious memories of childhood. They assume there isn't much to tell and that it couldn't possibly matter.

Bergler's approach, like Freud's, honors the perception of the child and gives the child an interior life, even as it explores the child's irrationality. Whatever disagreement one might have with Bergler's perspective of the child's experience, he does give the child a voice. He provides a child-centered narrative of that early experience and speaks to the richness of inner life.

Obviously, the child is experiencing situations and events very subjectively. How could it be otherwise? Even adults struggle to be objective about life and to see things clearly. The child is contending with a whirlwind of impressions, including helplessness and the drives of megalomania, aggression, and libido, as well as a world that is imposing its reality from without.[36]

Most of us presume that the child is trying his or her best to figure out reality. Not so, said Bergler. The child, instead, is interested in denying reality. The child especially does not want to recognize his or her helplessness, or to give up pronounced self-centeredness. The child associates reality with the requirement that he abdicate his illusory throne. "The child's entire inner development," Bergler stated, "is directed, not towards objectivity, but towards its opposite. It is hardly an exaggeration to reproduce the infant's inner battle cry as, 'Falsify reality!'"[37] Objectivity is a rare and precious attribute among adults, he said, because of the leftover effect of having managed with some success in early childhood to deny reality.

Societies, too, can have difficulty accepting unpleasant realties from the past. For instance, histories of the United States have not always given a full account of slavery or the displacement and killing of Native Americans.

 Residues of that infantile intention to falsify reality remain in our psyche and doom us to operate below our intellectual ability. Through our defenses, we also block from our awareness the dynamics of our psyche's operating system. The resulting self-sabotage, which includes adult incompetence, stems from *psychogenic restriction of intelligence,* which was Bergler's clinical term for widespread intellectual mediocrity.[38] An aspect of this failure of intelligence includes our resistance to peering into our psyche for fear we will discover evidence that we have no substance or value. Or we are fearful that what is inside us is not just worthless but possibly "bad" or forbidden. Hence, we stubbornly insist, in a display of restricted intelligence, that the unconscious mind couldn't be a significant influence in our lives.

The quest to falsify reality, Bergler believed, starts with the child's acute self-centeredness. This self-centeredness incorporates the baby's "belief" or instinctive conclusion that he or she is self-sufficient as well as all-powerful.[39] This perception is, of course, totally contrary to actual facts. Rather than being self-sufficient and all-powerful, children are entirely dependent on their mothers or caregivers. However, it's entirely logical that babies would prefer to be stabilized in a perception or experience of power, which is pleasurable, rather than in an acknowledged helplessness, which must be for them, as with adults, an unpleasant or painful feeling.

Feeling power also provides an illusion of safety. That illusion might be a psychological (or even biological) survival mechanism for babies that strengthens their will to live and bolsters their immune system.

What instinctive conclusions, given their ignorance of objective facts, can babies draw from their postnatal state of affairs? According to Bergler, babies soon begin to take everything for granted. Along with their sense of self-sufficiency,[40] they live in a state of oneness, meaning they don't or can't acknowledge that their mother or anything else exists or is operating independently of them. Nevertheless, onrushing reality keeps intruding, leading infants once again "to say no to reality" to protect their illusion of being all-powerful.

Months later the "outside world" breaks through. It introduces babies to the sense of their dependence on their mothers, thereby contradicting the fantasy of self-sufficiency. Forced to modify their distortions of reality, babies concede that things or objects do indeed exist outside of themselves. But now they believe these things are subject to their powers. Mother becomes an instrument of their magic power. Babies wake up hungry and cry, their magic signal, and mother appears with the breast or bottle, confirming their omnipotence. Babies lying in their crib reach up for an object and caregivers hand them a toy, again confirming it.

Babies and young children are constantly making inner modifications or reassessments in order to maintain the illusion of power. The process resembles the procedure in a court of law when a lawyer, without changing his intent, rephrases a question after his opponent objects to it and the judge sustains the objection.[41]

The next troublemaker to challenge the child is inborn aggression (I elaborate here on the earlier mention of the subject). Aggression is a natural drive and a survival requirement of our species. Early humans had to be very aggressive to protect themselves from dangerous animals, hunt wild game, and survive. The emotional intensity of a child's aggression is comparable to what he will feel as an adult.[42] When we become toddlers, our natural aggression starts to build up like water behind a dam. Toddlers can't release all this aggression into the environment, in part because of their undeveloped muscular system. The aggression requires an outlet, and, having nowhere else to go, turns against the child as self-aggression. This leads to the formation of the child's superego (commonly referred to as the inner critic), which establishes itself as an authoritarian inner voice.

Some of the baby's natural aggression, however, does erupt into the environment. The aggression is triggered when babies' "commands" are not instantly or at least quickly carried out by their caregivers. Bergler wrote, "The only controllable organ of any power is his [the baby's] mouth, and therefore he resorts to crying, spitting, or vomiting, in order to maintain his 'constitutional' right to object."[43]

Waiting for mother, as she hurries about the house with other work or attends to other children, seems like eternity to baby who has no way to assess the relativity of time. Affronted by a wait of just a few moments, the child's beleaguered self-centeredness erupts in frustration. His aggression builds in mounting fury. Each minute of waiting seems endless and is another attack on his fantasy of being all-powerful.

The child believes, through his acute self-centeredness and in his attempts to preserve it, that whatever happens is what he wants. This process of turning displeasure into pleasure—again, the verb from classical psychoanalysis is "to libidinize"—was first mentioned in Chapter 4 with respect to feelings of refusal. Here we see the process again, except now it is self-aggression that is libidinized or sugar-coated, hence made agreeable, acceptable, and even desirable (though, as mentioned, the second-rate pleasure is unconscious).

The aggression that the baby can't fully expend outward ends up flooding his psyche. His sense, at this point, is that the aggression rebounding against him must be what he wishes to feel. His acute self-centeredness excludes any other explanation. Through his pleasure principle, as constituted in libido, he uses the power of wish and will to make the self-aggression into a perverse but acceptable caricature of pleasure.[44] (*Perverse* is used in the clinical, not pejorative, sense.) This faulty inner processing is, in a sense, a kind of survival reaction—it's a way to manage and to survive the onslaught of self-aggression. Temporarily, it's a clever stratagem, but it's self-defeating in the long run.

Many adults are passive to the aggression and dominance of others, at the same time that they can react passive-aggressively to it. Such individuals feel controlled and threatened, anxious and fearful. This distress is precipitated by our defenses which cover up our underlying willingness to absorb both self-aggression and the aggression of others. When we absorb aggression, we "go negative" within ourselves.

90

We feel this negativity as a form of suffering (often as resentment or paralyzing passivity), while we convince ourselves that we're innocent victims of the malice of others.

The dynamic of projection, another unconscious psychic operation, comes into play. In *projection*, one expels an unacceptable feeling from oneself and attributes that feeling to another person. In the months before babies become aware of mother's loving kindness, they project their own aggression on to her. This creates the illusion that mother is the aggressive one. Babies now experience her as a dispenser of malice. This "wild distortion," as Bergler called it, creates the fantasy that everything "good" comes from themselves and everything "bad" from the outside, namely mother.

Many adults remain fixated on this idea that they need protection from something "bad" outside themselves, and they look for certain targets to identify as bad. In America, the effect of this lingering irrationality can be seen in the population who believe, on the political Right, that everything bad comes from the government and, on the Left, from private interests and corporations. Adults project their aggression to outsiders and experience them as being hostile or malicious. This lingering infantile mentality is marked by emotionalism, aggression, entitlement, and close-mindedness. In American society, certain media pundits gain followings by reinforcing this mentality, claiming that the "bad" (elites or the government, for instance) comes from outside us. Passive, naïve people gawk at these media theatrics as they absorb the aggression, negativity, and sense of victimization. On a broader scale, certain countries or states, under the collective influence of this infantile mind, see only danger and malice from the world beyond their borders.

The baby, now convinced that aggression is coming at him from mother, acquires baby fears, which include fears of starvation as well as fears of being devoured, poisoned, castrated, choked, drained, dropped, crushed, and flushed down the toilet. Bergler stated that, over time, the mother's smile and love were powerful reassurances to the child that she would not harm him or her.[45] Most adult fears, which can be relatively easily aroused by perceived dangers in the environment, are irrationally based inner fears left over from childhood. These inner fears can produce painful exaggerated fears of crime, terrorism, poverty, accidents, ill health, and damnation.

The child gradually experiences a grudging realization that mother is a generous provider upon whom he or she is dependent. However, this dependence continues to offend the fantasy of self-sufficiency. In addition, it becomes clear that mother expects gratitude and love from the child. The child faces three powerful forms of retribution for defiance of mother's authority: punishment, moral reproach, and inner guilt. The child suffers more, and is plagued with this retribution as well as the designation of being a "bad child," when he or she continues to deny reality. "It is the essence of the human tragedy," Bergler stated, "that the child is forced into making his 'masochistic decision' when his reasoning powers are still undeveloped, if present at all, and that all the countermeasures of love, kindness, friendliness, bestowed upon him by his mother have little influence upon unconscious events."[46]

Will the child compromise or not? To what degree will the child modify his or her fantasies? Most children will sublimate their aggression, modify the acute self-centeredness, and shift in diplomatic ways. Other children will not do so successfully. Even children who are shifting to reality still have struggles with the deadly flaw because it is established so early in life. However, children who do not make the shift, or who make it to a lesser degree, will be more entrenched in suffering.

At this point, genetics and the quality of parenting can be contributing factors in how successfully children shift to an acceptance of reality. Parents' tender love can help a child to "save face" when the child's narcissism is offended by incoming reality. "This does not mean," Bergler wrote, "that the parents can 'determine' by means of their own conduct whether or not their child will accept the reality principle, and choose normal rather than neurotic solutions for his infantile conflicts. A child can develop a neurosis in spite of a happy family life . . ."[47]

Those children who stubbornly maintain acute self-centeredness are likely to flagrantly violate parental edicts and be punished for it with guilt and moral reproach. The pleasure principle remains a strong instinct, even when such willful stubbornness produces suffering. Hence, children seek further masochistic "solutions" to their untenable situations. The weapons of parental authority—moral reproach, guilt, and punishment—are made perversely pleasurable by means of libido in conjunction with this deduction: "Mother may be punishing me, but I, through my naughty behavior, *cause it to happen*." Emotional satisfaction is generated through this perverse calculation. Children may consciously feel a kind of inner glee in this illusion of power, though as adults we remember little or nothing of having produced any such second-rate pleasure. This defensive maneuver preserves acute self-centeredness, as it produces the perverse pleasure-in-displeasure.

Sexual masochism, which is a conscious experience of displeasure becoming pleasure, is the tip of the psychological iceberg, a hint of the secret, non-sexual problem of the deadly flaw lurking beneath the surface.[48] The feeling of inner passivity is libidinized as overt sexual arousal by pedophiles, meaning they achieve some of their sexual pleasure through their identification with the helplessness of the victimized child. The sexual arousal of sexual masochists and pedophiles clearly reveals the libidinization of the negative emotion of inner passivity (see Chapter 16).

To repeat, children who refuse to compromise do find a solution they can live with. That solution is to take displeasure (which includes the guilt for their misconduct) and, by force of wish and will, turn it into a perverse pleasure that is registered semi-consciously. This maintains vestiges of the illusion of power, as the emphasis is shifted from the passively endured mother's punishment to the child's pseudo-aggressive provocations and naughtiness. The child feels that he or she still has the power and that mother is doing nothing but reacting to that power. Once again, the thought is, "She punishes me, but I *make* her do it!"

The child, by taking perverse pleasure in his or her alleged power, minimizes or nullifies the punishment rendered. Refusal, rejection, and guilt all acquire pleasurable undertones. Willing this perverse gratification into existence through libido constitutes the origins of the deadly flaw. Our flaw comes into being as a configuration in our psyche before the end of the second year of life. Our flaw is "wired" in our psyche, and it will reformulate itself into a sophisticated structure of accusations, vetoes, defenses, and compromises—all capable of producing behavioral and emotional self-defeat—as a person ages. Nevertheless, it can be "unwired," meaning we can update the old "software" or operating system, as we become conscious of it.

Bergler frequently argued in support of his theory that individuals who, as children, had experienced refusal and rejection from their parents would logically be expected to marry generous and loving partners.[49] The opposite is true. These individuals repeat the painful impressions of childhood, whether objectively or subjectively experienced, by marrying partners who are similar to their parents in this respect. Sometimes this arrangement is reversed, and the person who felt refused and rejected as a child becomes the adult who now refuses and rejects his partner. Either way, the individual suffers with feelings of refusal and rejection. Some experts have suggested we find such partners because we are interested in resolving the original hurt. But that is not so. Unconsciously, we do not seek resolution. Instead, we want to repeat and recycle what is unresolved, even when doing so is painful. Freud recognized this human trait and called it *the repetition compulsion.*

As adults, our negative emotions circulate within us, spilling out into our families and society. As we age, the suffering often intensifies as regrets, bitterness, and painful memories. Without the vital knowledge of the deadly flaw's existence and its modes of operation, we can't see into the heart of our suffering.

We are willing to live with this flaw, despite the suffering it causes, because it incorporates a substantial sense of how we know ourselves. We operate at a level where "our suffering and our symptoms are us." They are the ingredients of our identity, and they include stubbornness, righteousness, defensiveness, egotism, and a fear of (or aversion to) self-reflection.

We also suffer with self-pity, poor self-regulation, inner passivity, and sensitivity to refusal, criticism, and rejection. Meanwhile, we feel no benefit from the unconscious pleasure-in-displeasure we have created. When confronted with the evidence of it in a therapy process, we can feel both our (mental) willingness to accept it as true and our (emotional) reluctance to let go of it.

Our deadly flaw is our secret determination to recycle negative emotions not for resolution, but because we are compelled to experience repeatedly what is unresolved. This determination to suffer represents much of the resistance and the difficulty we have in achieving personal growth and social progress. The prognosis, though, is not grim. It's highly optimistic. Just a thin veil separates us from a higher level of consciousness.

Chapter 8
To Get or Not to Get

The pursuit of *un*happiness is often driven by oral issues. These issues compel us to feel that our needs and desires are constantly unfulfilled.

Adults contend with oral issues on a physical level—as in cravings for junk food, sugar, alcohol, and cigarettes. Oral issues also confront us on an emotional level—as when we feel deprived, refused, and distressed about "not getting" in relation to love, excitement, material objects, and social connections.

The more desperately we crave substances and experiences, the more anxiety we have about "not getting." It's the distress of "not getting," rather than the pleasure of "getting," that so often produces a materialistic mentality and bouts of unhappiness.

Oral issues creep around in economics, politics, culture, and lifestyles like spiders in the basement. These issues lurk behind drug addiction, alcoholism, eating disorders, and shopping compulsions. They're also evident in our general dissatisfactions with life. Someone's distress, for instance, that the stock market isn't favoring his or her investments isn't always solely about the money. The distress can be caused in part by a willingness to feel that the world itself is refusing to support one's needs or aspirations. This attitude is reflected in the sentiment, "Nothing works out for me, and no one cares."

Oral issues made it possible to produce economic systems in the United States and other developed countries that were based on consumerism. American marketing and advertising acquired its effectiveness from psychoanalytic insight, starting with Edward Bernays (1891-1995), a nephew of Sigmund Freud's, who was a pioneer of public manipulation. He had a long career in New York City and became known as the "father of public relations."[50] According to his obituary, ". . . he was instrumental in making it acceptable for women to smoke in public . . . on behalf of the American Tobacco Company's Lucky Strike cigarettes . . . The cigarettes were even called 'torches of freedom.' On behalf of Lucky Strike, Mr. Bernays also undertook to alter women's fashions. When surveys showed that women objected to Luckies because the green package with its red bull's-eye clashed with the colors of their clothes, he swung into action to make green fashionable. There followed a green fashion luncheon, green balls (at which green gowns were worn), and window displays of green suits and dresses. The campaign was a brilliant success, according to sales figures."[51]

Psychological manipulation that sells more cigarettes and junk food plays on a great human weakness. We have considerable issues and repressed memories involving oral satisfaction, dissatisfaction, stimulation, and eroticism. Feeding for most infants, whether by breast or bottle, is enormously gratifying. This is followed by huge disappointment, if not a sense of tragedy, when the breast is lost through weaning. As adults, we experience food as an oral pleasure, and often as a way to fill an inner void, provide emotional comfort, and repress anxious feelings. At the same time, many of us feel agonized and tortured with impressions of food deprivation and struggles with self-regulation. It is through the oral function, as well, that much sexual excitement is experienced.

Cigarette smoking is something of a parody on oral fixation. Smokers puff frantically on something that gives them decreasing satisfaction as it risks their health. On the surface, it appears they want to get oral satisfaction, but their compulsive smoking, while also a physical addiction, displays their apparent willingness to experience a situation in which their pleasures are declining in value. Cigarette smoking is driven by the illusion of getting. The behavior becomes perverse and irrational, providing little pleasure for its expense and its dangerous side-effects. It is also a passive way, as is alcohol or drug abuse, to commit aggression against oneself. Here it becomes entangled with the previously mentioned death instinct, the mysterious human capacity for self-destruction. Aggression against oneself is hidden behind the addiction. That means that an unconscious willingness to suffer from self-abuse is as much part of the problem as the physical addition itself. In other words, it may be that libidinized self-aggression makes cigarette smoking an emotional as well as a physical addiction. (To understand the concept of libidinized self-aggression, it helps to recall the child's perverse satisfaction when he or she claims, "I, through my naughty behavior, make mother punish me").

Smoking involves another self-defeating dynamic relating to the deadly flaw. Many smokers claim they get pleasure from their habit. But any "pleasure" that is so self-damaging is likely to be "libidinized displeasure." This means, in this context, that an illusion of pleasure is produced to cover up one's unconscious willingness to indulge in feelings of "not getting" or of inner emptiness. The defense of smoking proclaims, "I'm not interested in feeling orally deprived or emotional emptiness. Look how much I enjoy smoking."

This same mechanism applies to problems of weight gain and obesity. Because of plentiful, relatively cheap food, people can use food to produce the same defense: "I'm not interested in feeling orally deprived or emotional emptiness. Look how much I love my food." We produce defenses to cover up our indulgence in deep negativity, and they are typically self-defeating and self-damaging. Since our defenses are acts of desperation to cover up our participation in our suffering and self-defeat, the behaviors and feelings they produce tend to spin out of control.

Meanwhile, our unresolved oral issues induce us to see the world with want rather than with wonder. We become drawn to commercial images or messages that play on our unhappiness and inner dissatisfactions. Soon we're feeling entitlement instead of gratitude, as consumerism becomes materialism's religious observance. Consumerism's pervasive advertising can easily invade our emotional and mental space to serve its purposes. Instant gratification is the sweetener in oral craving. Consumerism's enjoy-now, pay-later ethos likely contributed to the "financialization" of the economy and conceivably to its instability.

The entitlement mentality is steeped in the acute self-centeredness of early childhood: "If I want it, I am entitled to it." Hence, to not have it, or to imagine oneself without it, feels like deprivation, refusal, and loss. Through our defenses, we need to get, or at least (in an example of how our defenses can befuddle us) we need frantically to want to get in order to "prove" that we don't want "to *not* get." The resulting materialism can entangle us in the frustration of shallow values and makes us more indifferent or oblivious of others.

The degree of *want* is directly related to our level of negativity and the problem of the deadly flaw. A person with less negativity is more attuned to inner value and goodness. This person does not experience this intangible want, this longing or inner emptiness, or else he or she experiences this negativity to a lesser degree.

To become free of this negativity, we expose how, in our own psyche, it is produced or generated by the deadly flaw.

An individual free of oral conflict is able to feel satisfied and fulfilled with simple things. He or she can generate a great deal of pleasure from inner harmony, a sense of connecting to a valuable authentic self, and an appreciation of life itself. We use and appreciate material things and the byproducts of technology, but these do not become objects of commodity fetishism. We do not surrender our souls to the products of our mind.

To understand oral fixation, consider some of the ways that personal unhappiness is expressed: "Nothing good ever happens to me," or "If only I had that (whatever), then I would be happy," or "Life is boring—nothing here interests me." With such shallow consciousness, money and merchandise often became our primary indicators of personal worth. Money, merchandise, food, and love can be indistinguishable to the psyche—it's easy to feel deprived of one and all. We often feel urgency or impatience about getting our desired object (the entitlement mentality), a longing that serves as "evidence" that we really do want to get rather than, through the deadly flaw, indulge in deprivation and refusal. This makes us prey to a financial system that sells us credit at exorbitant rates to facilitate these infantile conflicts.

It's not material abundance that's at issue here. Having abundance and prosperity is a good thing. However, when our unconscious attachments to deprivation, refusal, and loss remain unrecognized, abundance is more likely to be taken for granted, if it can even be achieved in a stable manner. When we crave material things to cover up our emotional affinity for deprivation, our cravings can override the need to protect the environment, be generous to one another, and maintain economic stability.

Many people believe that good feelings require the stimulus of outside agents, events, or situations. Their bad feelings, they also perceive, come from others or outside circumstances. The problem is a kind of "empty-plate disorder." Seeing one's life as an empty plate becomes even more painful when contrasted with the plates of others that are heaped, as our envy perceives it, with all kinds of benefits and rewards.

--

Larry's story illustrates oral conflicts as well as problems of low self-esteem. A 40-year-old real-estate agent, he revealed the following information about himself in our first session. He was depressed and crying a lot, feeling sorry for himself, and worried about his finances. A business he owned had failed a year or so earlier. His wife worked only part-time, since she had to be available for their young son. "I'm feeling like a deadbeat," he said, "and dreadful about not being able to take better care of my family."

His mother had died four months earlier, and he was "devastated." He cried daily over the loss of his mother. (Some adults idealize their parents, in part to make it easier to repress painful feelings unresolved from childhood.) He had experienced the same kind of feelings for two years following the death of his father several years earlier.

A friend of Larry's had lost his wife and child in a car crash the year before, and Larry was deeply involved emotionally in his friend's tragic loss. Larry said he also spent considerable time brooding about his own son, worrying that his son would grow up without the amenities and advantages of a financially secure family. "I want everything for him," Larry said. "But I'm afraid for him, that he will grow up being deprived." Then he added, "I admit that I have a crummy attitude about life in general."

His problem involved an unconscious fascination with the prospects of loss, missing out, and feeling deprived. He suffered more than was appropriate or healthy following the deaths of his parents. Essentially, he was not grieving so much for them. Instead, he was feeling sorry for himself as he indulged in his own sense of loss. Thus, these experiences of the deaths of his parents were almost entirely self-centered.

He identified with his friend who had lost his wife and child in the car crash, and he thereby slipped into the skin of his friend, vicariously feeling his (Larry's) attachment to loss in this indirect manner. In other words, his "sorrow" was contaminated: It was more about his own readiness to feel loss and to indulge in that feeling than it was an expression of true sorrow or compassion for his friend. When Larry brooded about his son being deprived (well in the future, if at all), he was entangled in the present moment in yet another way to accentuate his own affinity for deprivation and the bleakness of life.

A year earlier, Larry's business had gone into bankruptcy. Such financial loss and business failure are more likely to happen when an individual is flirting emotionally with the prospect of loss. With an attachment such as this, we secretly make use of situations or events to act out and make real the negative emotions we are willing to experience. Such issues obviously place us in greater danger of self-defeat and failure. Some people take greater risks with their investments because doing so "proves" how much they want to get—a defense that covers up their attachment to loss or to "not getting." Our defenses almost always cause us emotional distress and frequently they move us in the direction of self-defeat.

Self-defeat defies common sense. Why would someone like Larry ruin his own chances for success and happiness? Keep in mind that we are dealing with irrational processes and the need to falsify reality. For Larry, his unconscious problem with loss was like having a saboteur as a business partner.

With the feeling of being a "deadbeat," Larry blamed himself for his plight and felt terrible about himself. Frequently, as a defense, a person makes a claim to power ("I cause it to happen") to cover up his passivity, his willingness to indulge in the loss. Making this claim to be a deadbeat produced guilt and shame, and in this way he suffered all the implications of being "a dismal failure." But the root of the problem was his deadly flaw, which in this case was his attachment to feelings of loss and deprivation.

Larry used his emotional imagination to feed his oral conflicts. He occasionally drove through rich neighborhoods lusting after all the luxury he saw. The words *envy* and *covet* capture the essence of his negative peeping (see Chapter 6). A person often covets what he can't have or what is forbidden. The person consumes with his eyes that which is beyond his reach or is unavailable, thereby generating a desire, emptiness, or even an intense pain of longing. We can believe on an emotional level that we do not get the objects of our desire because we're undeserving, unworthy, not good enough—thereby further undermining our self-esteem.

Larry was my client for a few months until he stopped therapy with me. I don't know how much he was helped. With his issues, he would have had to have stayed on longer before I could make any claims to having helped him.

In other examples, a person who compulsively wanders into the kitchen several times a day to peer into the refrigerator is looking for what is *not* there in order to "take a hit" on feeling deprived. Men who gawk at attractive women are pining for what is likely to be unavailable, perhaps also recycling the feeling that they're unworthy of such a prize. A Peeping Tom, as mentioned, is apparently after the sight of naked women, but the bigger "turn-on" is his sugar-coating of their alleged refusal to show themselves. A compulsive gambler secretly has an addiction to the feeling of losing, and he has become (or is in danger of becoming) a *de facto* loser.

Oral issues are involved in the following case. Eileen, a woman in her late forties, was working hard at two jobs, one part-time in a publishing office and the other with her new start-up business, managing a coffee shop. Eileen liked both jobs and was excited to be in business for herself. She had three employees in her coffee shop who were dependable and hard-working, and she felt fortunate to be staying afloat in a difficult economy. Her financial situation, however, did require her to continue with both jobs.

Despite her long hours of work, Eileen was not feeling physically fatigued. Her growing unhappiness had to do with the feeling that she had so little leisure time and that her social life was inhibited and practically non-existent. "I can hardly find time for a movie or for dinner out," she said. The main source of her unhappiness, however, was not the fact that her two jobs prevented her from having more free time. Instead, the problem was her determination to feel deprived. She had recently ended a one-year relationship with a boyfriend, and she was missing his company and friendship. That longing made it easier to feel deprived in all aspects of her life.

Though many moments and situations to feel satisfied presented themselves, Eileen was not registering those opportunities. "I don't even think about doing that," she said. "It's funny how it doesn't occur to me to make a note of that." Her wish to feel deprived overrode the common sense dictum that advises us to appreciate whatever pleasures are available in imperfect situations. She saw the unconscious choice she had been making to conjure up impressions of deprivation. She started "catching herself" in the act of making such choices, and with her new ability to expose what had previously been unconscious she was soon feeling much better.

Another client was struggling with oral issues, as well as a rejection issue (from the later oedipal stage). "I'm beginning to see how, in every way, I set myself up to feel deprived," said Rose. She remembered being six years old when someone caught a rabbit and gave it to her as a pet. "You have to set it free," her stepfather told her, "but I will buy you a rabbit from a pet store." She set the rabbit free, but another one was never purchased. Rose didn't press her stepfather to fulfill his promise. But she never forgot his empty promise as she passively endured the feeling of being deprived and let down.

Another time, Rose's mother baked a delicious pizza. Rose had a piece and then, with her aunt, went off for the afternoon. On their way home, she told her aunt she'd had only one piece of the pizza and was looking forward to having more. At home, the aunt mentioned Rose's anticipation of the pizza to the mother. When the aunt left, the mother slapped Rose across the face and said, "How dare you suggest to your aunt that you are being deprived!"

As Rose grew up, she was always a dieter but was never fat. In fact, she was anorexic for a period, and her weight fell from 105 pounds to 85 pounds following the breakup of a six-year-long romantic relationship. Very occasionally she would binge, which for her meant eating a box of cookies during the course of a day. Mostly, though, she deprived herself of food, and dieted even when she was underweight. She had almost stopped eating completely following the breakup of her relationship. Her loss-of-appetite reaction to rejection was a defense, a way to take control over the rejection, punish herself through deprivation, and cover up her attachments to both rejection and deprivation. Unconsciously, she took this position: "I'm not passively attached to feelings of being refused, denied, and rejected. I'm bad. I cause it all to happen. I do it to myself (stop eating)."

Oral issues can also sabotage a dieter's efforts to lose weight. Losing weight becomes more difficult when, unconsciously, a person uses the reduced food intake as a way to feel deprived. In other words, the reduced food consumption is challenging enough *physically*, but the attempt to lose weight also becomes *emotionally* challenging if the dieter's deadly flaw includes an attachment to deprivation. This emotional challenge can easily be the harder of the two. Because of it, a dieter is going to need to establish a defense that tries to "prove" that he or she wants oral satisfaction, not oral deprivation. This defense, which attempts to "prove" that getting is the real intent, produces cravings for food. Self-defeat is now more likely.

One client used food to illustrate metaphorically the appeal of indulging in his suffering. "It's so tempting, like cookies and milk," he said, grinning sheepishly.

Another indicator of our secret taste for "not getting" is a person's feeling that someone is out to take away his wealth, possessions, loves, or accomplishments. One wealthy client complained harshly about how much his wife "cost" him financially, although he admitted that the cost was considerably less than he spent on himself for hobbies, travel, and entertainment. He realized, in fact, that his negative impression was illogical since his wife was relatively frugal. Nonetheless, he suffered every time he saw (or imagined) her spending a dollar, due to his secret attachment to feeling loss and deprivation.

This is similar to another negative emotion, the feeling of being drained or depleted. Often this attachment takes the form of excessive concern over money. One client, a prosperous businessman, would several times a day count the cash in his wallet, which usually amounted to several hundred dollars. He usually felt the impulse to do this immediately after he had spent a few dollars. He felt anxious about not earning enough, despite his substantial assets and income. Counting cash was his defense to establish how much he hated the feeling of being drained or depleted. The cash reassured him (in a fleeting, minimal way) that he was still solvent and complete. The fact that he would count it all again the next day meant he was continuing to experience this aspect of his deadly flaw, the feeling of being drained and depleted.

People who work hard to get by can make their situation more difficult by using their toil as an excuse to indulge in feeling drained of energy. Their hard work is a realistic drain on their energy, but their secret emotional indulgence in that drained feeling doubles up on the challenge facing them, creating not only less energy but potentially a state of chronic unhappiness.

Substance abusers sometimes say they are partaking of their substance as a reward for something such as "coping with the stress of the day." One compulsive overeater said, "What's the matter with wanting to reward yourself? Isn't that a healthy thing to do?" But when people reward themselves with a self-defeating behavior or substance, their "reward" is obviously double-edged. The need for such a reward is a cover-up or defense against some secret attachment.

One woman, noting that her boyfriend withheld affection and commitment from her, said: "I get the impulse to eat chocolate ice-cream after I spend some time with him." Her need for the ice-cream covered up her deadly flaw, in this case her attachment to the feeling of not getting emotional satisfaction or of feeling devalued. "I want to get (this ice-cream) and give generously to myself," her unconscious defense professes. "That proves I'm not looking to feel deprived or refused."

Chapter 9
The Trials of Being Two

I borrow an expression from paleontology, in reference to early man's ascent, to say that early childhood is also a "cradle of civilization." Knowing what we go through as young children provides a missing link from past to present, from being infantile and irrational to becoming a mature, civilized person.

We can't find happiness and bring peace to the world until we reform what is a primitive *inner* world of drives, defenses, and forbidden and perverse wishes. When our early history is revealed, we have a starting point for personal growth and social progress. Knowing and respecting what we went through as young children enables us to feel more self-respect. It fills in the blanks. We can see our humanity with more sympathy and find meaning in our suffering.

History tells us much about who we are and where we have come from. Psychology tells us that we can't always learn from history when we don't understand the dynamics of self-defeat.

The previous two chapters have examined the oral stage and noted the roots of our temptation as adults to live through feelings of refusal, deprivation, and loss.

Even when our physical needs are met, we can suffer with these negative emotions, and as adults become entangled in desire, want, entitlement, and dissatisfaction.

Now we come to the next stage of childhood development, the anal stage, from where lingering feelings of helplessness, passivity, stubbornness, and self-doubt originate.

As children move from the oral stage into the anal stage, they are still hanging on to their sense of acute self-centeredness. At about eighteen months of age, they enter the anal stage when toilet training becomes an experience involving feelings of control and submission. Children's inner battle cry—"say no to reality"—accompanies them into this stage and into the overlapping oedipal stage that begins at about thirty months of age. Now children have new conflicts to resolve involving their experiences of helplessness and control, along with rejection and criticism.

At this anal stage, parents begin socializing their children. *Socialization* is the necessary process of civilizing children and making them into social creatures. It includes the need for children to accept the reality principle, meaning the objective world beyond their private wishes and cherished illusions. As the outer world presses in, each child has to sort out a turbulent inner world in which he or she has been experiencing highly irrational impressions, likely involving hallucinatory sensations and episodes of the uncanny, that are gradually modified by language, reason, and developing relationships.

As the narrative of childhood continues, youngsters are feeling more ambivalence about mother. It is becoming apparent to most children that she is providing care and protection. Yet, the aggression they have projected on to her (in part to avoid being overwhelmed by self-aggression) leaves them fearful that she is an aggressive figure who feels malice toward them. The impact of the "evil" mother-image can be seen in the fascination and horror that children have felt for stories such as "Hansel and Gretel" and "Snow White and the Seven Dwarfs." The fictional Harry Potter, as another example, has a "bad" step-mother, magical powers (omnipotence), and a life-or-death struggle with the evil Voldemort (possibly symbolizing our deadly flaw), all of which would account for why the Potter books resonate so strongly with young people as well as adults.

Another experience that began in the oral stage is now flooding the child's consciousness. As Bergler stated, "All the child's experiences in early babyhood have one common denominator: passivity. The child is *completely dependent* on the mother; he feels *passively* "victimized" even in the matter of being fed (although the breast or bottle is also woven into the autarchic fantasy and considered by the child to be a part of himself); he is *passively* dependent on getting milk; he is *passively* subjected to a schedule for getting or not getting his calories; and worst of all he must undergo the *passively* experienced 'tragedy of weaning.'"[52]

In the anal stage, children become more conscious of waste elimination and experience it as something unnatural and uncomfortable—even frightening. They have, of course, no mature knowledge to evaluate the process and can't understand it. They feel at the mercy of some force that drains parts of their body. Even sleep feels like something that forces itself upon them. When toilet training begins, children feel they are being forced to submit to a program that offends their (illusion of) omnipotence. Through the "terrible two's" they enlist their store of natural aggression and typically react with passive-aggressive counter-measures against parental efforts at socialization. Many children go into open rebellion and resort to tantrums and a stubborn refusal to cooperate. This behavior is based on the contention, "I am not passive; I have the power of rebellion." This power to say *no* is obviously a very limited, reactive power. The *misplaced* stubbornness, defiance, and rebelliousness of adults originate from this infantile distortion. At a collective level, political parties that are out of power can resort, when operating in a dysfunctional manner, to practicing "the power of no."

The child, beginning at about the age of two, develops another misperception to maintain the cherished sense of omnipotence. The child identifies with the restrictions or requests imposed by parents, and he thereby makes these external requirements into a self-imposed behavior. The feeling is, "I'm not submitting to mother or father concerning this requirement. *I'm the one* who has decided what to do."

This "concession" to the parents' or educators' authority preserves the illusion of power. And once again, with a perverse joy at one's own "power" to modify reality, pleasure is extracted out of displeasure: "I don't want to submit or feel passive. Feeling power is what I like." In this process, the child learns and feels the "benefits" of identifying with authority. Later in life, some adults with low self-esteem or inner weakness are eager to identify with authority, no matter how irrational or illegitimate that authority might be. Others with inner weakness go to the other extreme and defy authority— even benign, legitimate authority—because their passive-aggressive defiance provides an illusion of power that covers up their readiness to experience, through their deadly flaw, legitimate authority in a negative manner.

As children enter the oedipal stage, the revolt against parental authority is gradually quelled by moral reproach, threats of punishment, inner guilt, and budding rationality. Boys begin to identify with father, with his power, and, as boys sometimes construe it, the cruelty of his power. By identifying with father as a figure of power, the boy also demotes his mother as someone to be feared. Girls identify with mother; the more power and self-esteem the mother exhibits, the better for the daughters. Rather than power or aggression, girls are likely to be concerned about finding or seeing kindness and friendliness in father.

A child's compulsion to "say no to reality" is reinforced by one aspect of a typical family experience. Many children begin to understand that truth in the family setting is only what the parents are willing to hear and consider. These children sense the existence of a silent pact whereby the parents agree to love them providing they become what is expected of them and go along with prevailing views.

Children can feel as if their parents don't really know them intrinsically, at their core. If their parents can't or won't see deeply into them, there must not be anything of any particular value to see. Or perhaps, the feeling goes, something within them is forbidden or bad. If they do look too deep, they will surely see something objectionable. It's better not to look, which is, after all, how their parents apparently managed.

Children still need an identity, however, and the pleasure principle requires that they find some satisfaction in themselves. As adolescents and teenagers, they can identify with their personality, their ego-ideal, their body, mind, or ego. As adults, we continue to form limited identifications—with our mind, country, possessions, class, race, religion, ego, and so on. These identifications can be satisfactory enough, though they tend to be unstable. However, they produce suffering when entangled in the deadly flaw.

The feeling can be: "My personality sucks," or "My body is ugly," or "My mind is inferior," or "My religion is being disrespected," or "My possessions are not as good as theirs." Our deadly flaw barges in upon these limited identifications and makes out of them a means of suffering.

We get a better feeling for how to identify and eliminate the deadly flaw by understanding the self-defeating behaviors of others. Several brief clinical examples are provided in this chapter to help readers understand how the deadly flaw operates in the psyche of adults. These examples primarily involve anal issues such as feelings or impressions of being controlled and helpless. Inner passivity permeates the psyche of the individuals discussed in these following cases.

William, a stout client in his sixties and a former CEO of a mid-sized company, could not stop his midnight raids on the refrigerator, even after doctors told him his added weight endangered his life. These late-night raids were conducted after his wife had fallen asleep. She had been trying to no avail to control his weight problem with vegetarian meals. The more weight he gained the more insistent she had become that he eat only what she prepared for him.

Even when he fell asleep early, he would awaken at the allotted hour to prowl about the kitchen. Whenever he managed to refrain from raiding the refrigerator, he suffered from insomnia. Several times he had completed his midnight raids with hardly any awareness of what he was doing, almost as if he were sleep-walking.

I told William he was emotionally attached to feeling controlled. He felt controlled and restricted by his wife, and so his midnight munching became a passive-aggressive defense to this effect: "I'm not looking to be controlled. Look, I do what I want. I go into the kitchen and eat and she can't stop me." Even though William had been a high-powered executive, he was acting out with his wife an infantile conflict relating to his mother.

"Your defense is self-defeating," I said. "First, overeating endangers your health. Second, the more you gain weight, the more controlling your wife becomes toward you as she further restricts your diet and scolds you adamantly. Third, you become increasingly helpless to the control and dominance of your compulsion. The more deeply you see and understand the origins and nature of your compulsion, the more it will lose its power over you."

Predictably, William left telltale signs such as crumbs and wrappers when he sneaked into the kitchen. Naturally, his wife knew he had been "naughty." This provoked her to try even harder to control him. In self-defeat, William thereby intensified the painful feeling to which he was attached, that of feeling controlled. Consciously, through his defenses, he protested how much he hated the feeling.

His mother had been a single parent, and he had felt especially constrained in accepting her authority and domination. His wife served as a mother-substitute by enabling him to recreate the old conflict. With his emotional attachment, William felt that when he was not the one in control of some person or situation, then he was *being controlled* by some person or situation. There is no middle ground with this either-or conflict. It is a case of either feeling the urgent need to maintain control *or* feeling out of control, with no room for experiencing the balance of these extremes.

Another aspect of William's deadly flaw was his attachment to feeling criticized and disapproved of. He had frequently felt criticized by his mother, and he remembered feeling guilt at her implications that he was a disappointment to her. More than fifty years had passed, and William was now repeating a close approximation of that old dynamic with his scolding wife, at much cost to his health and happiness.

Children are capable of becoming attached to the feeling of being controlled, whether they have controlling caregivers or not. If parents are truly controlling, their children are more likely to have submission and control as components of their deadly flaw. The feeling itself constitutes the passive experience of having to give up what one wants and having to submit to, or go along with, someone else's will. The feeling is also experienced as demands or obligations to carry out certain duties. As one client put it, "I'm always saying to myself, 'I *have* to do this, I *have* to do that.' It may just be the need to pick up some milk at the store, yet I make it feel like a heavy obligation. I feel I'm being forced to perform this task. I can't just do it in stride. I make it a burden."

This is the experience of a person who is recycling the feeling of being controlled. It's as if this person has a special "control" filter in his head. Unconsciously, he's on the lookout for encounters or experiences in life that he can pass through this filter. Once an experience is filtered in this passive way, the person takes on the impression that he is somehow being controlled. Instantly, his defenses arise to try to convince him that he hates that feeling. But, secretly, he's indulging in the feeling.

Consequently, he easily slips into feelings of helplessness and powerlessness. He often feels overwhelmed and manipulated, and he is resentful of the role certain people play in his life. He will sometimes be a rebel and resist authority, often passive-aggressively, producing defiance to cover up his attachment. Other times, he will allow others to direct and lead his life by being a passive follower.

Individuals often alternate back and forth between these extremes. They can "borrow" a sense of power by identifying with those who allegedly (or in reality) wield it. This identification, however, can make them passive to ideological or authoritarian forces or to people who would take advantage of them. Or they can become agents of abusive power themselves, and feel the strong appeal of having such authority as a defense to cover up their identification with the passivity of those upon whom they inflict their dominance. In other words, they become controllers themselves to cover up their attachment to feeling controlled. In the meantime, they also are vulnerable to the illegitimate authority of their superego, reeling from its frequent eruptions of self-aggression and inner control.

One client, a professional aged forty, was handsome and articulate, but quite immature, even boyish in his manner. He resisted doing the paperwork required by his profession, saying he hated feeling forced to do it. Emotionally, he felt that some conditions or elements such as legions of bureaucrats or "big, bad society" were forcing him to do paperwork. Of course, nothing was forcing him. His job required this documentation, and the time he took to do it was not unduly taxing. Because he felt forced, however, he rebelled through procrastination. The longer he delayed, the more intensely he felt he was being held accountable by outside forces. Anyone who procrastinates to a self-defeating degree is in a passive-aggressive protest (as a defense) against the feeling of being controlled, obligated, or forced. The individual is also likely attached to feelings of self-criticism (through the inner critic) or criticism from others, since his failure to be productive can evoke such criticism.

Jody, another client, was eating more than was healthy. She felt resentful that she "had to go" to work five days a week at a bank. She decided to work part-time three days a week. Soon she hated this arrangement because she was lazing around the house all day, either overeating or being tempted to. When she understood her attachment to feeling controlled, and realized how that attachment produced the impression that work was a grueling obligation, she returned to work full-time and felt good about it.

As a child, Jody had felt very controlled by a stepmother who required her to do a lot of housecleaning. At age thirteen, Jody weighed 160 pounds. Her stepmother "always pestered me about my weight." Feeling controlled by the stepmother, Jody had resisted unconsciously: "Don't tell me I have to clean the house, and that I can't eat what I want. I'll do and eat what I want!"

When she felt controlled by the need to work for family income and by supervisors at the bank, her compulsive eating became her defense, her "evidence" that she was not passively attached to feeling controlled and could do what she wanted: "I am the one who is deciding to eat." The self-deception and self-defeat in this defense are obvious: Her "decision" is to eat in a way that does her harm. This is not a true decision but a course of action compelled by her defense.

One client felt the power of this control issue in the supermarket. "I have to avoid certain aisles because it feels like the food talks to me," she said. "It seems to say, 'Take me! Take me!' I feel like it wants to jump into my cart."

Another client, Helen, a successful businesswoman who had recently retired, came to therapy to seek help for her addictions to cigarettes and alcohol. She revealed she was controlling with her sons, one of whom had bought her home-decorating business. She was trying to guide her other son through his tangled business affairs. She could see her controlling influence in their lives, but she felt her behavior to be justified because she was "helping" them.

"I just feel they would mess up if I wasn't there, checking up on them," Helen said. Her controlling behavior, however, was a defense against her attachment to feeling controlled. This attachment was triggered, or became activated, when she watched her sons flounder in business. She identified with them, which means she would imagine how helpless or overwhelmed they were feeling, and she would then take on those feelings and recycle them in herself. She was also quick to feel drained, another variation of the deadly flaw, as she took on the burdens of other people.

She acted out her own passivity and expectation of failure through her inability to stop smoking and drinking. Typically, addictive personalities are unconsciously willing to recycle feelings of helplessness and submission that go back to childhood. As adults, they find in substance abuse a new battlefield on which to experience inner passivity. Lacking the power of self-regulation, they succumb to the demands of their craving.

Helen also unconsciously expected other people to look at her as a failure (which is how she saw herself with respect to her addictions), and she consequently saw her sons in the same negative light, expecting them to fail. As she identified with their alleged helplessness, she felt compelled, as a defense, to rescue them. This dynamic strongly suggests that the sons themselves had an attachment to being seen in a negative light, and they were thus in danger of acting out being failures.

Brad was another client with an attachment to feeling controlled. He reported drinking excessively in order to relax. He felt pressure from the duties and obligations of his work and home life, and he said that drinking seemed to be tied in with his procrastination on important assignments. As a boy he had been required by his strict and dominating mother to carry out many of the farm chores. Brad had felt she forced him to submit to her, although in reality the chores did have to be done. He was the only one available, yet he was resistant to doing them. He internalized his mother's commands and, as an adult, experienced an inner voice that made him feel guilt when he was not doing his "chores." This way he became his "own" mother to himself, making himself feel forced to do chores.

To defend against this secret attachment to feeling forced, Brad allowed his excessive drinking to provide this defense: "I don't look for the feeling of being compelled to work. On the contrary, I try to relax with a few drinks in order to forget all the things I'm supposed to do." When drinking is used as a defense, there is more danger it will become excessive. The individual begins to act out what he is attached to, the feeling of being powerless to some external requirement. Brad's self-defeat consisted of declining health, loss of income, and guilt feelings about his drinking and procrastination.

Individuals who easily slip into helpless feelings often have fears around taking action and making decisions. Because of the attachment to helplessness, they can't feel their inner authority and are easily overwhelmed. One alcoholic client, in therapy with me following an in-patient five-week treatment program, said in his third session, "I've been out of the treatment center for two weeks now, and I don't like the feeling of being back in reality. I'm not liking dealing with work, and making decisions about finances, and having to do something about problems in my marriage. I feel like a child trying to do an adult job." This statement reveals that the helpless feelings that contributed to his addiction problem were still haunting him. I helped him understand that he was secretly willing to experience a feeling of helplessness and passivity with respect to the requirements of his daily life. "You will decline to entertain these negative emotions," I told him, "if you see your attachment to them clearly enough." Daily chores and responsibilities became easier for him as his deeper awareness empowered him to refrain from indulging in those feelings of helplessness and passivity.

The philosopher-mystic George Gurdjieff once said, "A man will renounce any pleasure you like but he will not give up his suffering." Now we have a better idea why this is so.

Chapter 10
Feeling Controlled

We can't really claim to be free people if we are attached to feeling controlled. Freedom isn't just about living in a democracy. Evolved freedom incorporates *inner freedom*, which is the measure of how free we are from internal conflict, behavioral problems, and unnecessary suffering.

In the unconscious, it makes little difference whether an individual is feeling controlled by friends, family members, bosses, events, situations, bureaucrats, oligarchs, governments, corporations, political parties, desires, compulsions, fixations, or the addictive capacities of certain substances. All of these are just different playing fields for the same game of feeling controlled.

For starters, we must distinguish between the secret desire to feel controlled and the actual problem of being controlled. To take a political example, an oligarchy might exercise abusive power over the people because the passivity of the people enables the abuse. Two interrelated circumstances need to be addressed: the passivity and the abuse. It's easy for people to complain about the abuse and ignore their passivity. Social progress occurs in a more enduring manner when we understand the relationship between passivity and abuse. If we take care of the passivity, the abuse will go away.

The child's first experience of feeling controlled begins, as mentioned, in the anal stage. An attachment to this feeling frequently lingers in the adult psyche. When we resolve the attachment, control is no longer an issue. Impressions of being controlled are no longer our emotional weakness. We stop looking for ways to feel controlled or to control others. We have no negativity around the issue.

Even if others are trying to control us, we don't react negatively. We can respond with power if abuse is occurring. To make that power more effective, we refrain from "going negative." We may get annoyed and challenge the controllers aggressively if their controlling behavior is out of line. Yet we remain largely free of negative reactions. We find appropriate responses that give us pleasure in our free spirit and our diplomatic powers. Sometimes we're just amused by someone's controlling behavior toward us, meaning we enjoy the freedom of not being influenced or triggered by it.

The pain of an oppressive situation stems largely from our attachment to helplessness, not just from the oppression itself. A person could be experiencing a truly oppressive situation, living, say, in a totalitarian political system, and yet be able to maintain his integrity and sense of personal freedom as, morally and spiritually, he resists the oppression. His political situation is, of course, far from ideal, but he's able to minimize the unpleasantness by resisting the temptation to embellish on the feeling of helplessness and oppression. He or she maintains inner strength and is able emotionally, when the time is right, to support the overthrow of tyranny.

We can possess equanimity, which requires some inner strength, even while oppression is being laid upon us. If we are submissive in certain situations, that doesn't necessarily mean we are passive. We may simply be acknowledging the reality that others may at times have oppressive power over us. We honor our integrity and protect ourselves to fight or to resist another day. However, when we are submissive because of inner passivity, we are likely either to lose our integrity and become pawns of the system or to suffer greatly in hopelessness and despair.

Many events and situations can't be controlled or changed by us. The healthier we are, the better we can accept that fact. Even when things are going well, it's not because we're controlling the situation: It's too egotistical to think in such terms. Perhaps the best way to have things go well is to live in harmony with reality, meaning with natural, spiritual, and psychological laws. This involves living with humility and respect for nature, which are other qualities that emerge when we expose our deadly flaw.

Some individuals repeat in a new context that old trick from childhood, when the child convinces himself that he's not submitting to the will of his parents but instead is making his own decisions. An individual experiencing some out-of-control behavior such as an addiction to alcohol or cigarettes often deludes himself with a claim to power of this sort: "I'm the one who is deciding to have another shot of whiskey (or another cigarette)." The reality is that passivity, not power, is "making" the decision to maintain the addiction.

Another claim to power that covers up out-of-control behavior goes like this (in conjunction with what psychoanalysis calls negative exhibitionism): "I make myself bad. I cause you to see me as bad. See, you can't control me." This defense might apply to a teenager who, rebelling against parental authority, develops a problem with drugs. It could also apply to someone who is being unfaithful to a partner.

Unconsciously, an individual can sugar-coat (libidinize) the feeling of being bad—in cases, for instance, of adulterers, gamblers, and drug addicts. This process often generates a manic excitement, a thrilling pleasurable-painful tension, that propels the individual toward self-defeat. Obviously, these intense, grotesquely pleasurable feelings are fleeting, and typically they are followed by plunges into deep misery. Trapped in this mode of operating, the individual does not manifest the power to succeed but only to fail and to suffer.

Some addictive personalities resist recovery because, stuck in anal stubbornness, they associate getting better with bending to the will of their parents, other

133

family members, therapists, or society. Sometimes they can extricate themselves from this self-damaging behavior by "formally" surrendering their will to a "higher power," as in the Alcoholics Anonymous program, thereby dropping their claim-to-power defense and coming under the "protection" of a benevolent or divine will. This approach can provide behavioral benefits, and I don't wish to disparage it. With this approach, however, individuals are not as emotionally stable, and certainly not as conscious, as they are when establishing "the higher power," for purposes of self-regulation, in their own self.

Drug addicts often say they engage in substance abuse to relieve boredom, to heighten a sense of aliveness, to enrich the imagination, to feel more potent, and to get "more" from life. Drugs can accomplish this, but temporarily and with dire consequences. Addictive personalities are under constant inner pressure to have fun or to produce highs in order to "prove" that they are not secretly attached to feeling refused, deprived, passive, and helpless.

Under the influence of some drugs, an individual experiences a kind of fascism of the ego that promotes the illusion of self-importance and power, restoring the old feelings of megalomania so prized by the addict's infantile side. The drug's high is a compensation for underlying attachments to feeling worthless, inadequate, and powerless in the world. The drug addict ends up being even more helpless and feeling more worthless as he is "taken over" or "possessed" by the drugs, as the drugs begin to harm his body and mind.

Are people really helpless and powerless over their addictions? They can be, indeed, if their self-knowledge is lacking. As our deadly flaw locks us into the unconscious recycling of negative emotions, this negativity weakens our will, our spirit, and our powers of regulation. Life is not felt to be so precious when we are weighed down by this negativity. Some of us can be quite willing to hurry life along and escape our suffering through premature death, even if we might adamantly deny doing that.

With the issue of control, we make an unconscious choice to hold on to the old negative emotions of feeling helpless and powerless. Drugs or alcohol can now have more influence over us, whether or not genes, biochemistry, or "disease" factors are also present. We unconsciously chose to feel weak, which gives drugs or alcohol the power to control and dominate us. We can also unconsciously wish to hurt and damage ourselves (and find perverse pleasure in the process), which stems from our attachment to inner aggression. The solution is to recognize the essence of our deadly flaw, in this case our affinity for helplessness and feelings of defeat.

People can misuse the emotional imagination to feel controlled. A woman in her forties reported lying awake at night, obsessed with her work schedule for the following day. It made no difference whether she expected the coming day to be routine or exceptional. She lay in bed with her insomnia, relentlessly visualized her day unfolding, minute by minute, worried about unpredictable possibilities. "I run through the routine of the day," she said. "I have to get the day's activities straight in my mind. I'd like to get into the day and get it over with, but I have to wait."

This person was feeling overwhelmed, which is a frequent symptom of feeling helpless and out of control. She was also indulging in feeling drained by the requirements of her work day. Once she realized her secret game of recycling those distressful emotions, she was able to stop doing so.

In order to learn more about their emotional attachment to control, members of a therapy group with eating disorders were assigned to write a letter to the weak part in them that was attached to control. One woman saw this part as a hairy monster with a huge gross mouth dripping with saliva and scum. "I kick at it, hate it, spit on it, yell at it, try to destroy it," she wrote. This woman's intensity is dramatically impressive, and her experience needs to be honored. Yet we benefit by seeing the ingredients of our deadly flaw in a more neutral way, with insight rather than hostility. We can't tame inner negativity with negativity of our own. Hostility toward parts of ourselves intensifies our inner conflict.

In this case, the woman was repulsed by the image, yet fascinated by it. She had built up rage toward this

136

"monster," which persisted for a few moments before she lapsed into passivity, into a feeling of being overwhelmed and controlled by it. This interaction revealed a frequent pattern in her life, to protest and rail against some power or influence that victimized her, and then to give in passively to it.

The compulsion to continue to experience control, helplessness, and refusal can produce the "dependee" personality. This is someone who maneuvers himself into a position of dependence on others and ends up complaining about (and being disappointed in) the "inadequacy" of the providers' care. The "dependee" is plagued with feelings of being incomplete and impotent, and he blames others for not doing their job, which, as he sees it, is to take care of him properly.

Underneath, this individual is turning his life over to someone who lets him down and fails to save him from himself. The "dependee" acts out the baby in all its entitlement, still not responsible for himself, wanting mother's or a substitute mother's constant care and attention, yet inwardly furious at mother for, as he sees it, still controlling, refusing, and disappointing him.

To cover up his attachments to control and refusal, he invokes the defense of blaming: "See what you made me, Mother. See how screwed up I am because of your inadequate care. I wouldn't be so helpless if you had taken proper care of me." This defense is unconscious. The individual is only aware of his bitterness and resentment toward the caregivers who he perceives to be as incompetent as he feels himself to be. He loves nothing more than to hear them confess to their "inadequacies."

One such individual, feeling crushed by some remark by his mother, said, "I can't help it—she robs me of my soul!" This is a very self-defeating defense and a most painful rationalization for passivity: "I can't help my behavior—Mom took away my power. This is not my fault."

The following list of personal weaknesses reveals whether a person has an emotional attachment to feeling controlled, dominated, or manipulated. One or more of the self-defeating consequences that an individual will encounter as a result of this passivity are in parentheses.

1. I can't say no (*hence, others will take control of your life*);

2. I can't make decisions (*others will make them for you, while you suffer with procrastination and other forms of self-defeat*);

3. I look to others for answers (*this lets them control and manage your life*);

4. I often feel powerless (*the vagaries of fate instead of the triumph of destiny will define your life*);

5. I fear being assertive (*others will be assertive toward you, as well as demanding of you*);

6. I blame others (*in not taking responsibility for your feelings and actions, you are likely to maintain your suffering and repeat your mistakes*);

7. I frequently feel like a failure (*you are entangled in inner passivity and have placed yourself at the mercy of your inner critic*).

As we participate in the circumstances of our lives, we give consent, consciously or unconsciously, to most of the pain we experience. As we accept responsibility for what has previously been unconscious, we see more clearly how we have been orchestrating the self-defeating reactions we have experienced.

It requires some courage to acknowledge that we are invested in maintaining our negative emotions. It also requires reflection upon the finding, long established in psychological literature but still fearfully denied, that much of our lives is run by unconscious conflicts that get played out in our life to our disadvantage. At the same time, we understand that turning inward to look for answers and solutions creates resistance, especially so when we are serious about dismantling the inner status quo.

One added benefit for doing this work is that we become much more perceptive and discerning about the intentions, motivations, and emotional health of others.

We need to understand that each of us has a mental side and an emotional side. Our mental side probably knows that nobody can control us unless we let them. Emotionally, though, many of us keep getting tangled up in feeling controlled, dominated, helpless, and submissive. In conjunction with those negative feelings, we're also likely to feel inadequate, not good enough, somehow defective, maybe even worthless.

These negative emotions have a life of their own. Even though these emotions produce much content that is irrational and untrue, we must refrain from "fighting" this negative side of ourselves. As mentioned, it's not our enemy. It's just us at our weakest point, where consciousness has eluded us. Fighting against ourself is futile. As we approach our deadly flaw for the purpose of understanding it, it's better to feel we're training with a sparring partner rather than fighting an enemy.

Chapter 11
Rejection: A Love Affair

Perhaps the biggest emotional hurt in human affairs is feeling starved of love. Many people have unwittingly erected a Great Wall of Rejection between themselves and others.

At that wall, people lament the absence of love in their life. How did they get stuck behind this wall? Many of us, out of misguided loyalty to our dysfunctional side, remain trapped in an infertile wilderness where rejection poisons the soil.

To trace this form of suffering back into time, we peer into the third and final stage of early childhood development. The child's consciousness has grown from "oneness" in the oral stage (involving just baby), evolved through "twoness" in the anal stage (incorporating baby and mother), to reach this third stage of "threeness" (baby, mother, and father).[53]

Rejection, betrayal, criticism, and abandonment are the negative emotions the child encounters as he or she moves through this oedipal stage from about two years to five years of age. These emotions can plague us throughout life, oftentimes painfully so, particularly in marriages, romance, friendships, and family relations.

Rejection issues arise even when we have good parents. A little girl, in longing for this emotional bonding with her father, may feel that "Daddy loves Mommy better than me." A little boy attracted to his mother can experience his version of this alleged rejection: "Mommy loves Daddy better than me." This feeling can extend to other family members; *e.g.*, "Mommy loves my sister Susie better than me." Soon it is easy for children, given their limited frame of reference, to begin to feel that they are not loved adequately by one or both parents.

The prospect of feeling rejected at this stage of childhood looms large for every child. Even when parents are decent and trying their best, some children still experience as insufficient what affection and recognition they receive. They can spend their lives pursuing love, all the while fated to avoid it or sabotage it.

As classical psychoanalysis contends, children in the oedipal stage become attracted to the opposite-sexed parent. This attraction is more erotic than sexual. It's also innocent and natural, involving a desire for bonding, a feeling of possessiveness, and a generalized eroticism associated with the pleasure principle. At times, children want to win the parent's attention exclusively and have the parent all to themselves. Since this is not realistic, we easily feel rejection.

Some children pass through this stage relatively unscathed. They soon accept that their hopeless longing for mommy or daddy is a fantasy. However, others do not fare as well. Some children are deeply wounded by the series of disappointments in which their yearning for the opposite-sexed parent was turned aside. Their failure to accept reality is due to complicated reasons that can involve genetics, the intractability of acute self-centeredness, and parents who themselves are entangled in the deadly flaw. These children can begin to believe that the "rejection" was their fault. They sense that, through some grievous deficiency of their own, they have caused the rejection. Libido, the drive behind the pleasure principle, is instinctively enlisted, and it enters the fray in order to salvage some comfort from the pain of the rejection. Perverse comfort is taken in the emotional conviction that, "I caused it (the rejection) to happen." The feeling of rejection becomes an emotional attachment, a pain we are unconsciously willing to experience. As adults, such individuals experience rejection in the everyday challenges of friendship and romance.

Typically, adults with an attachment to rejection try to deny or cover up that attachment with painful emotions and self-defeating behaviors that "prove" how much they hate rejection. Hence, even as they desperately go looking for love, they suffer from feelings or expectations of rejection, and their lives are filled with painful experiences of rejection that they act out with others.

An example of the pleasure-in-displeasure aspect of this dynamic is the reaction of some children to the birth of a sibling. Such a child feels displaced by the new arrival who is getting so much of mother's love and attention. He reverts to thumb-sucking, which had been given up months earlier, and he finds pleasure in displeasure, or libidinal satisfaction, in this regression. The thumb-sucking transforms the pain into oral comfort or pleasure. As an adult, he will potentially be driven to repeat experiences of rejection and then to cover up this secret game with painful defenses such as anger, jealousy, or depression—or, say, problem drinking—that "prove" how much he hates the feeling of rejection.

Some children can sublimate their hurt and become quite creative and successful in later life. Some who are good and well-behaved as children can later as adults be blindsided by the deadly flaw. Other children from an early age are operating on the premise that, "I, through my naughty behavior, cause you to reject me." This premise is fortified when they feel that the attention they get for bad behavior is better than no attention at all. These children appear to be aggressive in their naughty behavior, but this aggression is reactive (pseudo or passive aggression), and it serves as a defense against their underlying attachments to feeling refused, controlled, and rejected.

Most of the time, parents are simply trying to do what is best for their children. True, their parenting skills can be lacking, and they may not communicate the fact that their love is not conditional on how well their children behave or perform. However, even the efforts of the best parents can be discounted by children who are intent on denying reality. Certainly, some parents do find it difficult to love their children when their children don't excel or do the "right thing"—or even when they do. These parents are compelled, unconsciously, to repeat with and through their children the emotional memories of real or alleged refusal, domination, and rejection that they themselves experienced in childhood, which still circulate in their psyche. Such parents are not satisfied no matter how well their children do. At the same time, they may be eager to shift onto their children all the dreams and hopes they themselves failed to realize or achieve.

Even with kind, considerate parents, children can become emotionally attached to the feeling of being unimportant and insignificant. The feeling continues into adult years, following the principle that whatever is unresolved in our psyche is recycled compulsively, with our unconscious collusion, even when doing so is painful and self-defeating. So the problem is not simply one of feeling rejected by others but also of self-rejection. It doesn't make any difference in our psyche which form of rejection we experience. Both self-rejection and rejection from others have been sugar-coated (libidinized) in equal measure. People also "get a hit" of secret suffering by rejecting others: They take on, through identification, the hurt of those being rejected.

This suffering is sometimes experienced daily and hourly. Instead of establishing an inner conviction of our goodness or value, we become preoccupied with the idea that others perceive us as somehow deficient or flawed. We then acknowledge or "plead guilty" to being flawed in order to cover up our attachment to rejection. In the process we become dependent on others for validation. We swing back and forth between the comfort of being validated and our pain for allegedly being unworthy and insignificant.

We identify with that old, painful sense of self and can't let go of it. We become emotionally attached to this flawed sense of self: "If this is what I feel and what I want, it must be who I am." We are frightened by the sense that we would no longer be who we think we are if we leave behind our suffering. The unspoken sense is, "Better the little me I know than the better self I don't."

Our secret attachment to self-rejection, which is facilitated by our inner critic, is partly responsible for the epidemic of drug abuse. As mentioned, many drugs provide a temporary ego boost, restoring the grandiosity of acute self-centeredness. These drugs enable one to claim in the defense offered up to the inner critic: "This sense of my greatness and power is what I really want to feel, not that passive, worthless old me." The need for the defense, not the drugs themselves, can be the real imperative behind the craving or addiction. (Though biochemical anomalies are present in the brains of substance abusers, these anomalies can conceivably be of psychosomatic origin, meaning that intense psychological conflict can itself influence body chemistry.)

--

Egotism and its more pronounced variation, narcissism, are unconscious defenses against rejection, criticism, and passivity. The defense contends, "I don't want to reject myself; I want to exalt myself." Narcissism is like an antidote or a "high" that helps us cope with chronic feelings of being worthless or unloved. Once again, in an emotional predicament, we enlist the pleasure principle: We make ourselves an object of pleasure through our fixation on ourselves. The unconscious defense contends, "However much I am suffering in feeling worthless, I can compensate with comforting self-centeredness or a pleasing illusion of my superiority." Another variation of the defense contends, "Who says I am passively disconnected from myself. Look at how much pleasure I feel in actively validating myself."

This egotism is an unstable sense of self that leads us away from loving and being loved. Yet we do often find a second-rate pleasure in the experience of our egotism. For one thing, it compensates for our dread of nothingness, that impression that we are insignificant and without value. It can "buck us up" in superficial dealings with others and the world, though it doesn't provide us with the deep emotional support that comes through connection with our authentic self. Our ego won't follow us deep inside; it only keeps us at the surface of self-awareness. No one can love another's ego—we can only love the essential self behind the ego. This applies to our own ego, too—we cling to that false self more out of fear than love.

Deeper inside, some of us struggle to find a trustworthy substance, an object, a self, or an authority to rally around. An inner life doesn't even exist for some people. They can go for long periods without checking in with themselves in a way that provides emotional support. They fail to acknowledge and take note in a caring way of how they feel at any given moment. They show more emotional support for friends than for themselves.

Here, self-rejection has escalated to self-abandonment. These individuals are ignoring, rejecting, or abandoning themselves. They are missing a connection to their core self in just the way they felt their parents failed to connect with them. They can compensate with narcissism or obsessive self-attention. Alternatively, they may try to figure out through the eyes of others just who they are. Their love will be shallow, based on need or a sense of obligation or guilt, because of their own lack of self-appreciation. Obviously, some people feel this disconnect from self more intensely than others.

In any event, the deadly flaw is part of the problem. People become stabilized at the rejection level *and* also at the self-rejection level. They repeatedly experience their relations with themselves and with others in ways that activate their attachments to rejection, criticism, betrayal, and abandonment. This is how they suffer, and they are addicted to it in the sense that they're continually ready to feel it.

As mentioned, when we reject others because of our unresolved attachment to rejection, we identify with them in feeling rejected. That way, when we aim rejection at someone, it comes back and slaps us in the face. Whether we're absorbing rejection or dishing it out, we can't feel our goodness and value or that of others.

This difficulty we have in feeling our value is evident in our fascination with celebrities. Sure, celebrities are fun to have around, and they often bring great richness to our cultural life. But the emotional effect they have on certain people is revealing. When these people see a celebrity or even just think about a certain celebrity, they typically create a gap between their own sense of value and the value they accord the celebrity. This is true even with celebrities who have little to offer except their celebrity.

This emotional dynamic in our psyche happens in a flash. The dynamic can even occur when the celebrity is viewed remotely, as on the cover of a magazine, on television, or in our imagination. In this moment, many viewers (of the celebrity) first experience either self-rejection or a need for self-validation. This happens unconsciously. What viewers experience consciously is the feeling of either admiring the celebrity or disliking him or her. Sometimes their feelings are more neutral, though the famous person still has a mesmerizing effect. The conscious feeling toward the celebrity, whether of admiration or dislike, is a reaction to the self-rejection or the self-validation that happen first. For instance, an experience of self-rejection happens in a flash, like a static electric spark. These unconscious feelings can be described as, "He or she (the celebrity) is better than me. I am less than that famous person." Or, in the second instance, "I am as good as that celebrity, whose character is questionable. I'm probably even superior to that phony."

Our defenses now cover up the fact that we are doubting our own value and possibly rejecting or even hating ourselves. In the first instance, the excited viewers are unconsciously led to believe that, rather than feeling self-rejection, they are identifying with the god-like attributes of the celebrity. So they feel a jolt of grandiosity. This reaction "proves" to their inner critic that they are not attached to feeling unworthy and rejected: "This is how I want to feel! Exactly the way that celebrity must feel about himself or herself. This is what I want for myself!" Their daydreams of being a celebrity or having one as a friend are fueled by this contention.

This defense also works in reverse. Our society loves to peep at the trials and tribulations of celebrities and to see them in a negative light. That enables us to identify through them with how we imagine it feels to be reduced to nothing or to be seen as a lesser person. Now we are sneaking in suffering through the back door, and we defend against realization that we are "taking a hit" on feeling devalued with a sour-grapes defense that reads: "See how pathetic he is. Who says I should be like him?"

This problem also exists for snobs who exhibit their mentality as a defense against their secret attachment to the feeling of being excluded or rejected. They secretly identify with those who they themselves are excluding. When such a feeling of exclusion intensifies, it leads to hatred of the other. But the hatred is experienced in conjunction with self-hatred. The object and the subject are merged in the same grim negativity.

The fascination with celebrities involves other psychological aspects, as well. A sudden fixation on the god-like celebrity arouses in our psyche that old feeling of infantile self-centeredness. We're usually quite willing to get a jolt of that old grandiosity, as people do on drugs such as crystal methamphetamine and heroin, because it feels so "good," especially when we're dragging along impressions of being losers or failures.

Also, people are mesmerized by the narcissism of some celebrities. The narcissistic celebrity, it appears, is so full of life, and the dispirited people who flock around this figure are in pursuit of a few sparks to light their fire. Certain celebrities can feel their value through the admiration they receive from others. Such celebrities, especially those with little to offer, can create popular support for themselves with charm, personality, and intense narcissism. Their admirers are hoping their own smoldering narcissism or egotism can be ignited by proximity to the one whose self-admiration flares so brightly.

Healthy individuals are not fearful of rejection. They might feel some sorrow or concern at being rejected. But they don't take it personally. Their capacity for love is not impeded. Someone's rejection of them might be unpleasant, but it doesn't have to be painful. So-called rejection is often the compulsive behavior of the person doing the rejecting, which means it has nothing much to do with the qualities or virtues of the person being rejected. It's obviously pointless to personalize rejection of that kind.

When individuals have actually been rejected on rational grounds, they are, if healthy enough, more interested in understanding what happened than in suffering about it. They are open to the possibility that they have caused the rejection through oversight or lack of sensitivity. If so, they try to learn from the situation in order to repair the damage or to do better in future relationships.

Chapter 12
Exposing Our Defenses

In order to escape from suffering, we need to access vital self-knowledge and apply it to our life. This progress is impeded, however, by our psychological defenses. We want to move beyond our immature need for these defenses, but first we have to recognize them and understand how they operate.

To judge by the name, one might think that psychological defenses operate on our behalf. They do indeed protect us from feeling overwhelmed by anxiety and fear. That's because they affirm our self-image and ego, which constitute much of our limited and frequently painful sense of self. This sense of self is familiar, and so we cling to it.

Our defenses protect us from feeling overwhelmed by change. But they also end up protecting the inner status quo and blocking personal as well as social progress. Through our defenses, we lie to ourselves about ourselves.

To expose and eliminate the deadly flaw, we need to understand how our defenses work against our best interests. Being smart isn't always going to help us here. No matter how smart we are, our defenses can fool us. Sometimes the smarter we are, the more cunning we can be in erecting and maintaining clever defenses. It's our sincerity and integrity more so than brainpower that determine how quickly we break off our love affair with suffering.

The following examples portray individuals caught in cycles of suffering. These examples highlight the defenses they employ unconsciously to protect their inner status quo and avoid recognition of the deadly flaw. Their main issues involve rejection, betrayal, and abandonment.

For ten years, Marie had complained to her husband, Dave, that he always put their friends and his family before her.[54] She constantly felt excluded and rejected by him. She protested the situation, but essentially endured it and didn't seek remedies such as counseling. "I felt at the time," she explained, "that if I asserted my needs, Dave would leave me."

Her fear blossomed into a self-fulfilling prophecy. Her perpetual unhappiness became too much of a burden for Dave, and he left her for someone else. Marie said pensively, "I had a nagging awareness at the time that I was pushing things to the edge. It was as if I wanted him to leave me."

Marie's childhood had been permeated by feelings of being excluded and unworthy. She had been left in the care of a housekeeper, and she frequently felt abandoned by her parents' outside interests. As a child, she was convinced that, were she to assert her needs to her parents, they would abandon her and leave her to die. This expectation of abandonment was transferred on to her husband, at a terrible cost to her happiness.

For ten years, she had been secretly willing to feel that Dave's involvement with others represented abandonment of her. Her defense against seeing her temptation to suffer in this way consisted, in part, of her protests to Dave—she complained that he made others more important than her. Her complaints served to "prove" that she hated his "abandonment" of her. In her unconscious defense, the complaints proclaimed, "Look how much I hate it when he ignores me—that proves I don't want to feel abandoned. "But her complaints simply covered up her willingness during the marriage to continue feeling abandoned by Dave's closeness to his family and friends.

In another example, Oscar, a middle-aged man who had been on an emotional-disability pension for more than a year, came to counseling at the insistence of his wife. He had become emotionally distraught a year earlier after the death of his parents, both in their eighties. His parents had died within a week of each other in the same hospital, and he was convinced the hospital staff had not done enough to keep his parents alive. Oscar had doted on his father and mother and telephoned them daily from his home in another state. His wife had also come in for a therapy session, complaining of his obsessive and irrational jealousy.

In his dress and bearing, Oscar resembled an overgrown teenager. He was lacking in grace, poise, and dignity. He was living on his disability pension and trying to reconcile with his wife who was threatening to leave him because of his jealousy and increasingly erratic behavior. He was tormented by hatred for doctors and hospitals, and he was attempting to get an inquiry opened into the deaths of his parents. He was seeing a psychiatrist once every few months to maintain his disability status, as well as for drugs to treat his anxiety and digestive disorders.

Since the death of his parents, Oscar had lost his career, become seriously ill, made what looked like an unwise move to a new locale, and was on the verge of losing his wife. Yet he tried to devote the three sessions he attended (before deciding to end his therapy with me) to a recital of his litany of grievances against the world, especially doctors and hospitals. Nothing mattered to him emotionally as much as proving how justified he was in his disenchantment with life.

Oscar's relationship with his parents had been "close" because he had been trying (on the surface) to get love and validation from them. His wife had complained of how "he lived for his parents." (Parental idealization of this kind is often the result of repression of underlying, unresolved issues.) Oscar's mother had been quite negative, cold, and withholding. Unconsciously, he was attached to the feeling of being rejected and unloved, especially by her. He was consumed with rage against doctors and hospitals, ostensibly for "killing" his parents but really for "killing" his defenses. When his parents suddenly died, his defense system collapsed (his means of "proving" through his needy relationship with them how much he wanted to be loved), and he experienced an emotional breakdown. In another defense against his attachment to rejection, he flew into a rage when his wife offered a soda to a telephone repairman who had come into their house.

While Oscar had come to therapy out of emotional anguish and on the pretext of trying to save his marriage, he couldn't allow himself to get to the heart of his issues.

The next case illustrates another use of psychological defenses to cover up a secret attachment to rejection. Marion, a woman in her fifties, was a cynic and heavy drinker who had been unable to develop a solid romantic relationship. She felt that, as a child, she had been displaced by her younger brother. Her mother, Marion felt, had liked her brother better. Consequently, she saw her brother as depriving her of her share of affection. She resented her mother for this, and she blamed her mother for a multitude of alleged transgressions. In retaliation, Marion shut her mother and brother out of her life, while she acted out with others her expectations of rejection and refusal.

In therapy, Marion began to understand the psychological structure behind her bitterness. She had been secretly invested in seeing reality from a point of

157

view of rejection and refusal. She was willing to recycle these unresolved emotions, and her bitterness was the most painful consequence of her deadly flaw. Her defense required her to maintain bitter feelings toward her mother and brother. As long as she felt the bitterness, she could claim, in her defense: "See how much I hate them. That proves how much I don't like their rejection and refusal."

Now, as she saw what she had been recycling, the bitterness faded away. She was also able to let go of a lifelong resentment toward men, who she had perceived as likely to reject her. She began to realize she could experience her mother and brother in a neutral or even a pleasant way. Even if it were true that her mother had preferred her brother, Marion saw that spending her life as a victim of that situation was unwise and completely unnecessary.

Many people with rejection issues have an attachment to being seen in a negative light. They can be fixated, without being conscious of it, on how they look to others, and often they provoke others, through negative exhibitionism (a defense), to see them or to judge them negatively.

Victor came to therapy after a month-long program at a treatment center had stabilized his bulimic-anorexic eating disorder. He had started using street drugs and alcohol at age fourteen, stopped using "chemicals" in his late teens, and quit his heavy drinking about eight years later. After a blackout on a drinking binge, he quit alcohol completely a few years later, but he had then transferred his substance abuse to food.

His parents had separated when he was nine and divorced when he was fourteen. They had fought and quarreled viciously from the beginning of their marriage. "They married on a dare," Victor said, "and then they ended up staying together because their own parents wanted them to get the marriage annulled." Victor started to eat compulsively just as his parents separated, and, at one point, he weighed 210 pounds when he was only five feet, two inches tall. As a teenager one summer when he was heavily into drugs, he went from 210 to 145 pounds because he was determined to be accepted by the "bad" crowd he had fallen in with.

As a child, Victor felt isolated and abandoned. "My parents weren't expressive, I didn't get a lot of affection and comfort from them," he said. His father, an engineer, had worked long hours and had given him minimum attention when at home. After the separation, his mother became interested in boyfriends and frequently left him alone with his older brother. His brother, who as an adult was to have serious emotional problems, was verbally abusive to him and called him "Fatso" almost exclusively.

Victor felt "misplaced" at school. "As I got heavier, the kids really teased me. I would binge from the time I got home from school late into the evening, watching TV and eating until Mom got home." He had done well in school until he was about twelve, then he lost interest, skipped classes, and got in trouble with teachers. "I hated the school environment, not so much the classes as the other kids."

His primary emotional difficulty had its roots in attachments to rejection and abandonment. From an early age, he had interpreted his parent's deep unhappiness and general hostility to life as a personal rejection of him. Even when his father had been raging at Victor's mother or was furious for some reason, Victor nevertheless assumed these actions meant hatred and rejection of him personally. Victor also felt substantial insecurity and the prospects of abandonment because of the family instability and strife.

As a young adult, his personal appearance was extremely important to him. He was desperate to maintain an ideal body weight. This provided him with some confidence he would not be rejected. But it was also a defense, which went like this: "I don't want to be rejected. Can't you see how hard I'm trying to dress nice and keep my weight down!" In his desperation to maintain this defense, he would resort to bulimia and anorexia to control his weight. (This self-damage is evidence that his quest for weight loss was employed as a defense rather than simply being a healthy choice uncomplicated by psychological factors.) He had stayed within a ten-pound range of ideal weight in the year before starting therapy, but his bulimia felt out of control, creating stress and guilt, and he could feel control of his life slipping away.

He reacted with anger when he sensed people being "demanding and impolite" to him. This anger was also a defense—he served the anger up as evidence that he detested the feeling of being rejected or disrespected. "They're not thinking of me," he remarked of his friends and co-workers. "They're just out for themselves." In fact, Victor himself could be quite insensitive toward others. His attachment to feeling unloved locked him into a painful self-absorption. He also was tempted to reject others, in part to identify with how he imagined they felt.

Betrayal and rejection were the main issues in this following case. Leonard, a middle-aged businessman, was handsome but shy and socially clumsy. Depressed and feeling guilt, he had resorted to heavy drinking. He had recently experienced betrayal by business associates and was extremely bitter. He also had a pattern of being rejected and betrayed by women. In therapy, he revealed that he had felt (and was still feeling) betrayed by his parents, especially by what he perceived as their withdrawal of emotional support during his adolescence.

He told the story of how, when he was about ten years old, his father persuaded him to "squeal" on some friends with whom he had broken into a canteen and stolen sodas and chocolate bars. The father apparently had made Leonard feel that "father's love" would be the reward for this confession. But after the boy had told on his friends, the father betrayed his son (or so Leonard perceived) by failing to deliver the love in the months and years that followed.

With his attachment to the feeling of being betrayed, Leonard was a prime candidate to experience it repeatedly in his life. He became involved with individuals who, while pleasant on the surface, were untrustworthy. He acted naïve and overly trusting of them, providing them with confidential business information they used to their own advantage. Soon they conspired against him and almost drove him out of business. He also saw how he provoked women to reject him, mainly through his jealousy, withdrawal, and somewhat bland personality.

As Leonard realized his secret collusion in acting out his attachment to betrayal, he stopped using the defense of blaming his former partners. Even though they had indeed betrayed him, he saw that he had unconsciously been setting himself up for the experience of betrayal. His new awareness protected him from blundering again into this type of trouble. He now realized that, without deeper insight, he wouldn't learn from their mistakes.

Leonard had also been blaming himself for his bland personality and inability to sustain friendships. Self-blame is frequently a defense. Leonard was using it to cover up his attachment to being rejected and betrayed. "I'm not looking for rejection," his unconscious defense protested. "Rejection just happens to me because of my unpleasant personality." In pleading guilty to having a lackluster personality, he had to suffer with guilt, shame, and depression for this personality defect. Yet the defense "worked" in the sense that it covered up his attachment to rejection and betrayal. Of course, a "good" defense that remains unconscious is inevitably self-defeating.

Leonard's inherent goodness as a person was apparent, but his personality was degraded by his deadly flaw. His bland personality was itself a defense through which he could exhibit the cost to him of having been betrayed, as well as his ongoing sense of being a victim. This self-sabotaging defense goes like this, "Look at my social ineptitude! This is what you (father) have done to me with all of your betrayal!" Once this defense and the others were penetrated, Leonard eased off his drinking, improved his social skills, and was able to sustain and enjoy new relationships.

Our deadly flaw produces two kinds of dysfunction: *symptom dysfunction*, which includes emotional suffering, self-defeating behaviors, impairment of intelligence, and health problems; and *character dysfunction,* which produces disagreeable personality traits such as neediness, cynicism, hoarding, and shyness. Leonard's character dysfunction was visible through his shyness, while his symptom dysfunction included heavy drinking, relationship problems, and poor business judgment.

Compulsive overeating and obesity are other symptom dysfunctions that can be produced by an attachment to rejection. Sarah, a twenty-year-old, had just dropped out of college because of acute loneliness and insecurity. She had come to counseling to stop her compulsive overeating and to restore her self-confidence. She had been using cocaine but had stopped before beginning her therapy.

Sarah related in her first session a recent incident involving her father. Scheduled to meet him for lunch, she got to the restaurant ten minutes early and immediately felt that he would be late or not show up. Soon she was in emotional agitation and scanning the menu with an increasingly ravenous appetite. Her father showed up ten minutes late, and she could hardly bring herself to be civil with him. She ate a big meal and insisted on a high-calorie dessert, sensing his disapproval for her over-consumption.

Sarah's attractive mother and good-looking father were divorced. She lived with her father who, during her childhood, had frequently made note of his interest in attractive women but was not attentive to Sarah, his pretty daughter. She had felt as a child that he did not love her enough. Indeed, her father had been quite inattentive to her, which facilitated her attachment to the feeling of rejection. He had often kidded her about being "chubby," which frequently sent her crying to her bedroom.

Her difficulty controlling her impulses to eat produced painful feelings of guilt and regret. Those were followed by punishment in the form of self-reproach and self-loathing for being out of control with food. By getting fat, she extracted more indifference as well as disapproval from her father. Several times Sarah had lost twenty or thirty pounds, at which point, being more attractive, she became anxious about how to handle interest from men and possible romantic relationships. She associated relationships with negative emotions, having identified with her mother who, Sarah felt, had been "unloved, controlled, and cheated on."

As she came up against her own fear of rejection (a fear caused by her attachment to rejection), she found herself beginning to overeat and put the weight back on. Her obesity became a defense against her attachment to rejection: "I'm not looking for rejection. I'm rejected because I'm fat and I'm unable to lose the weight. Even my father rejects me because I'm fat." This defense made it harder for her to lose weight. In other words, she needed to stay fat to make the defense work.

At one point, she moved out of her father's house into an apartment with two other women. These women were popular and were out most nights with boyfriends. Sarah had difficulty controlling impulses to eat when she saw the other women having fun. That sight made her feel more deprived and more unlovable. She also felt rejected when her friends didn't take her along with them. The more she felt rejected, the more passive she became, which in turn impeded her self-regulation and made it more likely she would remain at home, prone to overeating and feeling sorry for herself.

Sarah came regularly to therapy and began to see the unconscious choices she was making to recycle the feeling of rejection. It was true that she had experienced rejection, but she realized that it did her no good now to plunge into that feeling. This process of gaining self-esteem didn't require her to forgive her father. Forgiving him was beside the point. Her growing power came from her awareness that her emotional predicament was held in place from within, and that she had the ability to liberate herself from her plight.

The therapy gave her the knowledge of inner dynamics, and helped her relate that knowledge to events and situations in her life. That enabled her to make much progress in feeling good about herself and getting rid of her symptoms. She saw her father more objectively and accepted him for who he was, with all his limitations. The self-knowledge she acquired enabled her to surpass her father in consciousness and become more evolved.

Rejection feelings are often accompanied by feelings of criticism and disapproval. One case involved Jack, a sales executive. At a meeting, Jack had an emotional reaction to a perceived criticism from his boss. Jack said nothing about it at the time, but he went back to his office and sat there angrily attempting to understand his hurt feelings. He knew from his therapy sessions that he was attached to feeling criticized, and he remembered how critical his father had been. Jack realized his still-unresolved attachment to criticism had been activated by his boss's remarks (objectively, he knew those remarks were intended as constructive criticism).

Jack saw the unconscious choice he had been making to activate the feeling of criticism. Since he was not interested in suffering in that old manner, he declined the temptation to "go there" and become entangled in those old feelings of criticism. He overrode the unconscious choice he would otherwise make to suffer with feelings of criticism (the old default position). He sensed through this awareness his ability to ease the feeling of being criticized. He was no longer feeling angry at his boss, which he recognized as a defense that covered up his indulgence in feeling criticized. Jack also felt relief and some pleasure at his new-found powers to curtail or minimize unnecessary suffering.

Chapter 13
More Defenses and Self-Defeat

Our deadly flaw invariably produces self-defeat, which is the psychological equivalent of stabbing oneself in the back. Sometimes the self-defeat is merely a flesh wound from which a person can quickly recover. Our quality of life is impeded, though, when this wounding occurs repeatedly. Other times the blade cuts deep and can lead to serious problems.

Self-defeat is inevitably what happens when we can't stop recycling painful feelings such as refusal, helplessness, criticism, and rejection. The damage can be measured in emotional pain, character limitations, inadequate self-regulation, relationship and career failures, lost opportunities, and health problems. Self-defeat is evidence that our deadly flaw is real and that it is an impediment to the expression and flowering of our intelligence.

It's truly amazing that we employ self-defeat or self-damage as a defense to cover up some important truths about ourselves. We actually hurt or sabotage ourselves to avoid the truth about our collusion in suffering. This behavior can reflect a certain tragic innocence. Because we don't understand how self-defeat works, we can't figure out what's happening. It appears as though some mysterious force hides within us and toils against our best interests. When things are going badly, we feel desperate to rectify our situation. But nothing we try works. We just keep sinking deeper in the spiral of self-defeat. To get to the bottom of it, we have to penetrate into our psyche, our unconscious mind.

This following example—involving emotional attachments to disapproval and criticism—illustrates self-defeat, and it shows how tempted we are to maintain our distorted impressions and deductions about what is happening around us. A middle-aged man who came to me for therapy said that he seldom stayed in one place longer than a year. He was wandering from city to city and town to town, unable to settle down and establish roots. He was miserable and professed how much he wanted to establish new friendships and settle in one community. But he quickly became disappointed wherever he happened to be.

In the one session I had with him, he told me stories of friends he had made in these places who had disappointed him. He felt he wasn't finding the kind of quality friends he expected or deserved. Nor did the cities and towns fulfill his expectations. I understood his self-defeat after he disclosed some childhood history—which was filled with the feeling that he and his father had been a disappointment to his critical mother.

I told him, "You can't make a choice of where to settle down because of your emotional attachment to criticism. You experience again and again the impulse to be critical of new friends and situations. You're convinced the problem is external, that this town or these people don't offer you enough, when the problem is your emotional inclination to "go negative" by being critical, and hence to feel disappointed and dissatisfied in yourself and others.

"You felt you were a disappointment to your mother," I continued. "Now you've reversed the emotional conflict and you have become like your mother, critical of others and disappointed in them and in yourself. One way or the other—whether you feel that you are the disappointment or that others are disappointing you—that attachment of yours to the feeling of criticism or disapproval is the primary troublemaker."

This wasn't what he wanted to hear. "No, no," he said. "I know that's not it! It's the fact that my new friends let me down, or it's something to do with my indecision, and how I make poor choices in where to go." He was now pleading guilty to being indecisive and choosing poorly in order to cover up his emotional attachment to the feeling of criticism. This defense required that he blame himself, which heightened his suffering. He left the session room not to return, disappointed again by his latest encounter and confirming what the sages have always known—that the secret intent and major life choice of many people is to take their suffering to the grave.

This man's self-defeat consisted of his chronic unhappiness and the effort and expense of his constant moving. It also consisted of what being rootless cost him in terms of family, career, and income. He threw the chance of happiness away in order to offer this pseudo-aggressive defense to his inner critic: "How can you say I want to be criticized. No, I'm the one who's aggressively critical of these places and people. They're the problem. To prove how disappointed I am in them, I'm going to have to move once again."

He fervently believed that external factors caused his misery. We frequently say of a painful situation, "He or she *caused* me to feel this way." For the most part, though, no one *causes* us to feel a certain way. We are the ones who take on those feelings based on our own determination to activate our particular varieties of suffering. It's true that others can *trigger* those negative feelings in us, but we ourselves are secretly willing to jump head-first into the negativity.

When a friend or acquaintance says something that we feel is offensive or provocative, we need to understand our negative reactions more fully and not take them at face value, as if we're justified in feeling offended or angry. We can say to ourselves: "Look how I'm feeling angry (sad, offended, and disgusted) after hearing what my friend said. Where does that feeling come from in me? I'm learning that I go to an old default position at such times as this, and doing so produces painful emotions, impulses, and actions that are self-defeating."

In that moment, we do the best we can to deal appropriately with our hurt feelings. Our friend might indeed have said something unkind to us. We can still avoid suffering if we recognize our deadly flaw. If we can't immediately avoid a painful "hit," we can at that moment do our best to avoid going "too negative." Later, we can attempt to understand the experience. At that time, as we see our own role in producing our negative experience, we prepare ourselves to do better in the future.

While physical actions usually cause a predictable physical effect (throw a stone in the water and it makes a splash), interpersonal actions do *not* have to cause a predictable effect. If someone yells at us, we don't necessarily have to absorb the aggression and feel fearful or angry. If someone ignores us, we don't have to feel hurt or offended. Our deadly flaw determines our *reactions*, while emotional strength through insight and awareness determines our *responses*.

As mentioned, our greatest strength is *not* in the ability to be assertive or aggressive in return when someone has allegedly (or in reality) insulted us. The greater strength is in our ability not to be offended in the first place. However, when people have too much inner passivity, it feels to them that their failure to be aggressive in reaction to a real or alleged insult is in itself passive. Then they are tormented by their inner critic for experiencing the situation through their passivity. Sometimes they feel better about themselves when they do become pseudo-aggressive and react to an apparent insult with some display of aggression, such as a verbal protest or complaint. But feeling better in this way is only a temporary fix. Pseudo-aggressive reactions are themselves defenses (see Chapter 17).

Another client, Tish, suffered with self-defeat. She was a bulimic who had rejection issues with both her father and mother, and she held on fiercely to a sense of being a victim of them. "Whatever I did was never good enough for them," she said. "If I got ninety-eight on a test, my father wanted to know where I missed on the other two points."

After losing considerable weight in a treatment program, she still continued to reject her body. Her negative body image now centered on the excess skin left from her overweight condition. Her secret attachment to rejection, not her excess skin, created her suffering. Even with a more appealing body, Tish would find an imperfection of some kind to use as a reason to reject herself. She made use of a defense called a *negative magic gesture*. In her unconscious, the defense was presented with ironic bitterness: "I am not attached to rejection. I am only doing to myself what Mom and Dad taught me. They rejected me, so now I am doing to myself what they did to me, only more so."

Her sense of victimization was heightened and the self-defeat elevated when she elaborated further upon her defense: "Through my self-image I want everyone to

173

see what my parents did to me, how bad it was for me, and what I had to endure because of them." This defense required that Tish continue to hold bitter feeling toward her parents. Eventually, these feelings were toned down somewhat by her ambivalence toward them, and she was able to have a decent (though not particularly loving) relationship with them. In any case, the therapy helped her considerably to acquire an appreciation for herself. She was able to stop identifying with herself through her body and using her body image for the purposes of suffering.

The next example involves George, a businessman who had a tendency to drink heavily at social events or parties. This client said he needed alcohol in order to "come alive" and really enjoy himself. However, before these evenings had run their course, he frequently became obnoxious and got sick from drinking too much. The next day George would often have forgotten much of what took place at the party, and his wife would complain that his conduct had embarrassed her. This behavior threatened his marriage as well as his social standing. "I don't want people to see me as a drunk," he said earnestly. "I want to be able to drink and not go over the edge with it."

I asked him, "How would you feel if you went to a party having decided not to drink?"

"Well, it hasn't happened for years. But I can tell you—I get bored. I look at them and see the same old faces and hear the same old small talk. I've heard it all before. I'm not good at it. 'Just let me go home,' I say to myself, 'and watch TV.'"

I told George, "I want to show you how you contribute to creating that impression that people are boring. As a child, you picked up your father's insecurity and lack of self-respect. As you've told me, your father felt like a nobody—completely insignificant and worthless. He would drink and become a show-off around others to compensate for that feeling. As it happens, you have some of that in you. When you go to a social event, you're steeped in the feeling that you'll be seen as boring and insignificant unless you make a big splash and become the center of attention. But by drinking and becoming obnoxious, you become like your father and create the impression of being a fool, which is how you saw your father.

"When you don't drink, you believe the problem is that the people you are with are boring and insignificant. You're seeing them as you really expect to be seen—as boring and insignificant—which is also how you see yourself, though much of this is unconscious. The solution is, first, to acknowledge your attachment to the feeling of self-rejection; second, to get in touch with your feelings of having seen your father exhibit in this negative way and the emotional effect it had on you as a child; third, to see that you are subjecting others to the same foolishness that you were subjected to and had to endure passively, so that you now can identify with their shame and embarrassment; and, fourth, to understand that harboring such ill regard for yourself blocks you from appreciating yourself and manifesting your authentic self."

As his defense, George pleaded guilty to negative exhibitionism and to his impression of being a fool. His defense became his self-defeating behavior: "I'm not attached to being seen as a nobody; the problem is I act up and look foolish." He did reform this behavior once he understood the driving forces behind it.

As children, we made conclusions about our circumstances that diverged greatly from reality. We saw rejection where it wasn't intended, we took neutral comments as criticism, and we felt betrayed when our sense of self wasn't fully validated by parents who were limited themselves. As adults, we're prepared to continue our misunderstandings. Liberation from the deadly flaw requires an understanding of how, from within, we "manufacture" our experiences of life. This means that we begin to take responsibility for the quality of our experiences. To do that, we have to uncover the part in us that's choosing to experience life in negative terms. With the benefit of this new intelligence, we see through the faulty impressions that are harmful and self-defeating.

Some mental-health experts say we can avoid self-defeat and suffering by making a concentrated effort to maintain our attention in the present moment, in the here-and-now. They are not addressing to what degree we conjure up old hurts out of our past, or foresee troubles in the future, for the explicit purpose of suffering in the here-and-now. Many people also experience the here-and-now as a "place" where their suffering is more intense. They're more interested in looking for distractions, entertainments, substances, and various such ways to avoid the here-and-now.

It is certainly healthy to be able to experience the present moment in a state of serenity or inner peacefulness. But an emphasis on the here-and-now as a means to mental health can be a way to avoid deeper issues, and the emphasis may in itself be a defense. A person can feel an illusion of wellness or power, for instance, in wholeheartedly practicing being present or mindful as the deadly flaw goes unrecognized and blocks real growth.

Chapter 14
Appeasement of the Inner Critic

Courtroom scenes are a staple of movie and TV drama, and their popularity may be due in part to our intuitive resonance with the courtroom in our psyche. The issues that confront us in the real or TV courtroom involving accusations, defenses, deception, guilt, innocence, and punishment are played out in our inner court of law.

Along with the similarities are some stark differences. In our inner courtroom, the proceedings are stacked up against the defendant, namely you or me. Like the presiding officer in a mock trial, our inner critic serves as prosecutor, judge, and jury. Meanwhile, our unconscious or subordinate ego, which serves as our defense attorney, is a wimp and a chiseler. It is afraid of the powerful prosecutor and rather indifferent to our wellbeing. Our timid advocate does bargain for tidbits of mercy on our behalf, but it never challenges the status quo, the corrupt inner power structure.

(These dynamics described in the following pages can be difficult for readers to follow. Don't worry about "not getting it." Instead, marvel if you can at the intricacies of human nature. If that doesn't work, skip to the next chapter.)

This court is a surreal place where the defendant can be tried for his fantasies as well as his deeds. In unconscious law, the thought is just as bad as the deed. Most of the so-called crimes for which a person punishes himself have not been committed. They are simply unconscious wishes, such as the willingness at any given moment to strike back aggressively at someone who has mildly offended us.

Moreover, in the mock trial of the inner tribunal the defendant is repeatedly tried and punished for the same "crime". For example, the jealous person is punished many times daily for his secret willingness to indulge in feeling rejected, unloved, or betrayed. The angry person is punished for his secret willingness to indulge in an insult or offense that provoked the anger.

This inner courtroom is a battleground between aggression and passivity, with the aggressive superego winning much of the time and the defendant required to accept punishment such as guilt, shame, remorse, reduced aspirations, anxiety, fear, depression, anger, loneliness, and the self-defeat of inappropriate behaviors. Essentially, our inner passivity or inner defendant operates like an enabler of the harsh inner critic or superego. The superego, Bergler wrote, is "the hidden but real master of the personality."[55] Our "defender," the unconscious ego (the overseer in our psyche of the no-man's-land called inner passivity) is the master of timid compromise, although at times— through sublimation—it works out a decent deal for us.

179

In this inner courtroom, the defendant is charged with harboring forbidden wishes and drives—a mixture of aggression, narcissism, the sex drive, and libidinized displeasure—that yearn to be satisfied, though they can be at odds with external reality and the requirements of civilized society. According to the inner critic, the worst crime of all is our unconscious wish to experience—whether in fact or in fantasy—our attachments to such emotions as deprivation, loss, refusal, helplessness, criticism, rejection, and betrayal (deep negativity). Our inner critic, which is anti-hedonistic and hence in opposition to the pleasure principle, objects to the pleasure—second-rate and miniscule though it is—that we unconsciously extract through the deadly flaw. Our secret "pleasure" is frantically covered up by our inner defender, who often claims that we are guilty of some "lesser crime" or that we are an innocent victim of circumstances or outside malice. This inner defender proceeds to plea bargain, and we end up with a deal that can be exceedingly disadvantageous to us. Such a deal frequently requires that we accept some manner of emotional and behavioral suffering that far exceeds what is appropriate for the "crime." In the meantime, we remain unconscious of our deadly flaw, as well as the plea bargain itself.

Let me try to say this more simply. According to the typical "plea bargain," we agree to accept some emotional and behavioral suffering and self-defeat providing that our willingness to entertain suffering is covered up. In other words, we suffer greatly to maintain the corrupt inner status quo. We choose suffering over inner freedom because we can't bring ourselves to evolve into the mysterious and admirable stranger we won't recognize. The idea of making such an inner shift produces too much fear. It feels as if we'll lose all traces of how we know ourselves.

This fear is an illusion, a scare tactic of our resistance. We do, in fact, grow very fond of the self that we discover.

Often in the plea bargain we make with the inner prosecutor, we are punished for "substitute or lesser crimes." The punishment itself for the substitute crime becomes a secret attachment, an experience of the deadly flaw.[56] For instance, the guilt the individual feels when he pleads guilty to being lazy (to cover up, say, the deeper "crime" of inner passivity) is itself libidinized or sugar-coated. In another example, the guilt a person feels when he pleads guilty to being an angry person (to cover up, say, an attachment to feeling criticized) is likewise sugar-coated. The guilt is often accepted with bittersweet resignation: "Yes, it's true, I'm a bad person for what I did. I submit to the feeling of being bad. This suffering is what I deserve."

As mentioned, the inner critic objects to pleasure, even second-rate libidinized displeasure. In psychoanalytic terms, the inner critic is anti-libidinous. Some strict forms of religion, which object to people having fun and being carefree and autonomous, display this feature of the inner critic's mentality. Children can feel, too, that

181

their parents' objections to their noisy boisterousness are objections to their having too much fun.

As mentioned, the inner critic exacts punishment for the "crimes" of forbidden wishes in the form of guilt, shame, depression, and self-damage. These punishments in conscious suffering (in what further signifies the primitive nature of the inner courtroom) far outweigh the seriousness of the "crime."

For those whose deadly flaw is less of a liability, our weak inner lawyer manages to construct satisfactory defenses that help us to cope with everyday life and to thrive in some of our pursuits. These defenses consist of workable *sublimations*, which are resolutions of inner conflict that direct us into creative and artistic expression, relative happiness with work, social pleasures, community involvement, and hobbies. When society approves of the activities that constitute sublimation, the pleasure gain can be considerable and the resolutions remarkably stable.[57]

Another player in our psyche, the previously mentioned ego or conscious ego that we know as "I," doesn't have much role in the inner courtroom. Our "I" is basically oblivious to the whole procedure. It is the puppet prince unaware of the Machiavellian minister of state's antics behind the throne. It is likely to puff itself up with self-importance, and it becomes offended when the operations of the inner courtroom are alluded to: "How could all this be happening without my knowing about it!"

Hence, like our unconscious ego, our conscious ego isn't up to the challenge of representing us effectively and wisely. It is blindsided by unconscious operations. It presumes that it originates most of our thought and that, in a rendition of the infantile mentality, it is self-sufficient in this manner.[58] Psychologically, we want to attain not just self-esteem but realization of oneself beyond the ego. This new sense of self is a kind of software upgrade that transcends "the little me," the infantile remains of our past. As it transcends our old identity, it moves us beyond all ego, class, race, sexual, gender, and national identifications. It represents the attainment of an inner maturity in which our ego, if it's still hanging around, peers from the back row, far behind our consciousness, wisdom, and peace of mind.

Some noted psychoanalysts have written about a self or true self that they say is an essence that needs to be recognized by others.[59] I perceive the self as a consciousness that is discovered when the deadly flaw is addressed and that needs no external validation or recognition from others.

Any discussion of the self is a departure from Bergler's work, and I mention my views on the subject briefly in passing.[60] Bergler's concept of a healthy person involves someone with a strong ego who has made progress resolving his or her inner conflicts and achieved a stable level of happiness and fulfillment with relationships, work, and leisure time. I believe, however, that the benefits of tackling the deadly flaw are more profound. The process enables us to transcend our ego and replace it with the self. This self is a benevolent inner authority that is perhaps our soul or spirit or a gateway to it. Through this evolved aspect, entity, or quality, we are capable of consistently accessing the pleasures of compassion, wonder, and joy. It is the foundation of our authenticity and the seat of our autonomy, In helping us to overcome incompetence, mediocrity, and self-defeat, the realization of the self constitutes an advance in our intelligence.

While it may be that this self can itself be transcended with further inner development (Buddhists, for instance, claim we experience *no-self* in states of higher consciousness), the discovery or attainment of the authentic self represents a vital stage of one's evolvement, as well as a personal triumph. In other words, we have to establish or discover the self (through self-knowledge) before we can transcend it.

Bergler believed that the harsh, negative energy of the inner critic "is beyond analytic reach."[61] I would agree with him if we had only the unconscious ego and the conscious ego with which to counter the inner critic or superego. However, as I see it, the self, this "better angel" of our nature, does have the power to overthrow the inner tyranny of the superego. This self is a personal attainment that results when inner conflict and the deadly flaw are being successfully resolved. This self not only transcends the ego, it transcends the psyche's primary conflict between inner aggression and inner passivity. I believe the self emerges out of inner passivity, and then becomes the power that subdues the aggression of the inner critic. The attainment of such a self is not exclusively a secular or a spiritual matter. This dichotomy, too, is transcended.

The inner critic, meanwhile, is an agent of our deadly flaw but not the essence of it. To repeat, the anti-libidinous inner critic objects to the libidinization of deep negativity.[62] To see this acted out, consider the compulsive gambler. The inner critic may not bother to object to this person's gambling in itself. Instead, it objects to the reckless pleasure (libidinized displeasure) the gambler gets from the forbidden thrill of anticipated passivity and financial loss. The gambler, meanwhile, falsely believes, as his defense, that his excitement is due to his prospect of winning. The excitement, however, is due to his embrace of the likely suffering that will follow his reckless behavior.

Once the typical compulsive gambler loses, he is then berated mercilessly by his inner critic. The accusation—"How stupid can you be!"—is a favorite of the inner critic's. The driving force behind a compulsive gambler is his emotional addiction to the feeling of loss, in combination with secret attachments to inner passivity and inner aggression. So his addiction is not to gambling per se. Gambling is just his preferred "playing field" for the experience of his negativity. His primary addiction is to libidinized displeasure (which, again, is a second-rate unconscious pleasure) involving loss, passivity, guilt, and self-aggression. For the gambler and for all of us enmeshed in whatever form our deadly flaw takes, the agony of conscious suffering far outweighs the thrill of perverse displeasure.

The same mechanism is at work in numerous situations, including the following: the jealous person is secretly willing to circulate feelings of being rejected and betrayed; the cynic is "into" the feeling of being helpless to influence or reform situations; the envious person wants to feel deprived of things that are either available or unavailable to him; the perfectionist is looking for the feeling of being criticized; the complainer is "taking a hit" on feeling deprived, devalued, or rendered passive by circumstances; the chronically lonely person is indulging in feeling unloved; and the procrastinator is eagerly imbibing the distaste of his passivity, along with his inner critic's condemnation of it.

In the above examples, the inner critic decrees that the wish to feel, say, rejected or betrayed is forbidden. As mentioned, the wish contains too much gratification to suit the inner critic, though that gratification is a second-rate pleasure that is not even recorded consciously. The individual, through his unconscious ego (his defense attorney), now begins a series of defenses to ward off the inner critic and, consequently, to keep himself in the dark as to the existence and self-defeating nature of his deadly flaw.

In other words, the unconscious ego is frantically producing defenses to "prove" that the individual is not secretly indulging in those negative emotions. Knowledge of the deadly flaw is considered forbidden, because, for one thing, this budding self-awareness initially instigates a fearful sense that something inherently bad exists within us. As mentioned, our infantile conviction is that the bad, in the form of enemies or malice, comes from outside us, not from within. This is one reason many people and societies need to have enemies, so they can project outward the negativity that they refuse to see in themselves.

Some people will refuse to accept this knowledge of the "bad" within because they feel they'll be overwhelmed or shattered by it. Their egos are weak and they are far from developing an authentic self. To protect the ego, they will deny the possibility of the deadly flaw or else forget that they ever encountered the idea of it. I have respect for where they're "at," having been there myself, and I guard against being impatient with my clients' resistance.

It's important to remember that the self-aggression from the inner critic has itself been libidinized or sugar-coated. Evidence of this is the incredible fact that we allow the inner critic, which is almost exclusively irrational and negative, to have such a powerful influence in our lives. It harasses us for failings or alleged failings committed—or allegedly committed, or allegedly about to be committed—in the past, present, and future. Even individuals who energetically pursue success can be driven above all by their fears of inner-critic reproaches for allegedly being unworthy or being a failure.

Why can't we just make the inner critic go away? It doesn't go away because we're willing, through our attachments to both inner passivity and inner aggression, to live under its sway. This hidden master of the personality is primitive in the sense that it functions as a pack leader or strongman that dominates the organization of life around it. What could be more self-defeating than to continue to live passively under this inner tyranny?

Even people who know they have a problem with self-criticism do not usually understand how venomous their inner critic is. For one thing, it mocks our failure to live up to our *ego ideal*, which is a part of the superego that develops when we are young as an offshoot of our megalomania. We see the presence of the ego ideal in children who boast that they will grow up to become someone very outstanding—the president, for instance, or a great writer or actor. They sincerely believe in their predictions, and adults graciously humor them. Of course, we don't typically live up to these grandiose assumptions. The inner critic, conveniently overlooking the childishness of those assumptions, assails us harshly for allegedly being losers and failures when our achievements later in life fall short of those grandiose aims. Typically, we feel painful guilt and regret associated with a sense of being a disappointment to ourselves.

The inner critic plays a dominant role in the inner process that regulates our happiness. Bergler said the successful sublimations some people achieve, as well as the self-defeat that others produce, are the end results of a five-layer structure of inner processing. This structure consists of accusations and vetoes by the inner critic, along with a wide range of possible defenses put forward by the unconscious ego. This structure in all its variations gets into another level of complexity,[63] and this text does not elaborate on it. In many of his books, Bergler provides numerous examples of clinical cases involving this five-layer structure.[64]

We have considered the human psyche as an inner courtroom or tribunal. At the risk of mixing metaphors, our psyche can also be understood as a primitive political system, with a tyrant in one corner (inner critic), a weak legal system in another corner (unconscious ego), and a passive populace that has few rights taking up the rest of the space (conscious ego). Human progress involves reforming this inner system and replacing it with a true democracy.

In this inner democracy, the individual, representing the people, establishes his authentic self as sovereign citizen. This sovereignty is not individualism. The latter is a limited mentality that emphasizes separation from others, displays infantile illusions of self-sufficiency, and

189

easily becomes entangled in the infantile impression that, "What comes from me is good; what comes from outside is bad." By comparison, true inner democracy is a state of freedom from the psyche's warring factions. In this state, the primitive inner critic has been tamed, allowing intelligence and wisdom to flourish. The resulting inner peacefulness permeates the nation itself, as we become responsible citizens who personify goodness, behave rationally, and represent the values and ideals of self and country.

Chapter 15
Neutralizing Inner Conflict

"Everyone is a moon," wrote Mark Twain, and "has a dark side which he never shows to anyone." People never even show, Twain might have added, this dark side to *themselves*.

Many people do catch glimpses of the dark side that's held in place by our deadly flaw. (As I see it, our deadly flaw is our dark side, or at least it's the superstructure that supports our dark side.) Usually people quickly draw the curtain before they see more of it. Even when we're smart enough to seek in-depth therapy, we usually aren't able to handle more than one little peep at a time. We readily see the dark side in Darth Vader or the Joker or even the neighbor next door, but not in ourselves.

Twain also stated that man's sole impulse is "the securing of his own approval." This approval is "evidence" that we use to fortify our ego against inner-critic assaults. We brandish this approval to the inner critic, and say, "Hey, Jane and Joe approve of me. They think I'm great! So back off!" The act of patting ourselves on the back can be employed to shield us from our inner critic, though admiration and validation from others are usually preferred.

Sometimes the effort in acquiring a large number of friends can be partly a process of gathering evidence of one's worthiness and importance. Our less worthy politicians are frequently into politics for recognition, validation, and power. This illustrates how people so often do the right thing (in this case, having lots of friends or being a public servant) for, at least in part, the wrong reasons (external validation and the quest for power to cope with an underlying disconnect from self). When we become stronger emotionally, we don't need such validation to repel our inner critic. We simply no longer resonate with the doubts and accusations expressed by the lingering, weakened inner critic. We have liberated ourselves from the inner critic's tyranny.

Let me emphasize again that the inner critic is not our deadly flaw. It is easy to confuse the two. Our deadly flaw incorporates the inner critic, yet it is bigger than the inner critic. Our deadly flaw encompasses the processes whereby we first become emotionally attached to certain negative emotions (deep negativity). It also encompasses the mechanisms whereby we continue thereafter to regenerate and recycle these painful emotions. The inner critic is just one ingredient of our deadly flaw, the one that supplies the aggression. Other ingredients are the unconscious ego (the defense apparatus), libido (the agent of the pleasure principle but also the means to turn displeasure into pleasure), and acute self-centeredness (the infantile illusion of grandeur and power that diminishes over time but is retained as narcissism and contained in our ego). This is all tossed into the mix with our early experience of protracted helplessness, our unconscious repetition compulsion,[65] the challenges of wayward genes, the disposition of our parents, and other tribulations and variables of life.

In one sense the deadly flaw may *not* be a "mistake" in human nature: It may serve a larger purpose. The pain produced by the flaw generates a great deal of self-reflection as we search for a way out of our suffering. So the flaw could be a catalyst that leavens our intelligence and fuels evolution, driving us onward to greater heights. With the flaw fully exposed, it ought to be easier for each new generation of our descendants to face it and resolve it within themselves.

Being conscious of the deadly flaw is vitally important, but being aware of our inner critic is not particularly helpful in itself. People are often conscious of their inner critic and will readily admit, "Oh yes, I am my own worst critic, my own worst enemy." They still don't know what to do about it. It's our growing insight into how our inner passivity absorbs the inner critic's aggression that liberates us from the harassment and torments inflicted by the inner critic. One way to neutralize the inner critic is to recognize and acknowledge that we are emotionally attached to the aggression that it directs our way. However, it may be that we can even more effectively neutralize or tame the inner critic by becoming aware of our inner passivity. This is the aspect in our psyche that enables, accommodates, and even welcomes that aggression.

In other words, we silence the inner critic by resolving our inner passivity. The inner critic gets away with its interference in our life because, through inner passivity, we allow that interference to happen. (This process is explained more fully in the next chapter, where much more is said about inner passivity.)

The inner critic is not always discernible. Some people don't register it at all. They can be anxious, fearful, guilty, shameful, and depressed without a clue that their inner critic is contributing to these painful feelings. We have to get to the stage of recognizing it, feeling it within us as a negative, unwarranted intrusion.

Here's what the inner critic often says: "You just don't measure up," or "You can't even do the simple things right," or Here you are, still stuck in this mess," or "What's the matter with you! You should have known better," or "It's no wonder they don't approve of you." In a person's mind, the voice is often registered in the first person, e.g., "I just don't measure up," or I can't even get it right," or "I can't believe I was so dumb."

As I tell my clients, the inner critic can't be trusted. It's not a moral conscience that tells us what is right or wrong. The inner critic doesn't know right from wrong, and it doesn't care one way or the other. It's only fulfilling its function, which is to dominate the psyche and, by extension, the personality. It's almost always belittling us. We ought not to trust an inner voice that is unkind or critical. The voice of our authentic self has kind and affectionate overtones. The inner critic, in comparison, is not so kind. It can be subtle, so that we hardly know it is around. Yet, whether conscious or unconscious, it's often harping, nagging, mocking, and relentless. It specializes in holding us accountable and enticing us to feel bad about ourselves. Figuratively, it's like having a demon on our shoulder, whispering detractions, gripes, insinuations—all pure negativity.

One step in silencing and eliminating this negative voice or feeling involves becoming aware that we're no longer willing to tolerate the negativity. A true friend or an advisor would never speak to us in such a negative manner. We are fooled by it because sometimes the voice does contain a shred of truth. However, even when it is harping on facts that might be true (*e.g.*, accusing a person of being overweight or unpopular), it uses facts in a misleading manner, suggesting in these examples that body weight and popularity are measures of one's value and that one deserves to be criticized, condemned, or punished for these imperfections.

Most of us also have another voice or inner experience, that of inner passivity. It says things like, "No matter what I do, it's never good enough," or "Life is too hard, I don't have any luck," or "Too many people let me down," or "It's all their fault." It greatly helps us to step back and be able to listen to these voices, or sense these impressions, with some detachment or some degree of separation.

Otherwise, we slip under the influence of one voice or the other, and we are hopelessly entangled in the conflict between the inner critic and inner passivity. We experience ourselves only within the limited range of the passive voice or the aggressive voice. Frequently, we don't even realize there is a conflict. Instead of hearing voices, we are just emotionally and behaviorally overwhelmed by the conflict. We remain at the mercy of how the conflict will get played out, like sad children barely conscious of the agonies of their silently despairing parents.

As we make the conflict more conscious, it's helpful to recognize which voice is which. Is it the inner critic we're hearing, or is it inner passivity? Acquiring this discernment means we're hearing or recognizing the voices more objectively, with more clarity. This helps us to transcend the conflict between aggression and passivity in order to consolidate the self.

The inner critic's harassment first becomes operational when children, in order to save face and preserve acute self-centeredness, begin unconsciously to identify with the expectations and rules that parents need to impose. As mentioned, children exchange the external warning voice of the parent—"don't do this, don't do that!"—for an internal warning voice—"I won't do this, I won't do that!" or "I shouldn't do this, I shouldn't do that." The prohibitions are inwardly reframed in order to save

196

face: "Nobody tells me what to do. I am the one who decides what to do and what not to do." This phony claim to power now places the child at the mercy of this internal warning voice that has no interest in being rational. As children and later as adults our inner passivity gives this critical voice license to be ruthless, instigating cycles of suffering.

The challenge is to bring the inner critic and inner passivity into focus so we can escape their clutches. They're almost always producing negative impressions about us. It's certainly not our fault they exist. We're seeking to acquire, in the case of the inner critic, the strength to go "eyeball-to-eyeball" with it, staring it down with the power of truth, the pleasure of exercising inner strength, and our growing sense of self. Turning the tables on our inner critic is indeed a pleasurable experience and a big step in overcoming our deadly flaw. This process of gaining self-mastery produces a feeling of personal triumph.

We need to be patient and accept that inner reform may take some time. Yet even at a slow pace, we can still feel much pleasure in the progress we know is taking place.

Another way to neutralize the inner critic involves observing our defensiveness. This requires us to be mindful and present to the moment. The defensiveness referred to here is the argumentative kind that we employ with others or in inner dialogue. It is on the surface of our awareness, in contrast to the defensiveness of our defense system that operates covertly. Even though this argumentative defensiveness is apparent to others, we ourselves can be quite unaware of just how defensive we are. My clients are often surprised when their defensiveness is pointed out to them in our sessions.

We operate on a hair-trigger defensiveness and can be quite unconscious of how we process the statements, insinuations, or accusations that prompt our defensiveness. Often, when one partner in a relationship says to the other, "We need to talk," the person hearing this immediately thinks defensively: "Yipes! What now! What have I done!" The priority of this defensive person is not to resolve a situation through dialogue but to protect himself or herself from any allegations of wrongdoing.

Defensiveness is irritating in relationships and marriages because it causes the person who is hearing the knee-jerk defensiveness to feel that he or she is not being heard. Defensiveness undermines communication and spins our words in circles. It's produced as reactive thinking or talking when one or both partners "buy into" or absorb implied or actual criticism. In other words, defensiveness results when we absorb the real or imagined aggression behind criticism or objective dialogue.

The problem is not our partner but our inner critic. We jump when our inner critic talks. When defensiveness happens, our partner is only mirroring the internal relationship we have with our inner critic. When our inner critic becomes active, our inner passivity instinctively begins its defensive inner dialogue. In fact, our inner passivity is doing the talking when we are being defensive with our partner or others. Our inner critic has the power to hold us accountable and to pose as our inner authority. This happens because our inner passivity creates an inner vacuum into which our inner critic aggressively intrudes.

As mentioned, the inner critic can be subtle. Often we can only detect it through our inner defensiveness, our self-justifying thoughts and feelings that indicate we're under an inner attack. We can also detect it when we begin to feel some revulsion at its chronic negativity. As decent and intelligent people, we don't have to be defensive to anything or anyone. If an innocent person gets hauled into court for robbing a bank, then he or she certainly needs a defense lawyer. For the most part, though, defensiveness (whether inner or outer) is not necessary. It only exists and persists as the voice of our inner passivity when we allow our inner critic to rule over us.

We can stop the inner and outer defensiveness once we realize where the defensiveness comes from. Keep in mind that our defensiveness mimics the voice or the "reasoning" of the unconscious or subordinate ego, the inner lawyer who serves us so poorly as the voice of inner passivity.

People often try to beat back the inner critic by repeating positive affirmations ("I am a success. I am a kind, loving person."). Affirmations are superficial attempts to resolve a conflict. In fact, they're little more than variations of inner defensiveness. At best, they're the equivalent of aspirins for arthritis. At worst, they can be used as defenses, as in: "Who says I'm a failure? In fact, I'm a success, just as my affirmations proclaim." The only thing this defense will perpetuate is endless conflict between aggression and passivity, along with the continuance of the deadly flaw.

The following is an example of dialogue between the inner critic and the unconscious ego (inner passivity). This inner dialogue may be conscious or semi-conscious. (Deeper levels of dialogue exist in other dynamics involving our defense system.)

Inner critic: You made a fool of yourself at the office today. How could you have asked such a stupid question at the meeting?

Unconscious ego: It wasn't that bad. Granted, it was a mistake to ask that question. But everybody's probably forgotten about it by now. (Note the unconscious ego's defensiveness.)

Inner critic: I disagree. They're probably still snickering about it. It only proves to them that you're incompetent.

Unconscious ego: Many of them have told me how important I am to the organization. This was just a little slip-up, and nobody's perfect.

Inner critic: Well, that's certainly true of you. Hopelessly imperfect! With no improvement in sight!

Unconscious ego: I try to do my best. This is a tough organization. If only I'd gotten more support from my parents.

Personal growth is represented in the following exchange of dialogue. When we are succeeding in resolving psychological conflict, inner aggression becomes less invasive. A shift of power is occurring. In this example, the voice of the unconscious ego has now been replaced by the voice of our authentic self, representing our inner authority. This example provides a sense of the feeling of the inner authority that enables us to represent our best interests on inner and outer levels.

Inner critic: You made a fool of yourself at the office today. How could you have asked such a stupid question at the meeting?

Self: Did I just hear some inner criticism?

Inner critic: Yes, you did! Do I have to repeat myself!

Self: Who invited you in? What's this nonsense you're babbling?

Inner critic: Don't think you can brush me aside so easily.

Self: You're silly. Go away.

Inner critic: No, I won't!

Self: Okay, stay around. I don't care.

Inner critic: Did you hear what I said?

Self: I heard you. But I can't take you seriously. I'm no longer in your thrall. I no longer have an emotional attachment to your aggression and negativity. Your power over me has greatly diminished.

Inner critic: Well, you'd better listen. I know what I'm talking about.

Self: (Silence)

Inner critic: (Silence)

Even if the individual did something at the meeting that was foolish or inappropriate, he or she doesn't have to answer to the inner critic. If a serious breach of decorum occurred at the meeting, the healthy individual chalks it up as a learning experience. He or she might need to answer to the group with an apology or explanation. But the inner critic is owed no explanation and ought not to have any voice in the matter.

As mentioned in the previous chapter, Bergler believed the superego or inner critic was hard-wired in our psyche. It cannot be "removed or weakened without analytic help," he wrote, "and must simply be accepted as a fixed fact in the human equation, like death."[66] I disagree with this assessment. In my opinion and experience, individuals can tame, defang, and subdue the inner critic as they become increasingly conscious of the inner passivity that facilitates it and as they establish the self that transcends the conflict between inner aggression and inner passivity.

We certainly cannot tame or conquer the inner critic by pretending, as much of mainstream psychology does, that it does not exist. One does not become enlightened by imagining figures of light, said Carl Jung, but by making the darkness conscious.

Freud shed light on some of the darkness when he fashioned his theory of the oedipal complex and child sexuality. His findings revealed the powerful influence of libido in that stage of early childhood. Several decades later, Bergler provided more illumination by revealing that libido is active in earlier (anal and oral) developmental stages. At those stages, libido helps to create low-grade pleasure from infantile impressions of deprivation, refusal, and passivity. This psychological process, this mischief of our deadly flaw, continues to operate in our psyche as we age, and it enlists other negative emotions such as feeling rejected, criticized, betrayed, and abandoned in the cycle of suffering.

It's conceivable that this process eases our suffering in our early years, as it helps us to survive the onslaught of self-aggression. But when, as adults, we remain unaware of the fact and the process of turning displeasure into perverse pleasure, we remain hopelessly entangled in inner conflict, suffering, and unhappiness.

Chapter 16
The Territory of Inner Passivity

Risking mixed metaphors again, I depict the deadly flaw as an outlaw, a wild scoundrel who hides out in our psyche. As in the Old West, this outlaw hightails it to the Territories to evade the law. We can flush him out if we "civilize" that territory, that no-man's-land where our awareness is largely excluded and where our infantile aspects howl in the night.

The law, as represented by our growing self-knowledge, is looking for a way into the arroyos and canyons of our psyche to install the benefits of civilized awareness. To track down the outlaw, we can use a good map, or at least a description of the features and landmarks of that part of our psyche known as inner passivity.

As mentioned, this area of our psyche is also known as the unconscious or subordinate ego. In this Wild West metaphor, this part in our psyche is played by a decrepit sheriff who can't shoot straight and who hates to stray more than a mile or so from his favorite saloon. The previous two chapters described how inadequately that part represents us and how, much of the time, it sacrifices our well-being for its own self-preservation. This chapter moves deeper into the territory of inner passivity to help us replace that incompetent sheriff with our own trusted upholder of the law.

Inner passivity defies all attempts to define it. It can, though, be explored by recognizing its features. For starters, it's not simply a place inside us that renders us passive. It's not specific to the introverted personality type—an extrovert can be just as encumbered with inner passivity. Nor is it just about wimps and weaklings. People who are apparently powerful and successful can be quite entangled in inner passivity.

It is a condition of nonbeing, a largely unconscious phenomenon that is equally a problem for men and women. We find it easier to recognize our inner critic than our inner passivity. We also have more resistance to seeing it than we do the inner critic. Typically, we are more offended when accused of being passive than we are when accused of being aggressive, cruel, controlling, rejecting, selfish, greedy, lazy, or angry.

We get an inkling of the intangibility and elusiveness of inner passivity when we consider the fact that passivity, not aggression, is the root cause of violence, and that criminals and terrorists are among the most severely passive of us all.

Inner passivity, a component of our deadly flaw, is both a measure of our lack of evolvement and a way to understand it. It's not necessarily painful in itself, yet it causes painful and self-defeating reactions such as guilt, anxiety, fear, irritation, procrastination, impatience, depression, hatred, and violence.

Inner passivity is often experienced as a sense of inertia or as a lack of foresight or vision. It hides out behind the problem and the pain of being indecisive, yet it can also be a factor in hasty decisions. One of its primary emotional symptoms is the feeling of being overwhelmed, while one of its common behavioral symptoms is procrastination. We can experience inner passivity as the sense of having no power, as the feeling of being stuck or unable to move forward in our life, as an inability to make something happen, as a feeling we're always playing catch-up or running late, or as an impression that life is a losing battle, or in our worrying and emotional preoccupations concerning the uncertainty of life.

Inner passivity also is the culprit in our failure to create a vision or a plan for our success, and it can also be an enemy that snatches defeat from the jaws of victory. Generally, we can say of inner passivity that it dictates and degrades our everyday experiences. More precisely, we can say that we allow it to do so.

We gain a distinct advantage when we identify inner passivity as a psychological condition or as a characteristic of our personal development. Once we identify it in this clinical sense, we're able to step back from the limiting, self-defeating symptoms it produces, thereby establishing some conscious separation from our symptoms. Otherwise the symptoms of inner passivity (unable to take charge of one's life, for one) feel so much like our nature, as if they represent who we are or who we think we are. Without separation from our symptoms, the symptoms can define us in our own mind and thereby limit us.

Inner passivity is experienced in such recurring thoughts as "What should I do?" and "What if . . . ?" In fact, inner passivity, like the inner critic or inner aggression, has a voice all its own, and it's important to be able to identify that voice or feeling. If inner passivity had a mantra, it would be, "What's the use." If it was a hit song, the refrain would be, "It's not fair, it's not right." When it's voiced in a forlorn or plaintive manner, its other favorite refrains include: "What if I fail?" "I promise to do it tomorrow," "Nobody appreciates or understands me," "How come nothing ever works out for me?" "What am I going to say to her?"

Inner passivity can appear in many guises. A religious person might express a sense of helplessness or futility through the words, "If God wills it," or "God only knows." If we are considering becoming, say, politically involved in a reform effort, that voice, fearful of the repercussions, might say, to this effect: "You can get in a lot of trouble. Let other people take the risk. One less voice won't matter."

Couples who bicker a lot appear to be aggressive with one another. But the aggression is usually fake, a cover-up for underlying passivity. Their bickering is ultimately passive because it involves being caught in a loop or going in circles, with no likelihood of resolution. Militaristic-minded people are also passive when they identify with military might to compensate for a personal sense of powerlessness. True power, in contrast, involves the willingness if not the ability to resolve conflict without violence or warfare, even in situations where that appears to be impossible.

People watching TV, surfing the internet, or gambling on the internet or on casino machines can easily slip into the feeling of being "spaced out" or taken over and possessed by the influence of the visual images and other sensations. Young people hooked on video games can go into a kind of trance or even depersonalization, as if they have slipped into the Matrix, a simulated reality that pacifies and subdues them. Instead of overcoming inner passivity, they become personifications of it. These above activities don't have to be problematic providing they're not compulsive and providing people maintain watchfulness, meaning a degree of presence to themselves and alertness to their surroundings.

In the case of gambling at cards, the compulsive player feels himself at the mercy of the luck of the draw. However skilled a player, he still sits helplessly awaiting the rendering of the deck. When losing, he passively and painfully endures the bad fortunes of the cards. When winning, he can feel intoxicated with power and joy, and he is tempted to believe (as a defense against inner passivity) that he gives to himself, out of his own powers, the blessings of good fortune. Though it is hidden from his awareness, the compulsive gambler pursues not Lady Luck but the phantom of passivity. Gambling is his means of acting out his psychological and emotional love-affair with the feelings of helpless anticipation and even of being a loser in both the emotional and financial sense of that word. Successful or professional gamblers, in contrast to compulsive gamblers, can also possess these emotional liabilities, even as they are able to prevail against weaker players.

Inner passivity may be integral to our biology, yet overcoming it is a psychological and a learning process. (Psychoanalysis is not so much talk therapy or a talking cure as it is a learning process.) The psychological origins of inner passivity can be traced to childhood. Despite the childhood sense of omnipotence, we become painfully aware of our helplessness and limited powers. The illusion of being all-powerful fights a losing battle against the reality of helplessness. Throughout childhood we are desperate to feel power to counter the reality of helplessness.

A child's passive experiences can include helplessness during handling and diaper changing, the burden of infantile fears, the "tragedy" of weaning, the feeling of waiting endlessly for someone to show up, "enforced" sleep and elimination, the requirements of toilet training, and submission to parental rules. Through childhood and adolescence we continue to be held accountable, usually appropriately so, to the authority of parents and adults.

This passivity lingers in our psyche, and it constitutes a part of ourselves that, over the years, we fail to detect let alone resolve. But we continue to react to it. A man or woman can be strong in one context and quite passive in another. A powerful CEO of a major company can be passive with his wife, children, or parents. A man or woman who resists feeling vulnerable emotionally, and who is unwilling to commit to a partner in marriage, can interpret the marriage bond as a restriction on his or her freedom. A macho person who makes a point of looking tough and powerful can be warding off the fear of being seen as passive.

For most people, their primary inner conflict is between their inner critic (inner aggression) and their inner passivity. We can detect the conflict by consciously registering the inner voices that represent one side or the other. As mentioned, the inner critic's voice is likely to be mocking or scolding. The inner passivity's voice is typically seductive or defeatist. The latter voice often tempts us: "Oh, go ahead and have another drink," or "It won't hurt to stay in bed and miss work today," or "Do it! She'll never have to know that you were unfaithful."

The voice of inner passivity often sounds warnings to us, insisting, for instance, that we are in danger of being betrayed, cheated, or physically harmed: "That boyfriend can't be trusted," or "That friend is going to knife you in the back." Certainly, an intuitive voice does sometimes represent our best interests. But if we have too much inner passivity in our psyche, we find it difficult to establish what is true. We are buffeted about by the aggression of our inner critic and misled by the defensiveness and seductiveness of inner passivity. We don't know which voice to trust and we can't trust either.

A controlling person is someone with an inner passivity problem. This individual feels the need to impose his will or wishes on others to cover up inner feelings of helplessness and powerlessness. In other words, he feels passive when he's not in control. The underlying feeling is, "I'll control them before they control me." He's only worried about being controlled because of his inner passivity. Through inner passivity, he's secretly attached to the feeling of being controlled, and his controlling behavior is a defense against awareness of this.

A common symptom of inner passivity is one's difficulty believing in oneself and feeling one's value. Inner passivity is getting in our way when, for instance, we say or feel, "I wish I could get to know the real me."

With inner passivity we accept our fate rather than believing in and creating our destiny. As one person put it, "It's the feeling that things happen to me rather than me choosing." It's also the condition of dreaming about future success but feeling unable to achieve it. Another person told me, "Sometimes I feel I'm all dressed up,

212

ready to go, but my shoes are tied together." Inner passivity causes us to fail to imagine, visualize, or enact the goals we could otherwise achieve.

Inner passivity's symptoms also include not knowing, not learning, and not caring about what's important to know about ourselves and our world. It impinges on our intelligence. The existence of inner passivity blocks us from accessing feelings of power, value, and sovereignty. It inhibits the expression of our higher human qualities of integrity, dignity, courage, compassion, and love. Literary critic Lionel Trilling described the essence of this inner condition when he said that inner development requires us "to retrieve the human spirit from its acquiescence in non-being."

The condition is universal and its influence can be seen throughout history.[67] One example involves the ease with which so-called normal people can be enlisted for evil purposes. In recent years, Jewish groups have been investigating hundreds of lesser-known killing fields in Eastern Europe where some 1.5 million Jews met their deaths during World War II.[68] Many of them were murdered by their neighbors. A spokesperson for the International Institute for Holocaust Research said, "In many cases, locals played a key role in the murders, probably by a ratio of 10 locals to every one German. We are trying to understand the man who played soccer with his Jewish neighbor one day and turned to kill him the next."[69]

The murderous behavior of these locals can be understood through the dynamics of inner passivity and the deadly flaw. Both of these aspects of our psyche degrade ethical and moral behavior and enhance our capacity to do evil. When German officers appeared on the scene brimming with officially sanctioned fascist authority, the locals would have had to access integrity and self-respect to maintain their dignity and resistance. At that moment, the inner passivity in human nature became the Achilles' heel of the local citizenry. In many of these individuals, inner passivity dissolved whatever will and sense of right and wrong they possessed. Once that happened, these locals, in order to somehow "rationalize" or defend against their passivity and murderous actions, could have clothed their behavior in sadistic gratification, making a pleasure out of displeasure: "I am not passively submitting to the fascists. I align myself with them out of my own free will, and I enjoy it. This is what I chose. This is what I want." At the same time, their aggression toward their victims could have served as a defense against their identification with the helplessness of their victims: "I am not helpless or wanting to feel helpless— look at the power that I wield as I destroy these Jews!" In this way, inner passivity and the deadly flaw facilitated their acts of murder. Of course, this in no way excuses them. We are ultimately responsible for our evil, however unconsciously it arises.[70]

To illustrate the conundrum of inner passivity, people with the capacity and responsibility to wield rational and legal authority can, because of a lack of self-knowledge, still be passive in unconscious ways that are harmful to them and to others. An example is the behavior of economic experts and government regulators, along with political and financial leaders, who stood by passively as the U.S. financial system was gearing up for a collapse in the years leading up to 2008. Inner passivity clouds discernment and wisdom, makes it easy to weave illusions and dreams, and makes it hard to stand against the crowd. It also makes us afraid of life, so that, in survival mode, we embrace a dog-eat-dog mentality and pursue self-aggrandizement as a means of protection.

Procrastination is one symptom of inner passivity, but so is hyperactive behavior. Inner passivity can hide out in people who become somewhat manic or overly busy when facing tasks or projects. Their busy behavior is a defense to fend off the inner critic: "I am not looking to be passive and submissive. See how energized I am. I want to do these things and get them done right away." With inner passivity at play, a life of so-called *action* is more accurately a life of *reaction*. So a person can be busy or active and, based on how he feels about himself and his relationship to work and others, still be plagued with inner passivity.

Sometimes constant, intense thinking or mental activity produces an illusion of power, but it can be a compensation for inner passivity and lead to fatigue, frustration, and, in severe cases, psychosis. This kind of

215

unregulated thinking often ends up producing an even more painful feeling of passivity, a condition of just "spinning one's wheels." Another indicator of inner passivity is the inability of some people to set boundaries on the behaviors of others, such as a parent with an unruly child. In another instance, people who have mood disorders and become manic can be swinging emotionally between infantile illusions of power and painful feelings of powerlessness or helplessness.

Defensiveness is an expression of inner passivity. With inner passivity, our defensiveness is on a hair-trigger setting. As mentioned, people can be both inwardly defensive and outwardly defensive, without realizing how defensive they are. So, a first step is for us to become aware of our defensiveness. Next, we need to know when we are likely to use it as well as the language with which we express it. Defensiveness is always part of the cover-up of our own collusion in inner passivity and other forms of self-suffering. When inner passivity is overcome, we *represent* ourselves (instead of *defending* ourselves) creatively and effectively.

People who are compulsively apologetic have a pronounced passive streak in their psyche. Instinctive passivity can be seen in people who are quick to apologize—"Oh, I'm sorry"—when they brush against someone in a crowd or when they inadvertently step close to another person. This can be rationalized as required politeness, and indeed politeness is a necessary social lubricant. Yet in many cases such behavior is instinctively passive.

Inner passivity is also visible in body language, in people who shrug their shoulders a lot, or tilt their head, jiggle their limbs, or walk with a lack of grace. A person does well for himself when he becomes aware of such mannerisms and, understanding their significance, makes a point to stop them over time.

One of the most painful consequences of inner passivity is one's inability to support oneself emotionally. This common condition involves a person's unconscious willingness to continue to circulate that painful feeling of inner emptiness or emotional helplessness. This individual is unconsciously attached to such feelings, and often he or she angrily accuses others of not being supportive. This anger is a defense that covers up the accuser's secret willingness to indulge in the pain of feeling unsupported.

People with this condition frequently employ the "magic gesture" defense, whereby they give emotional support and validation to others on the pretext that this is what they want for themselves. The defense reads, "How can you (inner critic) accuse me of wanting to feel unsupported. Look at how I am supporting this person in my life. That's exactly what I want for myself." Variations on this defense are used regularly by codependents or enablers.

A client, Carol, was struggling with her freelance writing career and having difficulty promoting and marketing her skills. In fact, her procrastination was extreme, and for several months she had not taken steps to find writing assignments from regional and national publications. Carol received occasional calls for her work from editors, and she performed their assignments well. But the amount of work was insufficient for her to support herself.

She told me that each morning for months she had been waking up and saying silently to herself, "Oh God, what will I do today!" This voice of inner passivity set the tone for her day. Typically, she shuffled around all day without direction or purpose. By the end of the day her inner critic was attaching her fiercely: "You blew the whole day! You have nothing to show for yourself! You certainly ought to be ashamed!" She did indeed feel ashamed, even as her voice of inner passivity mumbled excuses and offered defenses. Unfortunately, she was now primed to repeat the painful pattern the following day.

One morning when she had a lot of chores on her agenda, her exclamation, again of inner passivity, was significantly different: "Oh my God! I have so much to do today. Where will I start!" As she pondered the question, feelings of being overwhelmed and helpless swept over her, along with anxiety and fear. This unconscious expectation lay behind her anxious morning exclamation: "There is no way I will be able to get anything effective or creative done today." Deeper still was her readiness to experience herself in this helpless way.

Over several months, Carol made excellent progress working out her attachment to the feeling of inner passivity. Like a flower in bloom after a long drought, she moved through the conflict between her inner passivity and her inner critic, into the discovery of her emotional independence, her personal authority, and her authentic self.

Carol's example suggests we would have more workplace productivity, as well as higher high-school and college graduation rates, if young people were taught the features and nature of inner passivity. This learning would give them an excellent chance of resolving this inner blockage of intelligence and vitality.

Jenny, a college student in her twenties, was also struggling with inner passivity. She was having a hard time representing herself effectively as she sought to overcome feelings of being unimportant. She would sit quietly listening to her boyfriend talk at length about football, saying to herself all the while, "Doesn't he know I'm not interested in this subject?" Occasionally, she told him so: "You know I'm not interested in football." Before long, however, he would again be excited about the subject and be talking to her about it.

Jenny told me there were other subjects as well that he talked passionately about, to which she felt indifferent.

When she objected, he would ask, "Well, what do *you* want to talk about?" At this point, she said, "My mind shuts down and I can't think effectively. Even though I often do talk a lot, this is one time when I can't think, and of course I feel foolish and inadequate."

Inwardly, Jenny claims that her mental paralysis is her problem, to which she pleads guilty as a defense and subsequently feels guilt. But the deeper issue is her willingness to sit and listen to others speak passionately on a subject, while she sits dispassionately feeling empty, as if she is nothing but a sounding-board. Her deadly flaw produces her emotional attachment to this old, painful passivity. Her resulting self-defeat is seen in her inability to represent herself more effectively and in the suffering she experiences for allegedly being defective.

Inner passivity can come across as a worldly voice of experience that claims to have our best interests at heart. Like the voice of the inner critic, it presents itself in the guise of an expert. "It feels like a core voice," one client said, "and that's why I give so much credence to it when I hear it." The more we surrender autonomy to that voice, however, the more we are left feeling frightened, vulnerable, and overwhelmed.

Sometimes inner aggression and inner passivity use the same words or expressions, so the tone of those words becomes a clue to the source. Consider the statement, "You never do anything right." If heard or felt as an accusation, then the inner critic is speaking. If heard or felt in a softer tone with a sense of futility or self-pity, then inner passivity is talking. Either way the voice is negative. It helps to know which voice—aggression or passivity—is being heard. Clarity about these inner dynamics speeds up the process of overcoming our deadly flaw.

Chapter 17
Normal Aggression and Pseudo-Aggression

When we're trying to resolve our deadly flaw, we need to understand two different kinds of aggression. One is normal and healthy, while the other is phony and covers up our deadly flaw.

Normal aggression is easy to understand. It's the power we need in the world to stand up for ourselves and take care of ourselves properly. It's the ability to function in the world in an appropriate manner, with wisdom, courage, and emotional balance.

Pseudo-aggression, in contrast, is an entirely different kind of aggression. It is phony aggression, a form of action or emotional intensity that is strictly reactive. While normal aggression has a neutral or positive energy, pseudo-aggression is mostly negative. Pseudo-aggressive behavior is like passive-aggressive behavior, but the former is more overtly negative and can display more hostility.

In a simple example, a man trying to fix a leak under the kitchen sink yells at his wife, who has just expressed alarm that the kitchen floor is starting to flood, "Can't you see I'm trying to do this right!" The man has interpreted his wife's alarm as a criticism of him for causing the flooding. Through his deadly flaw, he absorbs the feeling of being criticized. The challenge of fixing the leak could also be triggering his inner passivity if he is feeling overwhelmed or up against the limits of his plumbing skills. He instantly retaliates with pseudo-aggression, in this case a harsh remark to her.

Frequently, pseudo-aggression provides us with a feeling of power or righteousness that covers up (defends against) our underlying passivity and our other attachments to negative emotions. Invariably, this aggression produces guilt and self-recrimination. The aggression is produced to serve a person's defense system. A typical defense goes like this: "How can I be accused of being passive. Can't you see how angry I am!"

Pseudo-aggression is not always expressed as an action or verbal outburst. It can be felt and contained by the individual as an intense negative emotion such as resentment, bitterness, hatred or the wish for revenge. The individual feels the pseudo-aggression inside of him where it can be very painful. Frequently, it emerges in the form of covert provocations aimed at others. Whether the negative emotions of pseudo-aggression are expressed outwardly or contained within, they can produce much suffering and self-defeat.

Many therapists take pseudo-aggression (in this example, a client's anger or desire to retaliate) at face value and even encourage it. They say, "You need to be more assertive." They see pseudo-aggressive anger as

223

a desirable expression of an individual's strength and right to stand up for himself. They don't see that such anger is a defense produced by the deadly flaw. While pseudo-aggressive anger produces suffering, it also covers up the angry person's entanglement in some variation of his own deep negativity such as indulging in feeling controlled or rejected.

Because pseudo-aggression is based on an inner distortion of reality, it can't be trusted as the barometer of a given situation. For instance, assertive or aggressive behavior is likely to be righteous, angry, or blaming when it covers up inner passivity. Of course, individuals do indeed have to stand up for themselves, and they feel better about themselves and avoid self-defeat when they do it appropriately. We more wisely and effectively use assertiveness and aggression when we are not reacting to the deadly flaw.

As well, acts of pseudo-aggression usually produce, as an aftereffect, painful guilt and regret because the inner critic objects to the pseudo-aggression as inappropriate or "bad" behavior.

The so-called "wise guy" is rife with pseudo-aggression. He appears on the surface to have an aggressive personality, but, like the cynic, he's a frightened, passive individual who feels much anxiety over the uncertainty of life. So he tries with his bluster to give a sense of certainty in his comments and observations. This aggressiveness is phony. Behind his pseudo-aggression, his inner passivity experiences life as a risky, uncertain business, while his ego fears the imminent exposure of himself as a phony. Through inner passivity, he experiences life's uncertainty with a sense of bewilderment or impending defeat. To cover up his attachment to inner passivity, he produces an aggressive personality along with an air of certainty.

Here are a few basic differences between normal or appropriate aggression and pseudo-aggression:[71] Normal aggression has a legitimate target or a real enemy, while pseudo-aggression is aimed at an artificially created enemy; in the former, no feelings of guilt are generated, while in the latter, guilt is always present; in the former, the amount of aggression is proportionate to the insult, while in the latter, the slightest provocation can produce an act of (or a wish for) extensive retaliation; in the former, the purpose is to disable the enemy, but in the latter, the purpose is often to provoke even more retaliation; in the former, the ability to wait patiently for retaliation is present, but with the latter comes an urgency to retaliate; in the former, aggression is not easily provoked, while in the latter, it is easily provoked; and, finally, in normal aggression success is usually expected, while with pseudo-aggression failure is unconsciously foreseen. (Once again, note that pseudo-aggression is very different from self-aggression. The former is a *defense*, the latter a *drive*.)

Pseudo-aggression can make its appearance simply as a figment of our imagination and in a manner that's relatively benign and devoid of hostility. For example, a person who encounters a situation in which his passivity gets the best of him could subsequently spend much time remembering that experience and reframing it to imagine himself acting with more power. One client of mine in his forties said he fantasized for years about two attractive women who had stayed overnight at his apartment one time when he was in his twenties. He said he knew that on the night in question the women were sexually available to him, but he had failed to muster up the male enthusiasm and power to do the deed. To compensate for that passivity, and in fact to continue to experience it, he had recurring fantasies in which he successfully, in full macho glory, seduced and ravished the women. He figured that, in his mind, he had completed the deed at least 1,000 times, usually with erotic satisfaction. But the fantasy was finally "old hat," he said, and he wanted to stop. He resolved the problem by understanding his secret wish to continue to experience the passivity of his failed conquest. He no longer needed to use fantasies of sexual conquest to cover up his enmeshment in passivity.

Cynicism is an example of how pseudo-aggression is used in a subtle, defensive manner. The cynic puts on a show of criticizing, mocking, or denouncing some venerated institution or idea. He appears to be witty and in-the-know, as he attempts to draw in allies for his points of view. But his fake aggression is simply a defensive measure to cover up passivity and fear. He defends against accusations of passivity by aggressively (pseudo-aggressively) ridiculing others. To make this defense work over a period of time, the cynic often has to become an increasingly negative person, with his cynicism becoming more bitter and hostile. He can also thwart his inner critic by making his cynicism more foolish or ridiculous, so that both his cynical observations and the accusations from the inner critic are reduced to absurdity. (Personality traits such as being cynical or greedy are often overtly pseudo-aggressive.)

Another example of pseudo-aggression involves the brutality of a spouse-abuser. This problem is directly related to inner passivity. A wife might get slapped in the face by such a husband for serving dinner five minutes late. The husband himself likely feels victimized in some fashion (misunderstood, not appreciated, not respected), whether at work, at home, or wherever. If he is unemployed or in a low-paying job, he can feel stuck, blocked, trapped, and hopeless. He lashes out at his wife as a reaction to alleged injustices against him in other venues, through which he feels passively victimized.

Being abusive gives him a fraudulent sense of power that covers up his passivity. To him, this destructive pseudo-aggression against his wife feels better than his passivity. The more abusive he becomes, the more he is also identifying with the helplessness or victimization of his wife. In typical cases, he is soon overwhelmed with guilt and remorse for his pseudo-aggression and comes begging for forgiveness.

Spousal abuse is viewed by most experts as solely the offense or crime of the perpetrator (which legally it is). For psychological purposes, though, we're more objective and more likely to overcome the problem of spousal abuse when we understand that the aggression has its roots in the inner passivity of both the perpetrator and the victim.

Studies have shown that many schoolyard bullies are verbally or physically abused in their home. Bullies sometimes also come from relatively healthy families, and are adolescents or teenagers who feel passive in that family system or who identify with passive people in it. They then go to school and defend against their emotional attachment to passivity by pseudo-aggressively going after weak peers.

The bully revels in his sense of power, yet at the same time he identifies with the person he is picking on. In this way he "sneaks in" his willingness to feel passive. He experiences his bullying as a testament to his superiority, a feeling that makes his defense against passivity more effective. Typically, pseudo-aggressive behaviors such as those of the bully can initially feel good, but that feeling doesn't last long and it is often followed by the pain of guilt and remorse.

As mentioned, pseudo-aggressive behavior can be subtle, becoming passive-aggressive in nature. A man who had a dominating mother grew up accustomed to being dominated by her. He was attracted to strong women, but, through his defenses, he began to withdraw emotionally from them and behave coldly when he felt controlled or pushed around by them. He married a forceful woman and, before long, had trouble feeling strong around her. At times, he did act more assertively with her, but usually in a reactive, angry manner that constituted pseudo-aggression.

Later, his defenses shifted. Instead of behaving coldly or aggressively toward her, he compulsively began to keep secrets from her. This was a revised attempt to "prove" that he did not like feeling accountable to her. Keeping secrets was an act of pseudo-aggression in passive-aggressive format. It was self-defeating because it blocked intimacy between them. The self-defeat was evident, too, when his wife became suspicious about the reasons for his secretive manner, then alarmed, and made him even more accountable to her.

We can understand pseudo-aggression by seeing it in the behavior of terrorists. Though their behavior is irrational, it can be understood according to psychological principles. Terrorists believe they have been violated and oppressed by the power and values of others, and they are steeped in a victim mentality. They resort to the ultimate psychological defense, the murder of innocents in a display of pseudo-aggressive rage, to cover up their unconscious entanglement in inner passivity.

The role of the deadly flaw is also apparent in the pseudo-aggression of terrorists. They are under the influence of an infantile pleasure-in-displeasure pattern. With this pattern, they feel a pleasure, thrill, or manic excitement when a defense works or is successful in covering up their deadly flaw. The pleasure may be experienced according to this inner formulation: "I am not helpless against those with power. I, too, have power. I enjoy the thrill of defiance, the power of destructiveness, and the certainty of my righteousness." Though the pleasure is completely perverse, it provides the emotional foundation for dogmatic, irrational beliefs and subsequent mayhem.

Other characteristics common to terrorists are also symptoms of inner passivity: profound denial, oversimplification of issues, lack of patience, desperation, self-righteousness, and an authoritarian mentality (they identify with militant and patriarchal power to compensate for their inner passivity).

Evidence of passivity and pseudo-aggression are seen in terrorists' suicide missions. Suicide is an ultimate act of passivity and a gruesome act of pseudo-aggression against oneself. (This does not include a discussion of assisted-suicide in cases of terminal illness or excruciating pain.) Suicide is an act steeped in helplessness, alienation, hopelessness, and despair, as well as in the conviction that no other alternative is available.

The one who commits suicide has "successfully" covered up his or her unconscious collusion or masochistic participation in feelings of being trapped and hopeless. Suicide is an ultimate defense: "I don't want to feel this way! I'm ending it all!" In the case of a terrorist's suicide mission, the defense contends: "I am not mired in helplessness and passivity. Look at the power I have to take the lives of others and to impact the world." Their extreme aggression says, in effect, "I am not passive. I have power! I can destroy you!"

Suicide is an option for terrorists because, through inner passivity, they are not connected to their essence or value. They feel pushed aside and rendered invisible. Their mind, taken over by dogma or by the agenda of others, is totally passive. They don't think for themselves, and they adhere to authoritarian forms of organization. In their search for orientation, they embrace a cause that makes them feel powerful and righteous. Right and wrong no longer matter. What matters is the effectiveness of their defense of pseudo-aggression. Religious dogma enables them to enhance the effectiveness of the defense and to find perverse pleasure in the contention: "I am not passive—I am a noble person who knows what God decrees and who is willing to carry out His wishes."

They are very sensitive to feeling disrespected, yet they have little respect for others and none for their own life.

231

Terrorists also have their own inner terror, created through their feeling of powerlessness or their impression of being at the mercy of some alien force (the Great Satan) intent on doing them harm. They do to others what they themselves fear—being terrorized, rendered helpless, and defeated. Such extreme inner passivity gives license to evil impulses and actions.

This understanding of the psychological roots of terrorism could conceivably be part of a strategy to suffocate the ideology that drives these extremists.

Criminals are cut from the same cloth as terrorists. Bergler believed that criminals are "the most passive of all neurotics."[72] (He likely would have said the same of terrorists had they been more visible in his era.) Every criminal unconsciously bargains for punishment, he stated. Evidence can be seen in their unnecessary provocations and in the "silly mistakes" they frequently make that lead to their being apprehended.

Consciously, the criminal wants to get away with his crime; unconsciously, he wants to be found out. Not only is his unconscious ego especially weak, his superego is particularly corrupt and demanding. The consequence is greater self-damage. The criminal recreates his inner dynamic: He is helplessly trapped and pinned down by his authoritarian superego, and he ends up in a prison cell trapped and pinned down by the authorities.[73]

The terrorist's and the criminal's aggressiveness is a force rebounding off their profound inner passivity. Theirs is not true aggression but fake or pseudo-aggression. Yet just about anyone who tries to cover up awareness of the deadly flaw will use pseudo-aggression at some point or other. The difference is the degree of self-damage.

In everyday life, pseudo-aggression, as mentioned, need not be violent. As an example, a fellow named Bill gets angry at his friend Jake because he believes Jake acted in a controlling way. Bill is reacting with anger because he's taking personally the real or alleged controlling behavior dished out by Jake. That means that Bill is filtering the impression of being controlled through his inner passivity. He's soaking up the feeling of being controlled, and now he's required, as a defense, to protest with pseudo-aggression (by denouncing Jake) to deny his own indulgence in feeling controlled.

If Bill were especially dysfunctional, he might feel controlled even if Jake's intentions were innocent. If Bill were emotionally strong, however, he probably wouldn't get angry at all. First of all, he likely wouldn't even feel controlled, even if Jake had really tried to control him. When we are strong, we don't easily get triggered. If Bill were stronger emotionally, Jake would not likely be able to make him feel passive or controlled. Meanwhile, if Jake did far overstep the mark, the strong Bill would be able to deal with the issue in an appropriate manner, perhaps by talking to Jake about what happened and trying to resolve the issue.

When we can't manifest the power of natural aggression, we will lack self-regulation, and we can become quite indifferent to our own health. We become sedentary and avoid exercise. We eat and drink food that has nutrients manufactured out of it. We trash our minds with trivia and commercial rubbish the way we trash the planet with garbage and toxic substances. When we don't care about our own health, we don't care about the health of the planet.

We don't know how to protect ourselves from toxic influences such as cynicism, dissension, addictions, and dogmatic belief systems. It follows that we won't be able to protect our planet from all the toxic effects of industrialization. When we can't establish the inner authority of the self because of inner conflict, we are likely to be lacking in self-regulation and healthy aggression. It is this aggression that enables us to act forcefully to reform the consuming lifestyle that threatens the planet. When we remain mired in our own suffering and preoccupations, the planet's plight becomes secondary to our own.

Inner passivity creates more fear in us. We can't support ourselves emotionally. Our irrational fears rebound in the psyche and are projected into the world. We create enemies when we could be making friends. We reverberate with many kinds of fear, including fear

234

of change, loss, helplessness, the unknown, abandonment, annihilation, and death.

To generate more courage, we often have to move through a fear left over from childhood—a lingering impression that we are powerless and helpless against the authorities who rule us. We have emotional memories from childhood that associate the act of speaking up for ourselves with the danger of being rejected, unloved, or even annihilated.

Public engagement is needed to save the environment, our natural resources, and plant and animal species. Responding appropriately to our plight is an act of normal aggression. We won't access this power if we are spinning our wheels in the many varieties of pseudo-aggression.

Chapter 18
Psychological vs. Medical Solutions

Mainstream psychology has not produced treatments that are consistently effective in resolving emotional and behavioral problems. So it's understandable that medical approaches have been attempted to treat such problems, including the three described in this chapter—depression, post-partum depression, and sexual impotency (male erectile disorder).

Medical solutions are widely touted for certain emotional problems and dysfunctional behaviors that can often be resolved with deep self-knowledge. In each of the three examples in this chapter, we can see how the medical approach may be undermining long-term health and inhibiting our personal freedom and our intelligence.

Let's start with the first example, the widespread problem of depression. The medical approach does frequently recommend psychotherapy as a treatment for depression, though the recommended therapy tends to be of the more superficial variety. In this approach, psychotherapy is used alone or in combination with pharmaceuticals. The two most commonly prescribed therapies are cognitive-behavioral therapy and interpersonal therapy, which teach techniques for improved functioning but do not penetrate the unconscious mind.

Antidepressant medications are divided into two different classes: selective serotonin uptake inhibitors and serotonin-norepinephrine reuptake inhibitors. Studies have shown that depressed individuals often do benefit from these treatment approaches. However, that benefit is usually taken to signify "not being depressed," which is not necessarily indicative of emotional strengthening, personal growth, enhanced self-awareness, or even a state of happiness. People who take these medicines can become dependent on them, sometimes for life. Relapse is more common when the core issues have not been addressed.

Bergler recognized depression as a defense mechanism, meaning that it is both a consequence of the deadly flaw as well as a cover-up for it. (Note that the following explanations are somewhat complex.) Bergler identified several different varieties and aspects of depression. The basic defense provided by depression goes like this: "I don't enjoy my suffering; look at how depressed I am."[74] One of the most common sources of depression involves the inner critic's particularly odious act of harassing us with any discrepancies it finds between the illusions of our ego ideal (naively established in childhood) and the later realities of our modest station in life. Punishment takes the form of both guilt and depression.[75]

Basically, depression results from the punitive action of the inner critic, which seizes every opportunity to demand more suffering from us, as it holds us accountable for our secret wish to indulge in, and perversely enjoy, various negative emotions. (Ironically, one of these perverse pleasures is our attachment to the aggression dished out by the inner critic.) Depression can be a fee or a penance offered by the unconscious ego to the inner critic that allows the individual to enjoy part of his unconscious wish in a disguised form in his neurotic symptom.[76] The individual is unconsciously interested in maintaining his neurosis. He accepts it because, secretly, he's not willing to challenge the inner status quo. However, he's willing to give up, under the pressure of the inner critic's objections, a few features of his neurosis.[77]

To illustrate, an individual who, faced in therapy with the first glimmers of understanding of his unconscious passivity toward his wife, hastens to give up the worst of his pseudo-aggressive reactions toward her and call it a day. Anxious to avoid the "humbling revelations" of psychotherapy, he decides he's now fine and the problem is solved. Prolonged depression could be the outcome of an incomplete solution of this sort. He is getting to keep the core of his neurosis (his attachment to experiencing his wife through his passivity) in exchange, say, for refraining from angry outbursts toward her. But in doing so he might have to pay a price in continuing depression.

Depression can also occur as an after-effect of a missed opportunity to suffer. For instance, a man is building up nervous anticipation of his mother's visit, based on unresolved issues concerning childhood experiences of rejection and passivity. He starts to feel depressed shortly after his mother announces she will *not* be making the visit. This depression is a kind of mourning of a lost opportunity to indulge in unresolved negative emotions.[78]

Another variation is "preventive depression." In this subdivision, the unconscious ego, anticipating punishment, produces the depression beforehand, thus presenting to the inner critic the offering of suffering already undertaken, but for the lesser "crime," not for the deadly flaw itself.[79]

Depression can also result when the inner defense attorney has "a nervous breakdown" and abandons the individual to the inner critic's cruel onslaught. This happens, as Bergler described it, when the unconscious ego can't cope, at least temporarily, with "its hopeless double task of converting punishment emanating from the superego into psychic masochism, and changing id wishes into substitute wishes more acceptable to the superego . . ."[80]

Sometimes depression serves the purpose of a rainy-day piggybank. Bergler called this the "making-a-case-type" of depression. It involves occasions when, while the individual is entirely guilt-free, a test case of innocence is produced. The result is a depression designed for hoarding, which can be presented to the inner critic as a "shield when a justified accusation in the identical sphere is leveled at a later date when the ego is really guilty."[81]

How can we resolve such complex forms of depression? The method involves recognizing and transcending inner passivity. The main way our inner critic can "get at us" is through our inner passivity. As mentioned, this is the unclaimed part of our psyche that prevents us from feeling our evolving humanity—our birthright in autonomy, authority, and freedom. It is through our inner passivity that our inner critic can hold us accountable and demand its pound of flesh in conscious suffering. In a sense, our inner passivity creates a vacuum into which the inner critic bursts in full regalia, bellowing its battle cry: "Time to answer to me—time to suffer."

We just have to see our inner passivity more clearly and feel it more consciously in order to outgrow it and evolve beyond its reach.

The depressed individual spirals downward into a helpless surrender to the burden of life. This descent into hopelessness and helplessness is facilitated by our unconscious temptation to maximize the pleasure-in-displeasure opportunity inherent in a deepening experience of passivity. At this level of misery one ounce of unconscious pleasure, to put it conjecturally, equals one ton of conscious suffering.

As mentioned, it's through our inner passivity that we absorb the aggression from the inner critic. Since we can't avoid feeling distress or pain from whatever is psychologically unresolved within us, we're stuck with the emotional suffering. Depression is one price we pay as over time we absorb the self-aggression. So we can understand depression as a consequence of our deadly flaw, as we see the roles that inner passivity and our inner critic play in this form of suffering.

Even though depression is a symptom of inner passivity, people can sometimes feel debilitating depression as a close approximation of the inner passivity itself. The anguish of depression can be a "pure," intense manifestation of inner passivity. At this stage, inner passivity is not just a mental or clinical concept. We can when depressed actually feel ourselves being swallowed up by it as our vitality collapses. Here we can see inner passivity more objectively—as pure depression. This is when a person painfully feels that, "I am my depression." Now it is particularly difficult to separate the depression from the essence of oneself. This impression can also permeate other emotional and behavioral problems including procrastination, indecision, worry, fear, self-doubt, defensiveness, complaining, cravings, guilt, and feeling overwhelmed. When we understand that inner passivity is the source of these negative feelings, we can see our situation in a more objective or clinical light. We create more separation from the symptoms. We begin to understand how we have the power to heal ourselves.

The more clearly we see and feel our inner passivity, the more we also make ourselves conscious of the illegitimate authority of the inner critic. With this new intelligence, we feel, with a new understanding of what we are feeling, the negativity of the inner critic and the negativity of inner passivity. We now are able to take responsibility for our negativity. We acknowledge our attachment to it. Understanding this, how can we blame someone else for our negativity? If we try to pin it on the cruelty of others, we see through this self-deception. The deception is just another defense covering up our deadly flaw.

Seeing this helps us to stop taking our negative feelings for granted, as if they represent intrinsically who we are. This realization compares with the epiphany that would grip a people who suddenly are able to peacefully rise up to overthrow a tyrannical or dysfunctional government because they can finally feel, as their birthright, the naturalness of human sovereignty as an Inner Bill of Rights.

It is not enough to expose inner passivity solely in mental or intellectual terms. We have to expose it through our feelings, our growing awareness, our self-trust, and our moment-to-moment observation of it in action. These are the building blocks of higher consciousness. When we take possession of that no-man's-land of inner passivity and depose the unconscious ego, our inner critic's power over us is broken. We have taken the concept of freedom to a whole new level.

The second everyday problem we have failed to understand is postpartum depression. Some groups have asked for federal legislation—the Mothers Act—to make it easier for women, either during or after pregnancy, to take antidepressant drugs and other psychiatric drugs for the widespread experience of post-partum depression. The true goal of this Big-Pharma advocated law, one critic wrote, is apparently to transform women into life-long consumers of pharmaceuticals and psychiatric treatment by screening them for a whole list of 'mood' and 'anxiety' disorders and not simply postpartum depression.[82]

Bergler addressed the subject of post-partum depression in an article, titled "Psychoprophylaxis of Postpartum Depression," which appeared in 1959 in the periodical *Postgraduate Medicine*.[83] He stated that "harmless" postpartum depression, though it can be painful, usually corrects itself in a few days or a few weeks. Whether the experience is mild or more severe, he wrote, depression can be avoided or mitigated with more understanding of its roots. Pregnancy and the art of giving birth mobilize, as do most dangers, repressed infantile fears. These fears are unconscious and irrational, yet they create quite an inner disturbance when aroused (see "baby fears" in Chapter 7.) Once they have been mobilized, they can't easily be dismissed. They inundate the personality.[84]

Bergler warned that such fears build up in anticipation of the dangers of birthing complications and the possibility of health problems for mother and child. The inner build-up of fears is not fully released, even when the birthing goes well and the baby is healthy. He stated that, "It is a lot better for the woman to bear in mind, after the child is born, that her depression corresponds to the discrepancy between prepared and used-up fears than for her to believe, in her depression, that her whole life is collapsing."[85] He contended that infantile fears are maintained in the psyche of adults, both men and women, and are ready to be experienced in various challenging situations.

In his article, Bergler recommended that doctors advise their women patients of these inner fears. "Reassuring statements that 'everything will be all right' are quite insufficient," he wrote.[86] He specifically recommended that these inner fears be mentioned in order that pregnant women are provided with more understanding of the psychological side-effects of giving birth. He also urged doctors to familiarize their patients "with the fact that in refusing to admit their fears to themselves, they are mortgaging their happiness in the period after birth of the child and will pay the price of postpartum depression."[87] He stated, "Only in severe and unmanageable cases should the woman be sent to a psychiatrist."[88]

Such awareness of repressed inner fears from childhood gives meaning to a woman's experience, and it empowers her to regulate her own emotions. She can more easily step back from the symptoms, and separate her sense of self from them. She can understand that the powerful depression does not represent any truth about the current state of her life. And the pleasures of motherhood are not diminished unnecessarily.

Infantile fears, which are as much a problem for men as for women, have been sugar-coated or libidinized. That's means that we're compelled to feel and recycle them. Why else are fears so hard to release or outgrow? We convince ourselves that our fears are warranted by dangers or hazards we see or imagine in the world around us. This is how we "rationalize" this form of suffering. Meanwhile, unethical individuals in politics and the media, as well as authority figures in our family and community, stoke our fears about alleged dangers and threats for their own purposes. We end up passively coming under their influence. This is what it means to be afraid of freedom.

The third everyday problem—male sexual impotence—is often not due to a physical or medical impediment. Its roots lie deep within the male psyche. Male impotence, as psychoanalysis termed it, is now called male erectile disorder, which serves to frame the condition as a medical problem rather than a psychological challenge. Treatments such as Viagra and Cialis are commonly prescribed for impotence and for sexually enhanced experiences involving older men.

Because the best psychological knowledge is not being circulated, younger men suffering from impotence are not informed of alternatives that carry the appealing side-effects of greater intelligence, personal independence, and emotional health. While many men might decline this alternative, we do people an injustice if this knowledge is not made available as an option.

Bergler wrote about specific types of impotence, including premature ejaculation, delayed ejaculation, absence of ejection, absence of normal orgasm, and lack of or insufficient erection. A psychological problem is often common to all of these types of impotence. The problem involves the unconscious *refusal* of the man to give to his partner the satisfaction she desires. The impotent male, according to Bergler, remains passively attached to the mother-image of early childhood.

In the oral stage, boys and girls tend to experience their mothers as "refusing" to some degree. This refusal can be experienced acutely at the time of weaning. We maintain at a deep level an attachment to this form of suffering. Consequently, the male can be unconsciously willing to refuse to give love, tenderness, and sperm (as mother's-milk equivalent).[89] This behavior is based on the previously mentioned repetition compulsion, whereby we are compelled to inflict on others some variation of what we felt we have passively endured. The abused child, for instance, is more likely as an adult to be an abuser of his or her own children, just as the one who felt refused becomes the one who refuses others.

"It is therefore not surprising," Bergler stated, "that both potency disturbances of oral neurotics—premature ejaculation and inability to ejaculate at all (technically, psychogenic aspermia)—are linked to a fluid. In both cases, fluid is refused. In prematurists, the 'milk is spilled before it can reach the mouth' (ejaculation occurring at the mere approach to the vulva—ante portas—or a few seconds after insertion, when even a normal woman cannot derive any pleasure from the sex act because of its minimal duration). In aspermists [those unable to ejaculate], the 'baby' is given no fluid at all."[90]

The male's refusal of pleasure to his partner is not real aggression and revenge, nor is it conscious. Rather, it is the defense of pseudo-aggression, and it covers up the passive hurt of feeling refused, which is circulated, however subtly, in the emotional life of the "refuser."[91] In this process, the adult male recreates this hurt by identifying with the refused woman. He feels guilt for this secret pleasure, which he shifts and attributes to the "lesser crime," his problem of impotence or erectile disorder for which he often feels embarrassment, guilt, and shame.

The man feels unconscious guilt in two ways: once for playing the role of the "refusing, bad mother" and once for his cruelty, which his inner critic accuses him of, in spoiling his partner's pleasure.[92] This psychological problem is not solved by taking Viagra or Cialis. The "refuser" who uses these substances remains ignorant of his dysfunction, and, though he now has solid erections produced from the drugs, he is likely to act out by withholding affection or love in other ways.

I know from my clients that many people are eager for the psychological solution when they understand its roots in their psyche. But in our modern world this knowledge is hidden—twice hidden, in fact. First, we repress the knowledge within our psyche so that we can continue living wearily but resignedly with our familiar suffering. Second, we do not find the knowledge in libraries, bookstores, or the halls of academia, and it is not discussed in public debate or forums.

Bergler's findings are available through his books and papers at research libraries and at a few websites. But with so few references to this knowledge, and with such little support for these ideas, only a small percentage is able to benefit. Yet no one is to blame. In collective collusion, we have hidden from ourselves the deeper origins of our distressing symptoms.

This self-knowledge constitutes higher learning. Still, it can be assimilated intellectually and emotionally by everyday people. Initially, this self-knowledge stymies our mind. While it is intellectually accessible, it is not necessarily emotionally so. However, we can patiently ease our way into this knowledge with open-ended curiosity and with trust in our ability to discern what is true and what is not true.

Chapter 19
The Twenty-One Rules

To assimilate the knowledge of the deadly flaw, we have to appreciate the ways we resist learning that knowledge along with the ways we can be confused about its essentials. To help us acquire this insight, Bergler wrote twenty-one specific rules that apply to the experience of learning it.

His rules apply specifically to the experience of working with a psychoanalyst.[93] Yet I believe these rules are helpful even when we don't have an analyst or a therapist. In themselves, the rules constitute important knowledge for understanding our resistance to learning about our deadly flaw. Bergler believed that individuals who are "not-too-neurotic" can benefit from practical psychoanalytic advice, and in one of his later books he outlined such advice to help his readers, whether they were in therapy or not.[94]

Here, with my paraphrasing and elaborations, are his twenty-one specific rules when confronting the deadly flaw in one's own psyche.

1. Don't misuse the analytic interpretations to denounce yourself. Your inner critic is eager to harass you for any alleged failure, including the insinuation that you should already know all this "stuff" about yourself. People are initially tempted to consider new revelations about themselves with a sense of despair, which activates inner passivity and serves as an unconsciously hypocritical cloak to cover one's willing participation in suffering.

2. Be as skeptical as you like about the interpretations. But remain open-minded as to the possibility of their accuracy. Considering the vital importance of self-knowledge, it would be tragic to dismiss what might be true. We like to think we're objective in terms of self-understanding, but our defenses easily fool us. We have a secret vested interest in maintaining the inner status quo. Be skeptical of your skepticism. Your obligation is to be honest. It can't hurt to err on the side of humility.

3. Interpretations can be difficult to comprehend, and it may take some time for the understanding to be assimilated. Try to seize hold of the core or basic interpretation, which hides out beneath the layers of resistance and defenses. Some of the more superficial layers require interpretation, but at these levels the understanding is not necessarily as important as it is at the core level.

A core interpretation might be: "I am secretly attached to the feeling of being passive to my wife." A less important understanding might be: "I can be passive-aggressive with my wife." Through resistance, we're *not* usually interested in keeping the most important interpretation in focus.

4. A person can have an emotional reaction in which two different external triggers are at play. It's important to know which external trigger is more significant. For instance, you can be upset about poor service in a restaurant and blame your sour mood on the feeling of being badly served, when the essential reason for your sour mood is related to some other situation that may have arisen earlier without you having realized its significance. The psychological factors at play in that earlier situation can be more important or decisive for inner understanding and resolution.

5. Begin to practice detachment from your symptoms. In other words, as Bergler put it, decline "to be taken in hook, line and sinker by the panicky feeling of being completely under the influence of the unconscious."[95]

Imagine that your symptom represents an image, form, or creature. Your anger, for instance, could be a big blob with flashing red eyes and swarming tentacles. Tell your symptom in silent dialogue that it has no power to torment you. The symptom may "hang around" or quickly come back in full force. Talk to it again, perhaps saying it has no business in your life. Each time you do so, you're detaching from it instead of being hopelessly entangled in its tentacles. The quiet strength with which you address your symptom represents your best intentions, and it can override your inner passivity. Also recognize that your symptom is just that—a symptom— and not the deadly flaw in itself.

6. Don't fall for the idea, proposed by your resistance, that interpretations are just words. We know the power of words when they convey truth, such as the news, say, that a dear friend has been injured in an accident. Words that convey the truth about our inner predicament are extraordinarily powerful. They can throw us into a tizzy, shake up our unconscious mind, produce vivid dreams during sleep, and help us to accept inner truth.

In this context, one word—indulge—has plenty of power. The idea that we *indulge* in negative emotions has conveyed a sense of truth to my clients. They can fathom the existence of the deadly flaw more readily when it's described as unresolved negative emotions in which they readily *indulge*. "That is how I resonate with it," said one client. "I can just feel that I do indeed *indulge* in those painful places." That word, applied repeatedly, has the power to liberate us if we use it to recognize and "own" our attachment to deep negativity.

7. Don't judge the truth of interpretations or insight by the measure of whether they succeed quickly in overcoming specific symptoms. A correct interpretation doesn't work at once, although it can begin in relatively short order to mitigate a specific symptom.

Keep in mind that many people go through their lives with symptoms that can get worse and become more painful. Anyone who overcomes a chronic symptom (being a cynic, for instance) in a year or two of understanding the underlying dynamics is usually to be credited with having achieved a remarkable transformation and a personal triumph.

8. Interpretations are not mere suggestions or advice. They constitute vital knowledge. New clients have occasionally said to me, "Thanks for that advice." Well, I don't usually give advice. Rather, through analysis, I help my clients discover self-knowledge. That knowledge will change the distribution of inner forces in the direction of mental or emotional health. You will discover that an emotional upset that once would have lasted for days or weeks, and possibly lingered longer to be "milked" for painful memories, is now dealt with and cleared from your psyche in a matter of minutes or hours.

9. Don't shoot the messenger for his or her alleged shortcomings. For this rule, Bergler stated, "Don't project your specific problems upon the analyst, thus escaping into unproductive anger."[96]

We can be tempted to see in the therapist what we refuse to see in ourselves. As you project, you convince yourself that your source of help is somehow lacking or deficient. Doing so, you are engaged in denial: "The problem is with him or her, not with me." The deeper we work in our psyche, as the therapist puts our feet to the fire, the more tempted we can be to demote the therapist as an authority. Take the focus off the therapist and turn your eyes and your intelligence inward instead. If you don't have an analyst or a therapist, you might be tempted to denounce the bearer of the knowledge or the knowledge itself. This is a primitive yet predictable attempt—based on our own fear of freedom—to denounce that which will liberate us.

10. At some point in the working through of your issues, you can start to feel bored by the constant repetitions of the interpretations. Repetitions are needed for deeper understanding and to penetrate our resistance. In the course of working out, say, an oral issue, a person might say to himself thousands of times over a period of months or years, "I am at this moment feeling my attachment to deprivation. This is what I'm unconsciously willing to feel. As I see this clearly, I am affirming my determination to escape from this form of my deadly flaw."

You might start objecting to the repetitions on the grounds they're just "senseless words." This is another of the many forms of resistance. You can stop repeating the interpretations, and not even have to reflect on them, once your symptoms are gone. (I used to repeat my interpretations silently to myself in the middle of the night if I had trouble sleeping: "I am secretly wanting to feel passive in such-and-such a situation; I am secretly wanting to feel deprived in such-and-such a situation." Since inner agencies do not like it when our consciousness is growing, this had the effect of helping me fall asleep.)

11. In situations involving depression, it's important to understand your depression and not take it at face value. You want to resist feeling that your depression is a measuring-stick of your value and goodness. Rather than feeling hopelessly entangled in depression, try to trace it back into your psyche. To provide some degrees of separation, imagine you are a scientist looking at it through a microscope. Depression feeds on our inner guilt, which itself is produced by our passive absorption of the aggression from our inner critic. You can escape from depression when you understand how it as a byproduct of the deadly flaw.

12. Don't confuse the flaw with its defense mechanisms. Our defense mechanisms are often seen as the problem in themselves. For instance, pseudo-aggression is often a defense to cover up one's attachment to passivity: "I'm not passive: Can't you see how aggressive I am!" The tendency is to believe that one's display of aggression (the symptom) is the problem, while its likely source—inner passivity—is overlooked. In the case of substance abuse, an addict tends to plead guilty, as a defense, to being weak-willed or to being a failure, while he harbors and covers up an emotional attachment to inner passivity as well as to self-rejection or self-hatred.

In another example, a person might interpret the condition of loneliness as the problem in itself. The loneliness, though, is the defense (and the price paid in suffering) to cover up one's secret willingness to indulge in feeling unloved, abandoned, or devalued. This defense reads: "I'm not indulging in feeling unloved or abandoned—my loneliness proves I want to be with people."

13. Some clients want to believe they are exceptions to the rule that the working-out process takes time. They would like to believe the solutions to their symptoms can be quickly solved. Bergler stated, "It takes one, two, or even three or more years to cure a complicated neurosis."[97] This estimate was based on a three-to-five-session a week program, which was the norm in Bergler's day.

I believe the "cure" (substantial progress in eliminating the flaw) can happen more quickly for some people on a once-a-week schedule of sessions, providing they show intellectual interest in this insight psychology, along with reflection upon the correct interpretations. As mentioned, progress can be made without therapy, involving self-study through written material, though in this format the time-frame for inner growth becomes less predictable.

In any case, therapists who want to do this form of analysis must do the inner work. Bergler wrote that, "The analyst who essays to analyze psychic masochism in a patient must first eliminate this scourge from his own psychic household. And this is practically impossible, without help."[98]

14. Bergler stated, "Don't look for contradictions, and don't use all your intelligence to reduce analysis to absurdity by playing off different layers of interpretations. Don't underestimate the complexity of the psychic apparatus. There is always the possibility that a new facet, not hitherto discussed, may appear."[99]

Of course, the patient is entitled to put up a fight and object to interpretations. But some patients doth protest too much. They try to get the therapist to soften up his or her interpretations. They hold on to their deadly flaw as if in a fight to the death. Many academics and critics have displayed this resistance, striving through their comments and beliefs to reduce psychoanalysis itself to absurdity.

15. Watch for the tendency to be self-critical because "progress isn't happening fast enough." The slowness of the process, as some subjectively perceive it, can produce distress and impatience. When we're working out our deadly flaw, we happily become aware that we're making progress. While the inner critic must concede that progress is being made, it shifts tactics and begins to claim that progress isn't happening fast enough. Try to understand that this claim by the inner critic is not objective. Note, too, that the inner critic never gives us positive credit for what we've achieved. It always seeks to undermine us.

16. Understanding that our inner courtroom operates 24/7, we can check on the accuracy of interpretations through our dreams. New clients can be quite skeptical

of these interpretations, because the operations of our psyche initially strike us as nonsensical. Clients can feel reassured when they have evidence from within, in the form of specific types of dreams, that the interpretations are correct.

One type of dream, called "a dream of refutation," is produced because the inner critic, always prepared to torment us, seizes upon a decisive analytical interpretation to say, to this effect, "Yes, it's true what the therapist says. You are passive. And you like being passive in such-and-such a situation." Even as we sleep, the weak or subordinate ego is forced to defend, and, in some melodramatic or surrealistic dreamscape, we deny or refute that accusation. We wouldn't have such dreams if the therapist wasn't hitting an important nerve deep in our psyche.

Other types of dreams, of a positive nature, indicate we're making progress overcoming our secret attachments. Here the dreamer plays the part of the hero, star, or admired person, as contrasted with one's earlier dreams of being a victim or someone who functions in a limited manner.

17. Some clients in the early stages of therapy concede in small measure to inner reality and give up one of their less significant symptoms in preparation for holding on for dear life to their basic neurosis. Such pseudo-success is an illusion. It involves a shifting of the dysfunction without its destruction.

A most impressive example of such "success," Bergler wrote, involved "a man who consulted me on Friday to start analysis the next Monday because of potency disturbance, only to call it off on Sunday since he was 'already cured.' The 'threat' of analysis sufficed in his case to give some semblance of potency for a few weeks."[100]

18. Beware the basic fallacy. That means watch out for your determination to blame your problems on some variation of a cruel father and cold mother. Blaming parents leaves us stuck in place, and it serves to maintain if not activate our suffering. Certainly, bad parenting is going to make for a difficult and painful childhood. Yet children brought up in the same family, and subjected to the same levels of cruelty or affection, often turn out quite differently in terms of their dysfunction or state of emotional health.

All of us experienced some sense of injustice and neglect in childhood. We don't have to be perpetual victims of it. Sometimes unjust or cruel upbringings have been launching-pads for triumphant lives. As adults, we have the option of growing our consciousness, which is an accomplishment that makes us very grateful for life, however difficult it has been at times.

19. High intelligence is not essential for benefiting from this process. It takes integrity, diligence, and courage—more so than intelligence—to break through the boundaries of resistance. The smartest people can be

the most resistant, the most cunning, when it comes to erecting inner defenses. Most of us are prepared to take the interpretations and use them as weapons of resistance against analysis. Let your integrity guide you when you track your thoughts to see if you're looking for ways to misuse the interpretations.

20. Be aware that your mind, in defiant resistance to insight, might refuse to work on your behalf. You will forget and fail to apply the new understanding that is being presented to you. Some of my clients leave my office and "conveniently" forget the high points of the session. They come back the following week without having given any thought to the interpretations and are blithely ignorant of the content of the previous session.

In Bergler's words, "Don't be naïve and don't relax for one moment your eternal vigilance against unconscious resistance. Sort out the relevant facts from a mass of irrelevant palimpsests. Refuse to be diverted by even the most ingenious red herring, which the unconscious may send into consciousness."[101]

21. Check in with yourself to see if you are using situations productively to fight your neurosis instead of your resistance. It's in the client's best interest to cooperate. Our resistance employs accusations, irony, and scorn to throw the hounds of heaven off our scent. If you sense that such mental tricks are at play in your psyche, identify them as efforts to cover up your deadly flaw.

Chapter 20
Society as Extension of Our Psyche

The first song written and directed by the Eagles when the band reunited after its fourteen-year breakup was "Get Over It." It's a song of protest against the constant whining and complaining of the victim mentality. These are the opening lyrics:

I turn on the tube and what do I see
A whole lotta people cryin' "Don't blame me"
They point their crooked little fingers at everybody else
Spend all their time feelin' sorry for themselves
Victim of this, victim of that
Your momma's too thin; your daddy's too fat
Get over it
Get over it
All this whinin' and cryin' and pitchin' a fit
Get over it, get over it.

We can "get over it" more easily when we understand our unconscious compulsion to experience ourselves as victims. We find it easy to play the victim role in life and even to indulge in the feeling of it.

Consider the economic crash of 2008 and the hardship and unhappiness that have followed. Was it the fault of bankers, Congress, regulators, the media, or the people? Blaming others feels good when it defends against our participation in the fiasco. Even though bankers may have broken the law and need more regulation, we're all part of the problem. Deficiencies in human consciousness caused the crash. The problem is at least partially due to the fact that our intelligence and awareness are impaired by unresolved negative emotions that produce collective occurrences of self-defeat and self-sabotage. This chapter provides some examples of that impairment and the consequential national suffering and collective self-defeat.

In the bigger picture, regulatory reform of our banks isn't sufficient in itself. Human nature has to be reformed as well, or we won't stand up for ourselves either individually or as a group when neurotic bankers and psychopathic speculators find new ways to cheat the system. Human dysfunction creeps into all our endeavors. We're in danger, for instance, of acting out our propensity for self-defeat with nuclear proliferation, genetic manipulation, and environmental degradation.

We're not to blame for being dysfunctional or neurotic. Human nature has a fundamental flaw, as this book contends, which can be resolved. What's different now is the urgency of our situation. It's obviously crisis time on planet Earth, time to answer the call to become more conscious. We can start by seeing and acknowledging our own contribution to the problem. We can't prevent institutional corruption or overcome passive inaction when we neglect to address personal dysfunction and negative emotions such as anger, distrust, dissension, envy, fear, greed, hatred, and overall lack of self-regulation. These emotions corrupt family, community, and national life, as they also block us from having the power or will to achieve reform.

Personal dysfunction manifests in two interconnected ways—through distress and suffering and through self-defeating behaviors. We're obviously dysfunctional when chronically unhappy, dissatisfied, or depressed. More symptoms of our dysfunction include being defensive, worrying a lot, feeling overwhelmed, messing up relationships, lacking self-regulation, neglecting our health, fearing change and the unknown, constantly criticizing, chronically complaining, and feeling like a failure. Many of us consider such emotions and behaviors to be more or less normal, as if we are fated to suffer endlessly. As long as our suffering is not excruciating, many of us don't consider the idea that our unhappiness is entirely unnecessary.

Society will weaken and crumble if we go on believing that our personal dysfunction is caused by defective genes or the malice and ignorance of others. That renders us helpless, like watching our fortune bounce randomly at an unlucky roulette table. Democratic society needs strong citizens who manifest enlightened values. Otherwise, the accumulation of ignorance and mediocrity produces national self-defeat.

An understanding of the principles of self-defeat has not been sufficiently integrated into the study of economics. That social science produced a trillion-dollar-plus bust when the American financial system went over the edge in 2008. The financial chicanery engineered by Wall Street was staged and directed by economists who graduated from (and taught at) America's top universities. How many of these economists have done the honorable thing and told us exactly how their so-called scientific discipline produced such falsehood and delusion?

We have a legitimate gripe with economics. But we can be even more disgusted with the field of psychology. It is producing its own brand of second-rate information and subprime factoids that are preventing us from getting to the heart of our personal and national dysfunction. Academic psychologists, to a large degree, have borrowed their knowledge from books. They haven't plunged into the unconscious to discover and champion essential truths about human nature. Instead, they have run off with their so-called scientific method to count all the correlations dancing on the head of a statistic. Hence, they flood the marketplace of ideas with second-rate and irrelevant information.

In the past century, psychology has produced many essential truths. These truths, however, have not been championed. Psychologists ought to have presented a united front in lobbying for human progress. But they have *not* insisted that the psychological dynamics of the unconscious mind be taught to students and the public. This failure has limited our intelligence and hindered our evolution. The world is desperate for deep understanding of human nature. People are suffering and dying every day (violence, war, psychosomatic diseases, and lack of self-regulation) because they do not understand basic tenets of psychoanalysis, including projection, transference, the death instinct, the negative repetition compulsion, and identification. People can feel substantial relief from suffering through an understanding of these tenets, even without delving into Edmund Bergler's more profound revelations.

Resistance is monumental. Sad to say, people don't necessarily change their minds when their erroneous assumptions are corrected. A University of Michigan study[102] found that misinformed people, particularly those loyal to their politics, rarely change their minds when exposed to corrected facts in news stories. Instead, they often become more strongly set in their beliefs.

Why are many of us so obtuse? We tend to create an identity—our sense of ourselves as individuals and as a group or nationality—that is based on certain beliefs. Those beliefs can be religious, secular, personal, cultural, and social. Beliefs are not just mental deductions: They carry a lot of emotional baggage. Many of us experience anxious turmoil and inner fears when our beliefs are directly challenged by opposing ideas and beliefs (or, even more distressing, by facts).

The emotional impact might be, "Who am I, who will I be, without my beliefs?"

Some individuals can feel a frightening cognitive dissonance, like a lost soul in existential panic, when confronted with facts that do not correspond with their belief system. To avoid this fear, they refuse unconsciously to assimilate the facts into their intelligence. With inner growth, however, we "know" ourselves and are comfortable with ourselves through human virtues such as integrity, honesty, empathy, courage, and a passion for truth. These virtues are not beliefs we hold but assets we embody.

As mentioned, psychoanalysis has an explanation for how our intelligence is restricted. An unconscious process of repression is active in our psyche, covering up old material from our past that's painful, shameful, and guilt-laden. Psychic energy, which ideally is used productively and creatively, is wasted in this process of repression and denial.

Psychic energy is also wasted in inner defensiveness. The energy is dissipated fending off the inner critic or superego. We waste this energy producing inner defenses that protect a delicate, idealized self-image or ego. Often the "logic" used in our defenses is completely irrational. All that matters is that the defense works as a cover-up. In this process, the individual sacrifices truth and reality to protect his self-image.

Take the example of greed, which appears to be Wall Street's driving force. If some greedy traders on Wall Street were to track this greed back to its source, they would discover a dark emptiness within their psyche. As mentioned earlier, they are entangled in feelings of loss, deprivation, not getting, missing out, helplessness, having no value, and fear of death. They are pawns of these largely unconscious negative feelings, and their compulsive striving for money serves as a defense or cover-up. Their main defense is to convince themselves they are superior individuals, "masters of the universe" whose superiority is evident through the money they make and the impact their decisions have in the world. As they embrace this defense, they have no qualms about destabilizing the world economy through their compulsive acquisitiveness.

We have only a specific amount of psychic energy at our disposal. The more we waste in inner conflict and the cover-up of our dark side, the less intelligence we'll have for the challenge of saving America and the world.

A similar impairment of intelligence affects people who can't separate church (or mosque) and state. With popular uprisings toppling governments in the Middle East, it's time to understand this rigid mentality more clearly. It's vital that democracy, not theocracy or new autocratic regimes, replaces corrupt Middle East governments that have fallen to popular uprisings. The growth of democracy is a measure of human evolution. Citizens of a democracy are more likely than their counterparts in a theocracy to value reason, the rule of law, cross-cultural exchanges, tolerance, self-respect, and environmental protections. Meanwhile in America, we won't be able to export the wisdom that honors the separation of church and state when we're in danger of being overrun by a theocratic mentality in our backyard.

Inner fear may be the main influence on those of us who can't separate church and state. Inner fear, which is an unconscious leftover from baby fears, is a common ingredient in human nature. The fear is evident in the widespread worry, stress, and anxiety that plague the human race. Inner fear causes the concerns of modern life to become fearful preoccupations, as when concern about terrorism produces a fearful populace willing to tolerate the suppression of civil liberties for alleged security.

Other concerns that are exacerbated through inner fear include fears of failure, impoverishment, rejection, and abandonment. Inner fear is also associated with looking bad in the eyes of others, being alone, feeling helpless, doubting one's value, and feeling controlled or overwhelmed. Ironically, we're also afraid of freedom, as social theorist Erich Fromm proposed in *The Fear of Freedom,* published in 1942.[103] Fromm's thesis states that people had not fully acquired a sense of being autonomous creatures directing their own future, despite the spirit of free inquiry and individual initiative facilitated by the Renaissance, Protestant Reformation, and Industrial Revolution.

How does all this relate to the separation of church and state? Having religious beliefs is perfectly healthy and appropriate. But because of inner fear, insecure individuals can misuse religion to prop up their weak sense of self. Such individuals believe they will experience less anxiety by adopting religious beliefs that place them in the mainstream or promise them salvation.

Basically, such people are entangled in inner passivity. When they try to break out of that passivity to develop a mind of their own, they are pushed back into it by the superego which assumes to be their higher authority. (Psychotics can experience the superego as the voice of God.) The danger is that they can now begin to process much of their cognitive functioning through religious belief. They start to weigh all their positions, interpretations, and decisions—whether personal or social—against religious convictions. They have surrendered too much of their autonomy in exchange for the security of a belief system. Now they can't access their inner self, and they're bereft of the wisdom and authority needed to stand outside of religious belief to make independent decisions. The superego objects when they try to make independent decisions. This produces self-doubt and anxiety. They are "let off the hook" when some "higher authority" makes decisions for them.

This doesn't resolve the inner fear, however. The inner fear is simply repressed. Often it can only be eliminated by consciously exposing its irrationality and its sources in our infantile past.

There are other ways to understand inner fear. Jumps or spikes in our level of anxiety and fearfulness occur when we're being accused or attacked by our inner critic. Inner fear hinges on whether the psychological defense we're presenting to the inner critic will suffice to keep it at bay. If one defense doesn't work, we might present another defense, one that is more self-defeating or involves more suffering (such as depression), to appease the inner critic. When our defenses are temporarily effective, our feelings swing between happiness and elation. However, a successful defense (and even successful sublimations) can weaken over time, at which point we drift emotionally toward anxiety, fear, and panic.

Inner fear is alleviated, or appears to be dealt with, through defenses that are effective temporarily but ultimately lead toward self-defeat. In one instance, the fear is projected outward, which makes the danger appear to be external. In other words, inner fear becomes "reality" fear. In this process, people can actually heighten their anxiety and fear as they create unnecessary enemies and personality clashes. The best way to rid the world of fearful and paranoid reactions, or at least to lessen their influence, is to recognize the existence of inner fear and to strive to eliminate it.

The lack in recent years of political civility is another expression of how determined we are to hold on to fear and negativity. Many political partisans are not interested in any resolution of political issues. The real purpose for the venom they direct at each other is to cover up their own unresolved negativity and to discharge that negativity on to their opponents. When civility returns to political discourse, these partisans will be left to bake in their own neurotic juices. They prefer a scorched-earth political climate to a true accounting of their distemper.

As a people, we are unable to outgrown regressive, reactionary, and violence-inviting political discourse when we don't understand the psychological dynamics clearly enough. A fanatical partisan, for instance, wants to believe that the (alleged) stupidity and malice of the other side are valid reasons for his negative feelings. This partisan doesn't see that political opponents have become, at least in part, convenient targets for the negativity that he is compelled to project or transfer on to them. This enables the partisan to pose as a blameless and innocent contributor to the debate instead of the dysfunctional participant that he is.

Partisans are quick to denounce this claim made by psychoanalysis that they scatter and dispense their own negativity under the cover of their passion, righteousness, and ideology. (Terrorists also do this, though with higher-caliber viciousness.) Were partisans to recognize this inner dynamic, they would also be obliged to acknowledge their personal need for

271

psychological insight and growth. Their ego and resistance say "No thanks" to that option.

Of course, passion and partisanship are perfectly acceptable in political discourse. However, passionate intensity can also be a feature of the individual who is dumping his or her negativity on to others. Passion is best moderated by wisdom and humility. Partisans without insight become self-righteous, judgmental, negative, and divisive, while putting forward a triumphant self-image that cons the naïve and pulls them into the pits of anger, hatred, and hopelessness.

Unrelenting partisanship, taunting, and overheated rhetoric serve as defenses that cover up each individual's own refusal to answer the call of human destiny, which is the realization of the oneness of humanity through a deep knowing of one's self. Meanwhile, the more stubbornly we cling to our ego, the more fiercely we end up battling what we experience as the arrogant, infuriating egos of others.

Inflammatory political discourse is just one symptom of the general ignorance of how our psyche works. Other symptoms include widespread narcissism, pervasive passivity, deteriorating mental health, and an entitlement mentality. All undermine the struggle for a better democracy.

We all have ways that we can grow psychologically and become more powerful in expressing the quality of our humanity. People on the Right need to address their hostility, irrationality, fear of change, and, ultimately, the deep unconscious fear of death that drive them to militarize the nation, stock up on handguns, and fantasize apocalyptically about salvation. On the Left, people can become more effective reformers by recognizing and addressing their forms of negativity, which include defensiveness, as well as feelings of victimization, oppression, criticism, and disappointment.

(Readers who are political partisans are apt to find this following content somewhat offensive—if they haven't already. Partisans very much want to believe that their political position is based on their sound rational considerations. Reading this material, they're likely to experience the irritation that depth psychology typically elicits when it pokes its nose into our political views and other cherished beliefs.)

Both the conservative and the liberal mentalities have psychological weaknesses that have been completely unconscious. (I start with the conservative blind spots, and then address liberal ones.) Berkeley professor and author George Lakoff encourages people to see more deeply into the psychology of rigid, dogmatic conservatives. We need to understand, he writes, how the conservative belief in individual responsibility, to the degree that it may exclude social responsibility, is based on the model of the strict-father family.

According to this model, the father's role in the family as "decider" and moral authority is required to teach kids right from wrong. Conservatives claim that father's superior moral guidance is needed, along with physical punishment if necessary, so kids can develop the discipline to become morally responsible adults. Why do conservatives think that father knows best? Psychoanalysis can provide insight.

According to psychoanalysis, the superego assumes an authoritarian, even a tyrannical, stance within our psyche. The superego is an aggressive drive that can function as an inner disciplinarian. However, it is usually negative and irrational. In less evolved individuals, the superego often decides what is right and wrong. As mentioned earlier, it makes this distinction solely to exercise inner authority. The superego is not interested in, nor can it even distinguish, what is truly right or wrong. Yet many individuals interpret the oppressive, impersonal superego as a guiding voice of inner conscience.

When people are inwardly weak and unaware, the superego can have the run of their psyche and dominate their personality. Often, it is critical, ruthless, mocking, and unforgiving. It frequently overpowers what little sense of autonomy and personal authority many people possess.

Unwittingly, hardcore conservatives plant their soul in the impersonal authority of the superego. Hence, they are enamored of the power of the impersonal, as evidenced by their emotional alignment with corporations, the market, and the military. These three impersonal forces impose their values and authority

274

often without sufficient wise oversight, as when the alleged self-regulating "invisible hand" of the marketplace destroys the environment.

Conservatives distrust government because it is personal, not impersonal. Though libertarians instinctively object to that assertion and conservatives decry the "nanny state," government is, ideally, the voice and protector of the people. A person battling a corporation over excessive charges on a credit card has nowhere else to turn but to the government. A democratic government is the strong father or mother who protects us from the bully next door. Through the government, the individual feels he can protect and represent himself.

However, according to the strict-father model, children (the people) are not supposed to represent themselves. Only some "higher" impersonal law or representative of that law (strict father) is allowed to speak for the child. Just as children of conservatives are expected to submit passively to the father, we adults are not supposed to have a mind of our own, nor a higher authority (the government) that respects us just for ourselves (for being citizens). This means that such conservatives (usually with no malice intended) do not expect or want people to grow in human consciousness.

Ideally, democratic governments express, on the external level, human consciousness at its best, just as on the inner level our *self* is the wise guiding authority that represents and protects us. But human consciousness is a discredited term in the conservative lexicon. That's because on an inner level, the consciousness of rigid conservatives tends to be somewhat frozen in place. The superego, the conservative mind's "decider," is hostile to human progress and inner freedom, and it's completely indifferent to our suffering and self-defeat.

Hence, the superego has no capacity for empathy. Yet empathy is a quality of higher consciousness, as well as a basis of American democracy. Empathy is built into the principle of one person, one vote. When each person's vote counts, each person is respected and valued. Democracy is an evolved system that practices equality and justice. Democracy is supportive of each person being strong and happy, and it's not, for instance, overtly hostile to labor's bargaining rights. Democracy and the wellbeing of all is served when as many people as possible have their dignity and personal power.

Rigid conservatives believe the government should not provide health care, environmental protection, and other forms of public service. Such rights, the feeling goes, gives too much respect and power to everybody. Such rights make each individual too important. Rigid conservatives rationalize their lack of empathy by claiming that the poor deserve their poverty because they're ultimately responsible for their own failings. But the poor haven't necessarily failed. Perhaps they're doing well with the weak cards they were dealt. We're the lesser ones if our hearts are closed. So we have no business being judgmental. But the superego's specialty is being judgmental.

The mental gymnastics that some people employ for disrespecting the poor enable them to practice guilt-free ruthlessness while feeling morally superior, which is precisely the stance adopted by the superego. The superego clings to its power like a dictator as it tries to keep down human consciousness. Meanwhile, the conservative embrace of individualism is derived from the righteousness and arrogance of the superego as a power onto itself.

The left-wing psyche has its blind spots, too. I believe that liberals and progressives—count me among them—are weakened significantly by a false article of faith. This false belief holds that national disharmony is caused by the malice, ignorance, and oppression of others, particularly the right wing and the oligarchy. On a personal level, we also blame our dysfunction and unhappiness on others, namely parents, employers, misguided friends, insensitive loved ones, and soul-crushing society.

Collective revolutionary action from the Left won't necessarily transform this country for the better when many so-called reformers remain psychologically naïve. The Left gets entangled in the infantile mentality that perceives all the bad that happens to be coming from outside sources. This left-wing belief is a kind of secular religion, and it causes us to collude unconsciously with the right wing in a political acting-out that maintains and enhances our sense of disappointment, oppression, and injustice.

In other words, liberals are looking unconsciously for external elements or circumstances of oppression and injustice, particularly in our relationship to the Republican Right, in order to recycle unresolved feelings from childhood of refusal, domination, and victimization. We haven't yet established inner freedom from these negative emotions that influence how we experience ourselves and the world. As we blame external factors and "oppressive" opponents, our acting-out enables us to deny and cover-up our own unresolved emotional issues and inner conflicts. Hence, we must continue to feel we're on the losing side. Over the years we may have lost many political battles or given up hard-won social progress for this reason.

The more heatedly we protest and complain about right-wing malice and ignorance, the more we are likely to be covering up (defending against) recognition of our own contribution to the nation's political, economic, and social distress. Conflicts, whether inner or outer, are typically unstable. They frequently deteriorate. Hence, in our self-defeat we could help to produce (or move towards) an authoritarian government. People invariably create the outcomes predicated by their emotional weakness.

Our deadly flaw, particularly involving inner passivity, is the source of the left-wing's collusion or psychological "acting-out" with the right wing. This self-defeating dynamic brings out the worst in conservatives, too. Conservatives are just as unconscious about inner processes as liberals, and the Right wing becomes more intransigent, irrational, and bullying as its members unconsciously treat liberals in the manner that liberals, through their provocations and passive-aggressive reactions, indicate they are unconsciously prepared and even eager to experience.

The modern Republican Party serves as the political arm of the rich for an emotional reason. It shares with the rich a mentality that fiercely desires the feeling of being superior and separate. The rich use wealth to feel this individual exceptionalism, while the Republicans use power. Republicans have matched the oligarchy's money grab of the past three decades with a burning desire for political power. (Obviously, many Democrats have also succumbed to this plague of civic indecency.) The lust for wealth and power is a kind of emotional addiction, and it's produced by inner poverty. Such poverty can be understood in a secular or a spiritual sense. Inner poverty is a measure of the degree to which a person is contaminated by unresolved inner conflict and is thereby disconnected from self, psyche, spirit, or soul.

Republicans want rich people to pay as little as possible in taxes, allegedly in order to help the economy through trickle-down benefits. This economic ideology covers up a hidden truth. Their allegiance isn't so much to the rich as it is to the mentality they share with the rich. Their ego knows how good it feels to be separate, superior, and powerful.

On a deeper level, though, they are not powerful. It is only in weakness that an egotistic or narcissistic person—through denial and resistance—seeks protection from the humbling truth about how he still lives substantially through old hurts of being unworthy, unimportant, and powerless. Many politicians on the far right tend to identify with the rich in this manner, and they have been willing, through tax favoritism, to provide them with more physical and emotional separation from their fellow citizens. This helps them and the rich maintain an artificial distance from their inner poverty. They don't have to deal with the moral, emotional, and psychological challenges of being one of us or one with us.

Ultimately, such individuals say "no" to what is good for society because they say "no" to what is good in themselves.

We need more self-awareness from the people running our country, and we can best achieve this by becoming more psychologically insightful ourselves.

Meanwhile, a lot of us fear that the big changes happening in America are for the worst. Many on the Left are convinced soft-core fascism has crept into our institutions and been smuggled into our laws. The fear is that such oppression will worsen.

There's plenty of evidence that democracy has been weakened since the 1980s, including the growing role of corporate money in politics, the rightward shift of the Democratic and Republican parties, the collapse of union power, the ascendency of the military-security state, the suppression of human rights under the Patriot Act, the high rate of prisoner incarceration, and the relentless pursuit of empire.

A tyrannical leadership could indeed seize power in America. But it's self-defeating for us to live in fear of that possibility. If we spend time in fear, we're in danger of facilitating that vile prospect. Fear arises, whether on the Left or the Right, largely out of a sense of powerlessness, passivity, and an expectation that the worst is going to happen.

It doesn't pay, for instance, to go around worrying about getting cancer. Worry and anxiety in itself can help bring on the disease. Instead, the wisest among us try their best to live a healthy lifestyle and keep cancer at bay through their vitality, sense of purpose, and ability to enjoy life, even with all its trials and imperfections.

What does healthy living involve in the context of our citizenship and our desire to defeat tyranny? Prevention, not fear, is the antidote.

Prevention is first and foremost a matter of how we feel about ourselves. Each of us can strive to cultivate the belief that we have the power to make sure fascism and tyranny in whatever form don't come to America. A reader might ask, "Are you talking about little, inconsequential me standing in the way of this?" Yes, you are possibly the most important person in America. Let me explain.

If you believe in the common good, you understand that a richer happiness depends on the quality of the relationships we have with one another. We know that each of us can contribute significantly to a greater good. When one of us realizes his potential, we all benefit. When he doesn't, we're all poorer for it.

The relationship we have with the ruling class is patterned on the relationship children have with their parents. We maintain in our psyche the emotional memories of how we experienced our parents. Passivity is a primary feature of that relationship. As young children, we were dependent on our parents, and we understood that they had the power and were, in a sense, our rulers. As children, we're mentally and physically unable to rule ourselves. We need the rule of parents. In an ideal world, parents would always practice benevolent authority. The rule of parents over their children is psychologically necessary, just as the rule of political leaders is socially necessary. We're not evolved enough yet to make our complex society work well without a hierarchy of authority.

Liberals and progressives often associate happiness with social progress. It's entirely reasonable for us to want the human race to practice higher levels of justice, tolerance, and peacefulness. Obviously, we believe in human evolution. It follows logically that we also believe in the importance of our own self-development and our capacity to grow in wisdom and generosity. We would be hypocritical if we were to insist that others make personal improvements while believing that we were somehow beyond that need.

We can't reasonably expect society to get better without our full participation. Evolvement requires that we discover sources from within us of our intrinsic value, goodness, intelligence, freedom, courage, integrity, and power. It all adds up to the fearless feeling that, if tyranny were ever to take root here, it would be over *your* dead body. In this manner of believing in yourself, you understand how important you are to the whole of society.

Now, obviously, not everybody in America or the world is going to acquire this kind of grounding in self-esteem. Don't worry that millions of Americans, possibly a majority, will go along with the old, weary paradigm as they continue to live through a wide disconnect from their personal value and power. We are more conscious. We're part of the revolution in consciousness. We're the ones who are stopping tyranny from coming to America. We will root out corruption by overcoming inner conflict.

If some evil were taking root in your family, you would know that you're the one who has to stop it. If evil were taking root in your community, you would also know that so much depends on how you respond. It's the same for the nation and the world. You have to respond with all the intelligence, courage, and goodness you possess or the danger becomes ever greater.

We can be hindered still by lingering passivity that goes back to our childhood. Those old emotional associations still live on in our psyche. Now, as we experience the ruling class the way we did our parents, we trust these leaders to know what is right for us. Yet childish traits accompany this arrangement, and we fail to protect ourselves when our leaders become untrustworthy, misguided, or dysfunctional. We can't find the words or take the actions that represent us effectively in the face of misguided authority. We think we have power because we can vote. But because of our immaturity and inner passivity, we often can't even discern who's going to represent us best in the political process.

A lot of us have been expressing negative, bitter, and even defeatist sentiments, as evidenced in the posts and comments at many political and social websites. The expression of cynicism and bitterness is a passive and painful use of our time. In contrast, the qualities that destroy tyranny are integrity, sincerity, generosity, fearlessness, and good humor. Thousands of the little things we do in daily life can express these democratic values.

How do you break through the illusion that you don't have what it takes? Having read this far in this book, you do have plenty of awareness and courage. If you so choose, you can feel pleasure in savoring these qualities. With your consciousness, you can libidinize your integrity, awareness, and goodness. This means that you produce pleasure by registering (becoming aware of) these qualities in yourself and appreciating yourself for being a person who represents (or is trying to represent) these qualities. Don't let your inner critic demean these qualities. Become aware of how your inner passivity serves as an enabler of your inner critic.

Before, in the old manner, you were tempted to let your awareness of how bad things are tempt you to feel helpless and defeated. Now, with new knowledge about your psyche, you make an inner shift and embrace the real you, the one who knows how to enjoy this crazy, wonderful life. In a nutshell, you generate this enjoyment through the quality of your consciousness and your being. The more you understand yourself, the more you can let go of negativity. The more negativity you let go of, the higher the quality of your consciousness and pleasure.

As you feel more pleasure in doing your best, steer clear of the temptation to dwell on the passive feeling that progress, whether in yourself or in society, is happening too slowly. This is a revolutionary time, and things are actually happening very fast. Don't cop out and don't be overwhelmed. It's your chance to be a hero and patriot who shows your toughness and persistence.

Chapter 21
Epilogue

Our psyche is a realm of chaos and mystery, a feature it has in common with the cosmos. Fortunately, we don't have to travel light-years to explore our psyche. Our intelligence can just turn inward to make the unconscious conscious. Our greatest discovery is the source of our unhappiness. We come face to face with our secret willingness to suffer, a condition that's maintained by a deadly flaw. We heal or repair this flaw by understanding its mechanisms and operations.

This deadly flaw is formed when the passive circumstances of the newborn child interact with psychological drives. A playwright might one day create a drama of the Three Wizards of Id—aggression, megalomania, and libido—who collide and collude on the stage of the human psyche. Here, inner aggression pursues elusive inner passivity across the stage, into the wings, and back behind the curtain. The ego—portrayed as the shadow of our self—flitters across the stage now and then for comic relief. The main character, the hero of the play, is initially portrayed as a weakling who keeps tripping over his shadow and catering to the whims of other players. Soon our hero breaks out of the Matrix, discovers the Self, and escapes from illusion and negativity to reveal the exuberance of inner freedom and the creative splendor of human greatness.

Human consciousness begins anew in the psyche of each infant. Natural aggression, megalomania, and libido unleash a perfect storm that each child experiences. The child can't expel all this aggression into the environment, however much he or she yells, kicks, and screams. What is not expelled turns inward and comes at the child as self-aggression. The child's megalomania (acute self-centeredness) is confounded: "Where did this powerful feeling (of aggression) come from? It must be what I want." The child's libido pipes up, "If it's what I want, it must be what I like!"

"It is a terrifying thought," Bergler stated, "that each of us, in earliest childhood, installs an internal 'misery-machine' in his superego [self-aggression or inner critic], and thereafter must—in self-defense—learn to enjoy suffering, once more unknowingly and unwillingly."[104]

So the deadly flaw is itself a defense, one intended to neutralize the self-aggression of our inner critic. The deadly flaw, as a living remnant from the oral stage, reconfigures itself for later childhood suffering and then carries on contaminating the circumstances of our adult lives. While it is manageable for most of us (meaning we don't self-destruct), it still degrades our quality of life. It also interferes enough in just about everyone's life to downgrade our intelligence and happiness.

Bergler emphasized the role of biology in shaping our emotional fate. Biology determines the long maturation time of the human child, which exposes our psyche to a longer period of enforced passivity. Biology also determines that the child's aggression and libido are powerful drives, perhaps as strong as the adult's. Summing up the situation at the end of *Principles of Self-Damage*, Bergler wrote that, "Biologically conditioned unfavorable depositions of rebounding aggression in earliest infancy result in the installation of the superego. Again in earliest infancy, unplaceable megalomania [acute self-centeredness], coupled with libido's rule of thumb, the pleasure principle, which tries to make the best of an impossible situation, results in the installation of the only possible defense against constant torture emanating from the superego—psychic masochism."[105]

Again, here briefly is how it happens. Acute self-centeredness, in combination with libido, produces a determination or conviction in the child's mind to account for the painful self-aggression: "If aggression is what I'm feeling, it must be what I want. If it is what I want, it must be what I like." Before long, in a twist of fate, the anti-hedonistic superego objects to this "liking" of the aggression. This compels our unconscious ego to scramble to produce a wide range of defenses. Some of these defenses involve successful sublimations involving career pursuits and the enjoyment of leisure time and hobbies. Other defenses, however, precipitate the loss of behavioral and emotional self-regulation, and they range from being mildly to severely self-damaging.

Bergler tried at different points to explain the essence of the process that creates the deadly flaw. Earlier in *Principles of Self-Damage*, he stated:

> The helpless immature ego is so flooded with offenses to megalomania, and with aggression that has rebounded because it could not be expressed, that libidinization alone prevents the ensuing debacle from becoming complete. Later on, when the pre-stages of the superego add to the conflict by vetoing libidinization of pain, the unconscious ego is forced to create new defenses. These supplementary defenses are included in the clinical picture of psychic masochism, in which extensive use is made of alibis [defenses] consisting of pseudo-aggression.[106]

Children have other experiences to sort out. They don't begin to experience their mother as a loving protector and provider until they are eighteen months to two years of age. As infants, they first experience her as an extension of themselves. In the following months, they feel ambivalence toward her and can regard her as a creature that represents danger. According to Bergler, it is in that early stage when the child is beset "with peculiar misconceptions about the kind of person his mother really is, that he constructs the picture of himself as the innocent victim of a witch who is capable of starving, devouring, poisoning, choking him, chopping him to pieces, draining and castrating him."[107] Here is the source of infantile or baby fears.

Mother can also be perceived by the child as an ogre or a "giantess of the nursery."[108] As mentioned, children's fairy tales and other literature provide evidence for this claim. The child tenaciously maintains the fantasy of the "bad" coming from mother. A duality is created in which "everything good comes from me; everything bad comes from the outer world." This misreading of reality may be a factor in egotism's emphasis on duality or the sense of separateness, which underscores the feeling that, "I must separate myself from the bad outer world." The consequence is apparent in world politics when certain governments or countries are demonizing one another or when in domestic politics heightened partisanship becomes self-defeating. Hence, in seeing others as enemies or aliens, our lingering infantile characteristics continue falsifying reality. Painfully, society does make progress, as when the Civil Rights struggle in the United States knocked some reality into us as it moved our consciousness along.

In my view, children can also experience mother as a queen. She is the one with the power to determine who is privileged to remain in her "court," at her side, as the good little boy or girl. She has the power to expel from her court the bad boy or girl who has not respected her "sovereignty." The yearning for mother's acceptance and love forces children into some degree of passivity, for it feels that certain precious aspects of oneself (acute self-centeredness and its accompanying determination to perceive mother as a "great refuser") have to be sacrificed in order to obtain maternal approval. This can produce an emotional association between approval and submission that is a factor in the sugar-coating or libidinization of inner passivity.

Inner passivity is frequently at play when men and women fail in relationships and marriage to establish loving intimacy. Inner passivity can compel them to grow resentful of one another because, in the give-and-take of life together, they experience the dominance, intensity, or demands of the other through painful submission or loss of one's self. Inner passivity also produces a disconnect from one's own sense of value. This form of suffering is frequently blamed on one partner's alleged lack of interest in the other partner or waning passion for the relationship.

The toddler begins to see mother as the "great refuser."[109] Once again the formula that originally created the flaw is applied: "If refusal is what is happening, it must be what I want. If it is what I want, it is what I like." Baby fears, which are created when the baby's inborn aggression is projected on to mother, become intense experiences of helplessness as the baby feels in peril from mother's alleged malice. These experiences of passivity and refusal are libidinized or sugar-coated to help cope with fear and to cling to acute self-centeredness.

To a considerable degree, our baby fears remain in our psyche and haunt us later in life. Usually, we project those fears into the environment and exaggerate the dangers posed by reality. We become convinced that our projections represent the truth of external dangers. Someone might own a handgun, for instance, because he believes external dangers require it, when his fears are solely the product of his psychology. Nations can refuse to initiate nuclear disarmament because the world's people, lacking self-knowledge, are likewise misguided about the nature of their fears.

Our fears become activated in challenging life situations, and they are experienced as anxiety and depression (as in postpartum depression). These fears, too, are libidinized in an unconscious effort to render them less excruciating. As such, they are entangled in the mix of the deadly flaw. The result is that we are more prone to be passive, to become worriers, to be plagued with anxiety, and to be less trustful of others and of life itself, as well as to be less trustworthy ourselves in our dealings with others. As a nation, we can be paranoid, fixated on national security, and thus more likely to elevate military power to something of a state religion.

Knowledge of our deadly flaw is indeed forbidden material. We try with all our might to cover it up. Accordingly, we covered up—in unconscious, collective collusion—the discoveries of Edmund Bergler. As mentioned, most overviews or histories of psychoanalysis or psychology fail to mention him at all.[110] Understanding the human psyche as I do, I take this extraordinary avoidance of him as evidence of the great significance of his findings.

Humanity has been stubbornly resistant to acknowledging the power our unconscious mind has over us. This stubbornness is its own kind of stupidity. The resistance is intensified when people approach Bergler's writings. His findings have remained esoteric because psychologists and psychoanalysts, like everyone else, are afflicted with what he called "the horror of self-knowledge."[111]

When we start looking for self-knowledge, we realize how little sense we have of our personal, developmental history. Imagine aliens visiting our planet and noting that, for such a technologically advanced species, we are incredibly lacking in objectivity and insight about ourselves. They are astounded that we know so little about the psychodynamics of our origins and the source of our negativity. They might conclude that we're doomed to extinction because our mental power and technical prowess outstrip our capacity to moderate and regulate our negative impulses.

Recorded history enables us to pierce centuries and millennia of our time on earth, but we have no sanctioned history of early childhood. How can that be? Do we continue to live in some dissociative state, afraid of our own selves, afraid of reality? Are we children terrified in a vast cosmos of being overwhelmed by our helplessness? Is inner passivity the emotional womb we still occupy?

If so, we are accepting inner tyranny and emotional chaos for a semblance of safety. Like a people resigned to dictatorship, we've been afraid of taking the steps required to feel our sovereignty more deeply and to know our authentic self. We have pretended such steps or options don't exist. We have to go through the "evil" of our deadly flaw to get there, and, like the "see-no-evil" monkey, we're disinclined to do so.

It's disappointing but not surprising we decline this call to greatness. The territory we must inspect teems with the taboos and forbidden knowledge of childhood. Children experience doubt and confusion about themselves when they're told or made to understand that touching and looking at certain things, such their own genitalia and mother's or father's nakedness, is forbidden. Sexual interest in brothers and sisters is also forbidden. In weaning, children are refused the breast. Next, they're not even allowed to look at it. To do so is bad or naughty. The peeping instinct is strong and children would like to look. But curiosity, especially related to genital regions, is discouraged and then prohibited. The taboo on childhood masturbation is all tied up in considerations of what is shameful and forbidden.

Soon children are aware that parents have secret lives in the bathroom and bedroom. Seeing what goes on there is not allowed. They would still like to look.

Forbidden erotic wishes drift through their consciousness. What are parents up to? Why are these sights forbidden to them? Using their imagination, children begin to peep. They peep into the darkness of what is forbidden, trying to shed light on this secretive world. It's thrilling to imagine what their parents are up to, though they feel wrong or guilty for doing so. When they grow up, their inner critic can veto introspection and creative use of the imagination because of original incestuous and sexual connotations.[112]

We start at an early age to repress and hide unconscious content in our psyche. The child discovers that certain wishes, thoughts, actions, and expressions of feelings are not acceptable. Mother first objects to any expression of this material, and later father. Parents have at their disposal the formidable powers of moral reproach, guilt, and punishment. The child, however, is not about to give up entirely these secret, forbidden wishes. He or she creates a Department of Secrets.[113]

In this private place in the psyche, which early on in childhood is fully conscious, the child stores a growing collection of vetoed wishes. In the child's psyche, however, the inner critic is also "coming into its own," and it has full access to all the content of the psyche. Being a "party-pooper" and fulfilling its function as a dispenser of punishment, it begins to object to the child's forbidden wishes. The inner critic has become a caricature of the parents, and it fills in as a misguided representative of the parents. Thus, the parent's prohibitions now apply to the Department of Secrets.

Bergler stated:

> Caught in this double maelstrom of external and internal prohibition, the child can choose either the path of complete renunciation, or that of compromise: pseudo goodness. Making the best of a bad bargain, the child chooses the second alternative, and *repression* enters the picture. The process can be described as a 'moving-van expedition' in which the child's secret wishes are moved from one storehouse to another which is more secure. 'Forbidden' material is moved from consciousness into regions that are not conscious, into the area described as the *unconscious*. Now infantile secrecy is victorious.[114]

The problem is that the repressed material is not expelled or even dormant. Instead, it's likely to create mischief in the form of anxiety, stress, and unhappiness. It's rich in material that is painful, shameful, and guilt-laden. It can simmer quietly, producing a low-grade state of unhappiness or discontent. This repressed material can burst into our life at any time with explosive power to precipitate out-of-control behaviors, emotions, and astounding feats of self-defeat. If we repress it too vigorously, it gets revenge, putting us at its mercy and making us helpless to moderate situations that can activate it more intensely.

We waste a lot of potentially pleasure-producing energy to maintain our repression. When the reality principle conflicts with our need to produce a defense to cover up our deadly flaw, the defense wins at the expense of our intellectual integrity and power. In other words, the deadly flaw forces us to create illusions and make mistakes—and we fall for it.

We can see that our intelligence may not be up to the task of managing this planet and its people. Emotional reactions and lack of foresight, planning, and wisdom have produced extraordinary dangers involving weapons of mass destruction, global climate change, fresh-water depletion and pollution, destruction and contamination of food sources, cravings for self-aggrandizement, pseudo-aggressive hostility among nations, and the proliferation of individuals and groups that embrace the death instinct. Perhaps our character suffers as much as our intelligence. That our moral character would deteriorate as we go on denying vital inner knowledge seems a reasonable expectation.

Wars constitute evidence for the existence of a powerful wish for self-destruction that we act out individually and collectively. Our self-destruction is forecast, too, in the predictions of global warming. In what may be an increasingly deteriorating situation, we could be passively acting out a deadly fate in a slow, inexorable drift. This is not a medical problem or a problem that neuroscience is going to solve for us. We have to delve into the mystery of our dysfunction and self-defeat as a challenge to our intelligence and as a way for that intelligence to grow. The solution requires us to become responsible for what has been unconscious. Underestimation of the psychological factor, Carl Jung warned, "is likely to take a bitter revenge."[115]

The knowledge that Bergler produced can facilitate the quest for world peace. We are less likely to be triggered by others and to become angry at them because we now understand that they're not the cause of our fear, insecurity, or unhappiness. As we lay down our inner defenses, our pretenses of being superior will evaporate. We'll have less fear and aggression to project, less need to use others for self-validation and gain, and fewer occasions to hide out passively in painful self-scrutiny and in the expectation of failure and defeat.

When Copernicus and Galileo discovered that the earth goes around the sun, not vice-versa, supporters of conventional wisdom fiercely objected to this truth. Like infants in acute self-centeredness, people wanted to be at the center of existence. The revelations of astronomy stimulated human intelligence and might have done much to inspire the Reformation and the Age of Enlightenment. Psychoanalysis and Edmund Bergler have explored inner space and made a comparable discovery: Our egocentric consciousness—the idea that the bad comes from outside us and we are exclusively good—is an illusion.

We're not the center of a universe that acts upon us arbitrarily and determines our happiness and our fate. God is not playing dice with us. We're not the little self that has been victimized and damaged by a cruel world. We're not suffering mainly because of what others have done to us. If bad things are happening to us, we might look to the possibility that we're still "saying no to reality."

We pass though this life on the flight path of conscious and unconscious choices. If we're unhappy, some unconscious pilot or pilots in our psyche are choosing our orbit. We find the best orbit by fine-tuning our inner compass and placing a conscious pilot—our self—in front of the controls. That requires us to recognize the deadly flaw and overcome it. Irrationality no longer spins inside us, sending us careening off course in pursuit of ways to suffer.

Appendix

Examples of Inner Dialogue

To become free of the major conflict in our psyche between inner aggression (inner critic or superego) and inner passivity, we need to bring the conflict into focus in the everyday personal experiences in which it appears.

The following examples of inner dialogue show the nature of the conflict in an instance of overeating or the eating of unhealthy food. This dialogue also shows how the conflict leads to self-defeat. (Other dialogue examples are provided in Chapter 15.)

Inner aggression: Why did you just eat that chocolate cake?

Inner passivity: It was so good. But I know I shouldn't have eaten it.

Inner aggression: Obviously it was good. But you promised to stay on your diet.

Inner passivity: I know. I was weak.

Inner aggression: Weak! It's worse than that! You're a hopeless slob!

Inner passivity: I went two days without eating anything sweet. That shows I can be strong.

Inner aggression: Who are you kidding! You didn't think twice about gobbling it down. I think you like the feeling of not having any willpower, of being a passive wimp.

Inner passivity: That's not true. I'm going to do better in the future. I know I will. I'm certain of it.

Inner aggression: What a laugh! Do you really think it's going to get any better in the future?

Inner passivity: (capitulating, and pleading guilty to being a hopeless failure rather than to the underlying passivity) It's true. I'm hopeless. I do it every time. It's never going to get any better. I feel terrible.

Inner aggression: (backing off, while accepting the punishment of guilt and depression) Look, just keep trying. You've got to stop being such a failure.

Inner passivity: I don't know if I can. Damn, I'm such a loser, I might as well just go and eat another piece of cake.

Note in this example that no voice is present to speak for truth, justice, or the rights of the individual. Sometimes we can detect a weak voice of the self in the background, but it can easily be drowned out by the voices representing the conflict.

We can see from this example that the inner critic eases up once inner passivity, represented by the unconscious ego, pleads guilty to some "lesser crime," such as being hopeless or being a failure, or once sufficient shame, anxiety, guilt, or depression is accepted as punishment. The problem for the individual, who accepts this punishment to cover up his emotional attachment to passivity, is that he is going to suffer the consequences. In other words, to make the defense work he must feel like a failure or a loser, and he will have to accept the accompanying guilt and shame. Or he will give up and capitulate completely to out-of-control behavior, leading to different forms of emotional and physical distress.

The following is an example of a dialogue in which the individual is *not* plagued by inner passivity. This time the individual speaks through his authentic self with power and authority:

Inner aggression: Why did you just eat that chocolate cake?

Self: It was good. What's it to you?

Inner aggression: You are on a diet! You told yourself you were going to eat healthier food.

Self: You're right, I did. But I made an exception in this case.

Inner aggression: Exceptions aren't allowed! A diet is a diet! That was bad what you did!

Self: Oh, give me a break. Go away! You have no say in the matter!

Inner aggression: I do, I do! You are bad!

Self: Good-bye.

Inner aggression: (Silence.)

This individual is not intimidated. His attitude to inner aggression is dismissive. He doesn't take the accusation seriously and he exhibits no defensiveness. Nor does he absorb the aggression. It's like dropping the rope in a tug of war or displaying a martial-art maneuver that throws the foe off balance. One client called the process "inner jujitsu." (Dialogues also occur between the self and inner passivity.) This individual knows he might suffer physically with weight gain or stomach upset for breaking his diet, but he is not going to suffer emotionally as well by letting his superego pile on.

People actively look for ways to suffer. Someone will eat a piece of chocolate cake allegedly for pleasure but in reality for the unconscious purpose of encountering his or her harsh inner critic and being verbally abused by it. We have a hard time believing that we actually do this. It seems so perversely stupid. Yet, this is the power of our deadly flaw. It is why humans still remain entangled in negative and vicious behaviors after so many thousands of years of evolution.

Our deadly flaw compels us to repeat and recycle whatever conflicts are unresolved, all in the cover-up of our indulgence in libidinized displeasure, no matter how self-defeating or painful that is. That sadness, grief, and misery can feel like old, faithful companions. Our affinity for suffering can be heard, for instance, in the bittersweet longing and plaintive melodrama of country music. "Melancholy," the French writer Victor Hugo said insightfully, "is the pleasure of being sad."

Accessing Self-Knowledge

Bergler believed we don't become totally immune to our unconscious attachments to suffering. "Such total immunization does not exist and cannot exist," he stated. "What successful therapy achieves is diminution of that scourge by forcing it out of truly dangerous deposits."[116]

He also believed that neurosis is a progressive disease, meaning that it is likely to get worse with age.[117] It was also his view that, "After adequate psychoanalytic treatment an ex-neurotic is better off than his allegedly healthy confrere."[118]

Bergler did state, as mentioned, that some people can get better without psychotherapy providing they consider relevant facts.[119] I agree with that. Effective psychotherapy can certainly speed up the attainment of emotional health, but only a small minority of people can access it due to costs and availability. Acceptance and dissemination of the true inner structure of the psyche will benefit society, if not necessarily every individual. We must start seeing ourselves more objectively. Ignorance is killing us. As vital self-knowledge is disseminated, I believe people will absorb it to produce a collective uprising of intelligence.

I have little hard evidence for being more optimistic than Bergler about overcoming the deadly flaw, though I do know that many of my clients live much happier lives as a result of the in-depth therapy they have experienced.

Intelligence is impeded, psychoanalysis contends, by repression, denial, and inner defenses. Bergler wrote that, "Holding down the repressed material—which is dynamic, not static—requires the *unproductive* expenditure of psychic energy. This means that the individual cuts down the total sum of psychic energy available to him for productive use, and to a greater or lesser extent leaves himself with an ego poorly equipped to deal with reality."[120] In addition, the expenditure of energy "required to keep in repression the 'painful, shameful, guilt-laden' infantile material has decisive consequences for the scope of the individual's intelligence."[121]

The Defense of the Pseudo-Moral Connotation

Once we identify our own particular methods of defense, we find it much easier to expose our appetite for suffering and free ourselves from it. Five of these defenses, previously mentioned throughout the text, are: the method of pleading guilty to the lesser crime ("crime" as defined by the irrational inner justice system); the use of the magic gesture; the technique of negative exhibitionism; the use of pseudo-aggression; and the technique of negative peeping.

Another important mode of defense involves *the pseudo-moral connotation*. This ingenious defense is built around the misuse of a moral principle or rule that has validity in an appropriate context.[122] When a moral principle is used as a defense, the principle is misinterpreted so that it sanctions the opposite of the original intention. These moral props, Bergler stated, "are literally reproduced where literal reproduction at the wrong time, in the wrong place, on the wrong or inappropriate occasion, out of context and with the wrong intention, does not reflect but instead totally distorts the meaning originally intended."[123]

Pseudo-morals are powerful weapons of resistance, and often the deadly flaw can't be undermined without identifying and dislodging them.[124] Here are five examples of such moral rules, along with a statement in parentheses that shows what each rule can cover up:

1. It is important to work hard. (*People who make this claim can be covering up passive submission to a boss, to the authority of a spouse, or to their inner critic.*

They can also be using work to cover up their attachment to the feeling of having little value.)

2. Helping others is the right thing to do. (*Those who claim categorically that helping others is the right thing to do can be enablers who, through inner passivity, sacrifice integrity and self-respect to cater to others.*)

3. I'm supposed to finish all the food on my plate. (*Overweight people who decline to practice self-regulation because it means emerging from inner passivity can avoid guilt by insisting that finishing all the food on their plate is a moral requirement.*)

4. It is necessary to act decisively. (*Someone who, through inner passivity, quickly submits to the will of others could claim to be acting decisively. Others can act decisively without sufficient reflection, producing self-defeat.*)

5. The most important thing is to love others. (*A person who chooses a romantic partner who has low self-esteem might claim to have done so in order to be a loving person—"What's the matter with being loving!" The secret intention, however, may be to identify with someone who feels unloved or is lacking in value.*)

The moral rule serves as a shield that is raised with defensive, sometimes mocking, irony: "This moral principle is what you (my parents) taught me. This is what you said was right! I'm only doing what I was taught!" The defense works because the inner critic cannot easily decree punishment for an act or wish that is approved by society or adopted as a moral principle.

Bergler cautioned that the pseudo-moral connotation "does not by any means represent the totality of the interpretation. It is an additional—though indispensable—element in the construction of the symptom."[125]

He also said the pseudo-moral defense infiltrates another semi-conscious mechanism, that of flawed rationalization. In such situations, the unconscious ego and the conscious ego team up for self-deception, with the conscious ego supplying the shaky logic. These rationalizations can be particularly hypocritical, for they ascribe moral or intellectual superiority to their promoters. He provided this example: "An agoraphobe patient told me once that he had not touched his wife for years, because she worked hard to support the family while he, because of his inability to leave the house, merely stayed home and did the chores. Could he be so cruel as to incommode the poor tired girl by subjecting her to the strenuous effort of intercourse? Wasn't gallantry a 'principle which every mother implants in her child'?"[126] This case certainly illustrates how our intelligence suffers from our entanglement in the deadly flaw.[127]

Another common defense is *injustice collecting*. Injustice collecting is found among cynics and chronic complainers, as well as among those who simply exhibit their unhappiness with stoic coldness or resigned depression. Invariably, they are full of righteous indignation and are easily offended. Such individuals are reproached regularly by their inner critic for their secret attachments to deprivation, refusal, passivity, and criticism. Their inner defenses offer up "evidence" that they are but innocent victims and that the "real" culprit is the malice and ignorance of the outside world. To make this defense work, they are obliged to be fixated on the real or alleged injustices that supposedly cause their suffering, as they bemoan these injustices to anyone who will listen.

From birth to death, we fight off inner reality and, hence, external reality. Even those mental-health professionals who see the extent of our self-defeat are reluctant to lay it on the couch. One psychiatrist, when asked why he didn't confront his patients with this knowledge, said, "It adds insult to injury to tell someone who is suffering, 'You're bringing this on yourself.'"

It sounds as if he is saying, "We must be careful not to offend anyone with allegations of self-defeat. It's better to suffer than to face up to such unpleasant facts." Sure, the knowledge offends our false pride and thus it is uncomfortable. But facing the knowledge of our unwitting participation in self-defeat is like lancing an infection. The initial hurt is soon replaced by healing.

Bergler's View on Homosexuality

I wish Bergler had followed Freud's counsel on the issue of homosexuality. In a letter to the mother of a homosexual son, Freud wrote: "Homosexuality is assuredly no advantage, but it is nothing to be ashamed of, no vice, no degradation; it cannot be classified as an illness; we consider it to be a variation of the sexual function, produced by a certain arrest of sexual development. . ."[128] Bergler, however, believed his psychoanalytic approach could cure homosexuality, providing a patient desired that outcome. He wrote five books that dealt directly with homosexuality,[129] so the subject obviously intrigued him.

It would be tempting to discredit Bergler's body of work on the basis of what he wrote about homosexuality. He believed that his work in general constituted a scientific advance of great importance,[130] and I agree with that view. However, he was somewhat of a zealot concerning homosexuality. I won't try to defend his views on this subject, but I will very briefly report what they are. (I am reminded that Albert Einstein apparently didn't get it all right either.[131]) The following paragraphs provide the essence of what Bergler wrote on male homosexuality and lesbianism. He believed this knowledge could help young people who, in doubt about their sexuality, wanted to be heterosexual or believed that their best interests lay in being heterosexual.

Like heterosexuals, male homosexuals and lesbians also have issues with mother as the "great refuser" and the "giantess of the nursery." Bergler considered homosexuality to be a defense against lingering secret attachments to feelings of having been refused, disappointed, and dominated by mother. While other children struggle with these feelings, the male child who later becomes a homosexual has a pronounced narcissistic structure that accentuates his struggle. His acute self-centeredness is more problematic and so are his infantile fears centered on the mother image.[132] "Precisely because of their narcissistic substructure," Bergler stated, "the blow caused by incapacity to maintain the infantile fiction of omnipotence hits children who become homosexuals so severely. They recover only partially from the defeat of weaning, and even then only with narcissistic recompense."[133]

That recompense involves the establishment of a desirable substitute, the penis, for the breast. According to Bergler, the homosexual's unconscious defense states, "I am not emotionally attached to mother's refusal or control. I have nothing in common with her and I am not even interested in women."

The homosexual, Bergler stated, was particularly traumatized by the process of weaning. "He singles out the disappointing organ (breast or breast-equivalent), finds on his own body (in his penis) a replica of it, and throughout his life runs after the copy of the replica—the penis of the other man."[134] The defense contends: "I don't want that old breast. This penis is what I want. It is what I like." The greater the pleasure in the penis, the more convincing is the defense. The homosexual's main character trait—injustice collecting—belongs to his original sense of having been victimized by mother.[135]

For the homosexual who is particularly promiscuous, the impersonal nature of many of his sexual encounters and his quick turnover of partners also represent pseudo-aggressive defenses against his unconscious interest in continuing to feel the injustice of mother's alleged malice.[136] According to Bergler, homosexuals have difficulty being truly happy because they are compelled to continue experiencing disappointment, whether in a sexual or nonsexual context, in everyday situations.[137]

The conflict for the female child who later becomes a lesbian is aggressive rather than erotic.[138] Typically, he wrote, in families producing lesbianism, the mother is aggressive and dominating and the father is weak. "The child," Bergler wrote, "hates the mother and is incapable of splitting off the pre-Oedipal ambivalent attitude toward her." Hence, the Oedipus complex, whereby the girl achieves sexual interest in the male represented by the model of her father, never reaches mature resolution.[139] Bergler stated, "Under female homosexuality lies a savage defensive hatred" toward the mother that is warded off or covered up by a libidinous defense: "I don't hate her, I love her sexually."[140] This defense is unconscious and is subsequently shifted to other women. Lesbians replay the passive baby, active Giantess game.[141]

"Officially," Bergler stated, "one partner plays the role of husband, the other that of wife. Under that Oedipal family fiction is hidden the baby-mother relationship. This fact accounts for the passive (baby) and active (mother) types in female homosexuality."[142] He added, "These persons consistently construct, unconsciously, situations in which they are unjustly treated.[143]

Again, I wish that Bergler had followed Freud's counsel—but there it is.[144] Sometimes people do need to address psychological issues involving their sexuality, but usually only when they become obsessive about it, or abusive of others, or when they use it promiscuously for self-validation or as a desperate substitute for love.

A Self-Help Technique

Overcoming our deadly flaw requires some technique as well as self-knowledge. I conclude this appendix with some instructions on how to counteract the influence of the deadly flaw. This self-help technique involves witnessing oneself from a position of detached objectivity, to the extent that is possible, while in the throes of an upsetting situation.

As one example, such a situation might involve strong cravings that typically lead to substance abuse or behavioral self-defeat. To resist the cravings, we try to recognize the underlying forms of negativity—frequently an attachment to deprivation, helplessness, passivity, or rejection—that are fueling the cravings.

Let's say we find ourselves in a situation where it appears that our boss has been trying to control us. At the time, we may not have objected to that allegedly controlling situation, but soon we're feeling resentful about it. Now, suddenly, cravings arise to overeat or to shop compulsively. If we're willing to look inward, we can establish an inner perspective from where we become a witness to our cravings. (At some point in our development, the cravings themselves will not arise in situations where they once did, because we have reduced the influence of the deadly flaw.)

As we're trying to resist the cravings, we can be accessing knowledge that leads us to the source of our difficulty. We might say to ourselves: "I'm feeling this powerful craving. I would prefer not to act on it. Where is this craving coming from? I know I'm feeling controlled by my boss. Today he was especially hard on me. If I give in to my craving, I will feel even more controlled and start to spin out of control. What is going on at a deeper level? I'm feeling controlled right now, and this is apparently what I'm attached to feeling. This is what I'm willing to feel and what I'm willing to indulge in. My boss is not causing me to feel this way. He only triggers what I myself am prepared to feel. Since I'm willing to feel this, it's my own negativity. I felt passive with my boss, and now I'm prepared to feel passive with myself, as if I'm being forced to give in to my cravings. My cravings are arising as a way for me to continue to feel passive. I need to look at this carefully. This is my own willingness to feel controlled. As I see this clearly, I can handle the situation better. It appears that I'm tempted to go on feeling controlled. The more I can acknowledge this, the more I'm making a powerful intention to avoid that feeling and to step clear of it. If I do that, I'll feel power coming back to me, because I'm taking control emotionally at this difficult moment. When the power comes back, the cravings should go away. As I continue to acknowledge my attachment to feeling controlled, I'm confident I'll get stronger. I'm responsible for this negativity—this temptation to go on feeling controlled—and I don't have to submit to it, especially now that I see where it comes from. This is not about fighting against the cravings—it's about seeing clearly where they come from. That should clear them from my system. I just have to see them clearly enough as symptoms of my deadly flaw, which in this case is my attachment to inner passivity. That's where I focus my attention right now—on my willingness to experience myself through this passivity."

That is a lot for a person to think about in a few moments. As well, it's difficult to have this kind of clarity when we're feeling rattled by cravings or negative emotions. As we're learning about our deadly flaw, however, all these thoughts become a deep knowing, a sense of truth, that's instantly available for our benefit.

Note that the emotional reactions we have in encounters with others don't always register at the moment. In other words, we might get triggered in an encounter with our boss and not even know that we were triggered. The only clue is that hours later we begin to feel cravings, anger, hopelessness, guilt, or shame. When feeling a disturbance, we often have to become a detective in our psyche, tracing our distress back to an external event or situation that triggered it or is continuing to trigger it. (Note also that our attachments to negative emotions can cause us to become triggered very subtly and very easily, sometimes just through a recurring memory, speculations about the future, or some other misuse of our imagination.)

Instead of cravings we often feel anger toward someone. In situations that are confrontational, we should, as a first instinct, seek to minimize both our suffering and the potential for self-damage. If angry, try not to say something you'll be sorry for. Often we're unable in that moment to do or say what is best for ourselves. We will get stronger over time if we understand the deadly flaw. Once we examine in hindsight the underlying dynamics of a challenging event, we can expect to do better the next time we face an emotional challenge of that sort. Meanwhile, being patient is a way to support ourselves emotionally.

The learning process described in this book doesn't emphasize the need for people to *do* something other than to acquire specific self-knowledge about one's involvement in suffering. Our intelligence and good intentions do the work for us once we have absorbed the knowledge of our particular variations of the deadly flaw.

Endnotes

[1] Elio Frattaroli, M.D., *Healing the Soul in the Age of the Brain: Why Medication Isn't Enough* (New York: Penguin Books, 2002) 6-9. Frattaroli writes, "In the pantheon of important questions that human beings can ask about themselves and the world around them, *only the very simplest questions can be answered in a laboratory.* Only in physics and chemistry are the relevant variables few enough that scientists can potentially know and control all of them in an experiment. For anything as complicated as a biological organism— especially a self-reflective biological organism—there will inevitably be many variables that cannot be controlled in a lab. In fact, for the study of human consciousness, it is highly unlikely that we can ever know for sure what all the relevant variables are!" 163-164.

[2] Edmund Bergler, *Selected Papers of Edmund Bergler, M.D. 1933-1961* (New York: Grune & Stratton, 1969) 953-966. This section at the conclusion of *Selected Papers* lists Bergler's published works.

[3] *Selected Papers of Edmund Bergler, M.D. 1933-1961.* 953-966. See also: Edmund Bergler, *The Talent for Stupidity: The Psychology of the Bungler, the Incompetent, and the Ineffectual* (Madison, CT: International Universities Press, Inc., 1998) xiv-xv.

[4] Bergler was in private practice as a psychoanalytic psychiatrist in Vienna from 1927 to1938, and in New York City from 1938 to his death. He was a graduate of the Medical School of the University of Vienna, and from 1927 to 1937 he was on the staff of the Psychoanalytic Freud Clinic in Vienna, serving as assistant director during the last four years of that period. In 1942-1943 and 1944-1945, he was a lecturer at the Psychoanalytic Institute of New York. From *Selected Papers of Edmund Bergler M.D. (1933-1961)* 953.

[5] *The Talent for Stupidity* was apparently written in early to mid-1952. Melvyn L. Iscove, M.D., says in his Introduction to this book that "the trustees of the Edmund and Marianne Bergler Psychiatric Foundation had to choose from over two dozen completed book manuscripts found among Bergler's working papers after his death. These manuscripts date from 1936 to 1962 and even include several still untranslated works in German, from his Vienna period. . . . Above and beyond Bergler's completed book manuscripts the Foundation has identified and catalogued dozens of unpublished scientific papers in different stages of completion, from preliminary jottings and partial drafts to completed papers typed and ready for publication. We have also catalogued well over one hundred unfinished book manuscripts, ranging from jottings or preliminary outlines to manuscripts at various stages of completion."

[6] Edmund Bergler, *Principles of Self-Damage* (Madison, CT: International Universities Press, Inc., 1992; New York: Philosophical Library, Inc., 1959; New York: Intercontinental Medical Book Corp., 1974) 328. In *Principles of Self-Damage* along with his later book, *Curable and Incurable Neurotics* (1961), Bergler provides the most comprehensive coverage of his body of work. His most comprehensive earlier works were *The Basic Neurosis* (New York: Harper and Brothers, 1949) and *The Superego* (New York: Grune and Stratton Inc., 1952).

[7] Edmund Bergler, *The Basic Neurosis* (New York: Harper and Brothers, 1949).

[8] Eckhart Tolle, *Oneness With All Life (Treasury Edition): Inspirational Selections from A New Earth* (New York: Dutton, 2008) 117.

[9] *Oneness With All Life (Treasury Edition): Inspirational Selections from A New Earth* 118.

[10] Throughout the text I use the term *emotional attachment*, as well

as (meaning the same thing) the words *attachment* or *attachments*. The term or words refer to our unconscious willingness to experience deep negativity. For instance, our willingness to recycle an unresolved negative emotion such as rejection means that we have an *emotional attachment* to the feeling of rejection.

[11] Barbara W. Tuchman, *The March of Folly* (New York: Ballantine Books, 1985).

[12] Daniel Gross, *Dumb Money: How Our Greatest Financial Minds Bankrupted the Nation* (New York: Free Press, 2009). Gross writes that the great financial crisis of 2008 was "a man-made product that turned out to be immensely toxic and damaging." It was not, as so many in the smart-money crowd insisted, "a random once-in-a-lifetime thing that fell out of the sky."

[13] *Principles of Self-Damage* 416.

[14] According to most experts, no one theory adequately explains or describes childhood learning and development.

[15] Edmund Bergler, *Curable and Incurable Neurotics: Problems of Neurotic versus Malignant Psychic Masochism* (New York: Liveright, 1961). This is one of Bergler's more technical books. In it he differentiates between typical cases of psychic masochism and more severe malignant-schizoid psychic masochism.

[16] Bruno Bettelheim. *Freud and Man's Soul* (New York: Vintage Books, 1984) 6-7.

[17] See "Psychoanalysis" at Wikipedia.

[18] Joseph Schwartz. *Cassandra's Daughter: A History of Psychoanalysis* (New York: Viking, 1999) 3.

[19] James Ridgeway, "Big Pharma Psychs Out the Shrinks" (CommonDreams.org, April 6, 2009). A recent example of the ethical lapses in the multi-billion dollar effort to promote the widespread use of drugs concerns the revelation that most of the authors of the *Diagnostic and Statistical Manual of Mental Disorders*, which is the American Psychiatric Association's clinical guideline, have financial ties to drug companies. Summarizing the findings, which were compiled by researchers largely from public records, the *Kaiser Daily Health Policy Report* states: According to the study, 18 of the 20 authors of the guidelines had at least one financial tie to drug companies. Twelve authors had ties in at least three categories, such as consulting, research grants, speaking fees or stock ownership, the study found. In addition, the study found that all of the authors of schizophrenia and bipolar guidelines had relationships with the drug industry, while 60% of the authors of the depression guidelines had such connections. According to the study, more than 75% of the authors received funding for research from drug companies. In addition, one-third of the authors served on the speaker bureaus of drug companies, the study shows. Another report stated that, "Six of the top medical journals published a significant number of articles in 2008 that were written by ghostwriters financed by drug companies, according to a study released Thursday by editors of *The Journal of the American Medical Association*." Duff Wilson, Natasha Singer, "Study Says Ghostwriting Rife in Medical Journals," *The New York Times*, 11 Sept. 2009: B5.

[20] http://www.salon.com/books/feature/2010/04/27/interview_whitaker_anatomy_of_an_epidemic/index.html

[21] http://www.counterpunch.org/levine04282010.html

[22] Psychoanalysis called this *infantile megalomania,* which most people consider a strange if not bizarre idea. Since the concept is not

considered relevant by most psychologists, it is not widely taught or understood. However, there is much evidence that it does exist as a significant mental/emotional state. Jean Piaget (1896-1980), the renowned Swiss psychologist and researcher of early childhood, wrote that children are markedly egocentric up until the age of seven. This does not mean that children are selfish but that they are unable to fathom any viewpoint other than their own. "The child is born into egocentrism. The child sees himself as the center of the universe, with everything revolving around him and occurring solely for his pleasure." Dorothy G. Singer, Tracey A. Revenson. *A Piaget Primer: How a Child Thinks*. Madison, CT: International Universities Press, Inc., 1997) 13-14. Up until the age of two, the child doesn't realize that objects can exist apart from himself. The child believes that everyone sees the world exactly as he or she does. Not until the age of seven does a child's language and behaviors become less egocentric and more socialized. Even after that age, children are emotionally attracted to superstition, the illusions of magical thinking, and omnipotence of thoughts and words. Classical psychoanalysis, seeing that regressed obsessional patients exhibited fantasies of omnipotence (being all powerful), traced this misperception back to the unconscious mental life of the fetus. Under the influence of the pleasure principle, the fetus presumably feels an agreeable sensation in the notion that its existence is allegedly self-maintained and self-sufficient, hence autocratic. In early infancy, the child discovers pleasure through the oral functions. The child also discovers pleasure in the emotional antidote to its state of physical helplessness, which is hallucinatory wish-fulfillment, the impression that whatever happens is what he or she wants. This misperception is further fostered when parents attempt to fulfill the child's wishes concerning food, sleep, and attention. The developing ego of the infant can also be the object or the recipient of pleasure, since the child cannot imagine sources of pleasure other than himself (*i.e.* he assumes that his mother's breast is a part of his own body or existence). This is the basis of childhood and adult narcissism. Bergler wrote that the infantile ego is reluctant to recognize objects and the

323

outer world as a whole, and is even quite resentful of the object, because the independent existence of the object infringes on his megalomania. Bergler's primary paper on megalomania is titled "Thirty Some Years after Ferenczi's 'States in the Development of the Sense of Reality'" (*Selected Papers of Edmund Bergler, M.D. 1933-1961*) 123-139. In this paper, after crediting Sandor Ferenczi's 1913 paper with the "highest originality," he produces "ten sets of facts" that broaden Ferenczi's understanding. Bergler wrote in a footnote, "It seems to me that the fact that the child does not make any distinction between *animate* and *inanimate* objects, both of which he considers living, has its affective basis in his assumption that the whole world is a part of his own body. Moreover, since the child considers the 'good' things which come from the outer world, for instance, the breast, to be a part of his own body, and the 'bad' things which come from the outer world only gradually to be external, he eventually regards with hostility everything coming from without. Here we have perhaps the kernel of hostility toward everything foreign so pronounced later in life. . . ."

[23] Benedict Carey, "Psychoanalytic Therapy Wins Backing," *The New York Times,* 1 Oct. 2008: A20.

[24] Peter Gay, ed. *The Freud Reader* (New York: W.W. Norton & Co., 1989) 612-616.

[25] http://www.enotes.com/psychoanalysis-encyclopedia/moral-masochism

[26] *The Freud Reader* 754.

[27] *The Freud Reader* 755.

[28] *The Freud Reader* 755.

[29] Mainstream psychology's understanding of jealousy is expressed in

the July, 2009 issue of *Psychology Today*. In the cover story on the subject, the author, Hara Estroff Marano writes, "No one can say for sure what jealousy is; attempts to define it are elusive for a reason. As a complex emotion it involves, at a minimum, such distressing feelings as fear, abandonment, loss, sorrow, anger, betrayal, envy, and humiliation. And it recruits a host of cognitive processes gone awry, from doubt to preoccupation with a partner's faithlessness. It may take much of its primal force from activating the attachment system of the brain, a genetically ingrained circuit that is the foundation of our social bonds and that prompts widespread distress when they are threatened." Modern psychology frequently attributes our emotional challenges to genetics and "ingrained" circuits in the brain.

[30] *Curable and Incurable Neurotics* 310-311.

[31] Edmund Bergler, *Laughter and the Sense of Humor* (New York: Intercontinental Medical Book Corporation, 1956) viii.

[32] *Laughter and the Sense of Humor* viii.

[33] In *Curable and Incurable Neurotics*, Bergler wrote a 180-page chapter titled, "How Does the Visual Drive, the Least Explored Chapter in Psychopathology, Contribute to Therapeutic Failures?" In this chapter, he discusses at length 22 "disease entities belonging to this [visual drive] orbit."

[34] Bergler coined the term, "writer's block." He proposes a cure for this dysfunction of the visual drive in his book, *The Writer and Psychoanalysis* (Madison, CT: International Universities Press, 1986; New York: Doubleday and Co., 1950). Bergler noted that Freud had earlier expressed his hope that one day the "metapsychological" mystery of artistic creation would be unraveled and clinically put to use. That solution "did actually materialize only ten years later," Bergler stated, "when I presented the theory of artistic creativity,

proving my contention with cured cases of 'writer's block'." See, *Curable and Incurable Neurotics,* 435, 276.

[35] *The Talent for Stupidity* 181.

[36] In contrast, conventional views of the emotional and cognitive development of early childhood generally ignore these inner drives. They focus instead on preferences and recognition, capacity for empathy, anger, frustration, learning, remembering, problem-solving, trust, autonomy, shame, doubt, and language. Much of the conventional literature deals with the child's relationship to his or her parents, caregivers, siblings, and others. The significance of the child's impressions of reality is downplayed, as if these impressions are secondary to outer reality. There is little regard for the idea that any consciousness in the first months of life would matter to us as adults. This corresponds with a tendency of parents and educators to impose their sense of reality upon the child without having much respect for the child's inner world.

[37] *The Talent for Stupidity* 23.

[38] *The Talent for Stupidity* xxxv.

[39] Again, the existence of infantile megalomania is a basic principle in classical psychoanalysis. Bergler discusses it fully in Chapter One of *Principles of Self-Damage.*

[40] *Principles of Self-Damage* 2-3. See also: *The Talent for Stupidity* 24.

[41] Edmund Bergler, *Tensions Can be Reduced to Nuisances: A Technique for Not-Too-Neurotic People* (New York: Liveright Publishing Corp., 1960) 91. This may be Bergler's least technical and simplest book, written in hopes of reaching a wider audience with his ideas.

[42] Edmund Bergler, *The Superego* (Madison, CT: International Universities Press, 1989) 11.

[43] *The Talent for Stupidity* 25.

[44] Classical psychoanalysis, when overlooking Bergler, describes this moment of childhood experience differently. "Such experiences of frustration, which are inevitably repeated over and over in a variety of ways during infancy, Freud considered to be a most significant factor in the development of a sense of reality. Through them the infant learns that some things in the world come and go, that they can be absent as well as present, that they are 'not here,' however much he may wish them to be so. This is one of the starting points for recognizing that such things (mother's breast, for example) are not 'self' but 'outside self'." Charles Brenner, *An Elementary Textbook of Psychoanalysis* (Madison, CT: International Universities Press, 1955, 1992) 64.

[45] *Principles of Self-Damage* 8.

[46] *Principles of Self-Damage* 7.

[47] *The Talent for Stupidity* 114.

[48] Edmund Bergler, "Crime and Punishment." *Selected Papers of Edmund Bergler, M.D. 1933-1961,* 764. (First published in *The Psychiatric Quarterly Supplement*, 1947.) See also: Edmund Bergler, "A Short Genetic Survey of Psychic Impotence (II)." *Selected Papers of Edmund Bergler, M.D. 1933-1961,* 587.

[49] Edmund Bergler, "Use and Misuse of Analytic Interpretations by the Patient." *Selected Papers of Edmund Bergler, M.D. 1933-1961,* 319. First published in *The Psychoanalytic Review*, October, 1946.

[50] http://www.nytimes.com/books/98/08/16/specials/bernays-

obit.html

51 http://www.nytimes.com/books/98/08/16/specials/bernays-obit.html. The obituary also says, "In his later years, beginning in the early 1960's, he was a public opponent of smoking and took part in anti-smoking campaigns."

52 *The Talent for Stupidity* 30-31.

53 *The Talent for Stupidity* 31.

54 Sandra Michaelson. *LoveSmart: Transforming the Emotional Patterns That Sabotage Relationships* (Santa Fe, NM: Prospect Books, 1999) 148. This example is taken from this book written by my late wife, Sandra Michaelson (1944-1999), a psychotherapist who wrote three books based on Edmund Bergler's theories.

55 *The Superego* 46, xv. Bergler said the superego is divided into two parts: The first part is the harsh dispenser of self-aggression, what he called "Daimonion," a term Socrates used in addressing the judges of Athens for "corrupting the youth." The second part is the ego ideal, described in Chapter 6.

56 *Curable and Incurable Neurotics* 79.

57 *Principles of Self-Damage* 107-111.

58 Even the highest achievements of the human mind can be outcomes of mysterious dynamics in the unconscious mind. Norman Mailer was sensibly modest about the origins of his creative talent. The title of his book on writing, *The Spooky Art,* refers to the mysterious, even uncanny, process of writing literary fiction. In that book he wrote that, "*Barbary Shore* might as well have been dictated

328

to me by a ghost in the middle of a forest. Each morning I would sit down to work with no notion at all of how to continue. My characters were strangers to me, and each day after a few hours of blind work (because I never seemed to get more than a sentence or two ahead of myself) I would push my plot and people three manuscript pages forward into their eventual denouement, but I never knew what I was doing or where it came from. It's fortunate that I had heard of Freud and the unconscious; if not, I would have had to postulate such a condition myself." *The Spooky Art: Thoughts on Writing* (New York: Random House Trade Paperbacks, 2003) 238. Bergler had much to say about this process in his book *The Writer and Psychoanalysis* (Madison, CT: International Universities Press, 1986; New York: Doubleday and Co., 1950).

[59] Donald Winnicott and Heinz Kohut.

[60] After many years of pondering Bergler's work and seeing its influence on my clients and on my own development, I am not entirely clear to what degree some of the statements and points I make in this book are my own ideas, as influenced by Bergler, or are in fact a straightforward retelling of Bergler's work. If the distinction is important, it would probably be apparent to anyone studying the two authors. I believe, for one thing, that I have brought original ideas and clarity to the existence of inner passivity. In any case, the comments on the self at this point in the book are not attributable to Bergler.

[61] *Curable and Incurable Neurotic*s 122.

[62] One explanation for the inner critic's anti-libidinous stance is found in Brenner's *An Elementary Textbook of Psychoanalysis.* Brenner wrote, "Thus the original nucleus of the prohibitions of the superego is the demand that the individual repudiate the incestuous and hostile wishes that comprised the individual's Oedipus complex. Moreover, this demand persists throughout life, unconsciously of

course, as the essence of the superego." 123-124.

[63] *Principles of Self-Damage* 100-111. Bergler's five-layer structure describes unconscious masochism as a defense against a defense. See: Bergler, *Parents Not Guilty of their Children's Neuroses,* 115-116; and Bergler, "On a Five-Layer Structure in Sublimation." *Selected Papers of Edmund Bergler, M.D. 1933-1961* (94-109).

[64] Just one noteworthy aspect to the structure can be mentioned briefly. (I explain this as simply as I can, yet readers will see the complexity involved. As mentioned, the understanding is made easier when the knowledge is applied to one's own issues.) In this five-layer structure, two of the layers are defenses put forward by the unconscious ego. The first defense (to offer a simplistic example) might involve pleading guilty to a lesser crime when the inner critic "indicts" a person for his attachment to passivity: "I'm not passive and I'm not looking to feel passive—the problem is I'm angry." This defense, however, is deemed unacceptable by the inner critic: "Being angry is bad." The unconscious ego scrambles to offer a second defense. This second defense involves a willingness to suffer with guilt (or shame) and to accept certain disadvantages that constitute some degree of self-defeat (or that, in ideal cases, constitute sublimation): "It's true, being angry is bad. I feel guilt (or shame) for being an angry person." The inner critic accepts this defense since the shame (the punishment) now greatly outweighs any secret pleasure. Over time the inner critic typically finds the defense unsatisfactory and requires a modification involving greater shame or depression and more self-defeat. (Even sublimations can require modification. Productive writing would be a successful sublimation, while writer's block could arise were this sublimation to weaken.) All symptoms and personality distortions, as well as successful sublimations, appear at the fifth layer, and they constitute the defense against the defense. *Principles of Self-Damage* 112.

[65] *Parents Not Guilty of Their Children's Neuroses* 23-25. The

repetition compulsion, or "repetition in reverse," is the tendency to repeat actively what one has endured passively. This means that children, feeling passive in relation to their parents, feel a powerful need to express themselves, or at least imagine themselves, with some sense of power. That power can be simply an illusion of power, as in, "I cause the punishment to happen to me through my naughty behavior."

[66] *The Superego* 351.

[67] *Principles of Self-Damage* xxix. In the Forward, Bergler stated: Psychic masochism is "the basic end result of the infantile conflict and . . . the center of psychiatric-psychoanalytic investigations of all individuals: normal people, neurotics, psychopathic personalities, criminotics, and psychotics."

[68] Ethan Bronner, "New Looks at the Fields of Death for Jews," *New York Times*, 20 April, 2009: A6.

[69] Bronner.

[70] Conventional wisdom says that people do evil things because they come under the influence of social or situational forces acting upon them. This view is expressed in Philip Zimbardo's *The Lucifer Effect: Understanding How Good People Turn Evil.* (New York: Random House, 2008). "By now," Zimbardo writes near the end of his book, "I hope you are willing to accept the premise that ordinary people, even good ones, can be seduced, recruited, initiated into behaving in evil ways under the sway of powerful systematic and situational forces" (P. 443). It's true that people are influenced by outside factors, but human evolvement still requires an understanding of the inner dynamics that occur when an apparently decent person becomes a perpetrator of evil.

[71] *Principles of Self-Damage* 69.

[72] *The Talent for Stupidity* 141.

[73] *The Superego* 22-23.

[74] *Curable and Incurable Neurotics* 81.

[75] Edmund Bergler, "'Making a Case'-Type of Depression—A Predictable Test-Mechanism, in Psychotherapy." *Selected Papers of Edmund Bergler, M.D. 1933-1961. P.* 349. First published in *The Psychoanalytic Review*, July, 1954.

[76] Edmund Bergler, "Five Aims of the Psychoanalytic Patient." *Selected Papers of Edmund Bergler, M.D. 1933-1961* 295. First published in *The Psychiatric Quarterly*, October, 1946.

[77] *Selected Papers of Edmund Bergler, M.D. 1933-1961* 288.

[78] Edmund Bergler, "Depression as After-Effect of Missed Masochistic Opportunities." *Selected Papers of Edmund Bergler, M.D. 1933-1961* 949. First published in *The Psychiatric Quarterly Supplement*, 1957.

[79] Edmund Bergler, "'Making a Case'-Type of Depression—A Predictable Test-Mechanism, in Psychotherapy." *Selected Papers of Edmund Bergler, M.D. 1933-1961* 349.

[80] *Selected Papers of Edmund Bergler, M.D. 1933-1961* 349.

[81] *Selected Papers of Edmund Bergler, M.D. 1933-1961* 350.

[82] Evelyn Pringle, "Just Say No to the Mothers Act." 27 April, 2009. http://www.scoop.co.nz/stories/HL0904/S00255.htm

[83] Bergler, "Psychoprophylaxis of Postpartum Depression." *Selected Papers of Edmund Bergler, M.D. 1933-1961* 360-366.

[84] *Selected Papers of Edmund Bergler, M.D. 1933-1961* 364.

[85] *Selected Papers of Edmund Bergler, M.D. 1933-1961* 366.

[86] *Selected Papers of Edmund Bergler, M.D. 1933-1961* 364.

[87] *Selected Papers of Edmund Bergler, M.D. 1933-1961* 364.

[88] *Selected Papers of Edmund Bergler, M.D. 1933-1961* 364.

[89] *Neurotic Counterfeit-Sex: Impotence, Frigidity, 'Mechanical' and Pseudosexuality, Homosexuality* 81.

[90] *Counterfeit-Sex: Impotence, Frigidity, 'Mechanical' and Pseudosexuality* 81.

[91] *Counterfeit-Sex: Impotence, Frigidity, 'Mechanical' and Pseudosexuality* 81.

[92] *Counterfeit-Sex: Impotence, Frigidity, 'Mechanical' and Pseudosexuality* 85.

[93] Edmund Bergler, "Use and Misuse of Analytic Interpretations by the Patient." *Selected Papers of Edmund Bergler, M.D. 1933-1961.* 301-322.

[94] *Tensions Can Be Reduced to Nuisances* 210-232.

[95] *Selected Papers of Edmund Bergler, M.D. 1933-1961* 308.

[96] *Selected Papers of Edmund Bergler, M.D. 1933-1961* 310.

[97] *Selected Papers of Edmund Bergler, M.D. 1933-1961* 315.

[98] *Principles of Self-Damage* 410.

[99] *Selected Papers of Edmund Bergler, M.D. 1933-1961* 315.

[100] *Selected Papers of Edmund Bergler, M.D. 1933-1961* 318.

[101] *Selected Papers of Edmund Bergler, M.D. 1933-1961* 320. Bergler used many anecdotes to illustrate his points. With rule number 20, he wrote: "A very intelligent scholar with a scientific reputation was in analysis because of impotence. He was, he believed, rendered very skeptical about analysis by his 'specialized training.' At that time my monograph on impotence was published in Switzerland, and was displayed in the windows of some bookshops in Vienna. On his way to my office the patient had to pass a street in which many medical bookstores were located. He took great delight and gained confidence in seeing the book in the windows. I asked him ironically: 'Why are you so impressed by printed paper? If your statement is correct that my interpretations are 'fantasies,' then the book is just a collection of fairy tales!' Being trained in publishing scientific papers himself, he did not see the irony and took the whole thing seriously. One day he came to me in a fury and said: 'Today I came to the conclusion that analysis is just nonsense. Your book is no longer in the window of my favorite bookstore. Not even the owner of the store believes in analysis!' The sheer stupidity of the argument that bookstores sell books because the owner 'believes' in them was not enough to warn the patient that he was being taken in by his resistance. 'What have you to say in your defense?' shouted the patient. 'Well,' was my reply, 'there are different possibilities. Perhaps the owner of the bookstore is impotent himself and is reading the book. Or perhaps he sold the last copy. Or perhaps he doesn't think it is a good idea to display a book on sexy matters in reactionary Vienna.' It took the patient a few appointments to figure out his resistance."

[102] *http://alternet.org/story/149262.*

[103] It was titled *Escape from Freedom* when published in the United States.

[104] *Principles of Self-Damage* 448.

[105] *Principles of Self-Damage* 449.

[106] *Principles of Self-Damage* 67.

[107] *The Superego* 33.

[108] *Principles of Self-Damage* 12.

[109] *Principles of Self-Damage* 36.

[110] Bergler is not mentioned in Morton Hunt's *The Story of Psychology* (1993), or in Peter Giovacchini's *A Narrative Textbook of Psychoanalysis* (1987), or in Joseph Schwartz,'s *Cassandra's Daughter: A History of Psychoanalysis* (1999), though these books discuss the contributions of scores of lesser lights. He was referred to in a few sentences, in reference to his views on homosexuality, in Eli Zaretsky's *Secrets of the Soul: A Social and Cultural History of Psychoanalysis*. (New York: Alfred A. Knopf, 2004) 300. However, he is mentioned at several points, at some length, in Arnold M. Cooper's *The Quiet Revolution in American Psychoanalysis*. (2005).

[111] *The Talent for Stupidity* 180.

[112] *The Superego* 25.

[113] *The Talent for Stupidity* 177.

[114] *The Talent for Stupidity* 178.

[115] C.G. Jung, *The Undiscovered Self* (New York: New American Library, 1958) 105.

[116] *Curable and Incurable Neurotics,* 18.

[117] *Curable and Incurable Neurotics* 16.

[118] *Curable and Incurable Neurotics* 16. When people work out deep negativity, they become more insightful about the psychological challenges the people they encounter are dealing with. In other words, they can read people more easily. The working-out process involves a distinct elevation of consciousness. Some individuals who have worked out their issues are in a position, with appropriate training, to become skilled psychotherapists. No psychotherapist can take clients beyond his or her level of consciousness.

[119] *Tensions Can be Reduced to Nuisances* 211.

[120] *The Talent for Stupidity* 179.

[121] *The Talent for Stupidity* 179.

[122] *Principles of Self-Damage* 112.

[123] *Principles of Self-Damage* 112.

[124] *Curable and Incurable Neurotics* 132.

[125] *Principles of Self-Damage* 122.

[126] *Principles of Self-Damage* 123.

[127] A pseudo-moral defense was mentioned earlier (in Chapter 3), though not identified as a pseudo-moral for reasons of simplicity. It said, "What's the matter with wanting to reward yourself? Isn't that a

healthy thing to do?" Since this statement involves "rewarding" oneself with some self-defeating substance or activity, it obviously incorporates flawed rationalization.

[128] Robert P. Cabaj, Terry S. Stein, *Textbook of Homosexuality and Mental Health* (American Psychiatric Pub., 1996), as quoted on p. 178.

[129] *Neurotic Counterfeit-Sex* (New York: Grune & Stratton, 1951); *Fashion and the Unconscious* (New York: Robert Brunner, 1953); *Kinsey's Myth of Female Sexuality,* written with William S. Kroger, MD (New York: Grune & Stratton, 1954); *Homosexuality: Disease or Way of Life?* (New York: Hill & Wang, 1956); *1000 Homosexuals* (New Jersey: Pageant Books, 1959).

[130] *Principles of Self-Damage* xxi.

[131] *Scientific American.* March, 2009. http://www.scientificamerican.com/article.cfm?id=was-einstein-wrong-about-relativity&page=6. "The status of special relativity, just more than a century after it was presented to the world, is suddenly a radically open and rapidly developing question. This situation has come about because physicists and philosophers have finally followed through on the loose ends of Einstein's long-neglected argument with quantum mechanics—an irony-laden further proof of Einstein's genius. The diminished guru may very well have been wrong just where we thought he was right and right just where we thought he was wrong. We may, in fact, see the universe through a glass not quite so darkly as has too long been insisted."

[132] *Curable and Incurable Neurotics* 66.

[133] A.M. Krich, ed. "Homosexuality and the Kinsey Report." *The Homosexuals: As Seen by Themselves and Thirty Authorities* (New York: The Citadel Press, 1954) 233.

[134] *Neurotic Counterfeit-Sex* 193.

[135] *Neurotic Counterfeit-Sex* 194.

[136] *Neurotic Counterfeit-Sex* 194.

[137] *Neurotic Counterfeit-Sex* 193.

[138] *Neurotic Counterfeit-Sex* 341.

[139] *Neurotic Counterfeit-Sex* 327.

[140] *Neurotic Counterfeit-Sex* 327.

[141] *Neurotic Counterfeit-Sex* 318.

[142] *Neurotic Counterfeit-Sex* 327.

[143] *Neurotic Counterfeit-Sex* 327.

[144] http://rogerhollander.wordpress.com/category/rogers-archived-writing/autobiographical-essays-roger/. Roger Hollander, who underwent Berglerian analysis, wrote the following on his blog in December, 2008: "Because I am a gay positive individual and have a long time involvement with the gay and Lesbian community and gay liberation, being an advocate of Berglerian psychoanalysis presents a problem for me. Several years ago, I had the opportunity to meet with the novelist Bernard Wolfe, who had been a patient of Dr. Bergler in New York. Wolfe, who at the time I met with him in Southern California was in the twilight of his life and career, had also been a secretary to Leon Trotsky during the latter's exile in Mexico. I asked him about Bergler's questionable position with respect to

homosexuality. Wolfe's response was that Bergler was a socialist and a humanitarian, and he opined that in light of the movement for gay liberation, he was confident that Bergler would have revisited and revised his stance if he were alive today."

25463866R00197

Printed in Great Britain
by Amazon